CompTIA®
Project+® Practice Tests

CompTIA®
Project+® Practice Tests

Brett Feddersen

Senior Acquisitions Editor: Kenyon Brown
Development Editor: Gary Schwartz
Technical Editor: Vanina Mangano
Production Editor: Dassi Zeidel
Copy Editor: Liz Welch
Editorial Manager: Mary Beth Wakefield
Production Manager: Kathleen Wisor
Executive Editor: Jim Minatel
Book Designers: Judy Fung and Bill Gibson
Proofreader: Rebecca Rider
Indexer: John Sleeva
Project Coordinator, Cover: Brent Savage
Cover Designer: Wiley
Cover Image: ©Jeremy Woodhouse/Getty Images, Inc.

I dedicate this book to my parents, who have given me laughs, wisdom, experience, insight, and love...

Acknowledgments

Holy cow! Do you know what's involved in writing a book? The team of dedicated professionals who helped to create this resource for you in order to advance your career in project management has to be the best in the business.

The spark for this effort began with Kenyon Brown, the senior acquisition editor who assembled this great team. Gary Schwartz was the development editor who served as a mentor throughout the process and at times strangely resembled my college composition professor. His efforts made this tool the very best product it could be to assist you in passing the CompTIA Project+ exam. Vanina Mangano helped to ensure the technical viability of this book. Her talents and dedication in the project management field are globally known, and she is a terrific collaboration partner. The rest of the production team, led by Dassi Zeidel, ensured that this text made it into print in a readable form. Thank you all for your collaborative efforts!

I would also like to acknowledge Kim Heldman, who has been a professional mentor to me for over a decade. One of the most courageous leaders I have ever met, Kim got me started down the path of project management certification, authorship, and speaking. Kim is one of the great leaders in public sector information technology. She brings order and structure to a scary and complex area.

Most importantly, I would like to thank my wife April and my children Kayla, Marcus, and Adric. They endured the opportunity costs of building Legos, helping with homework, or watching a movie throughout this process. The sacrifice in writing this book was mostly felt by them, and I couldn't do it without their smiles, love, and support. If I didn't have April in my life, my days would be dull and I wouldn't have such a cheery audience for life's little animations that we share together. She is my best friend forever, the world's greatest cheerleader, a creative and talented teacher, and the model for the person I want to be. I love you all.

About the Author

Brett Feddersen holds the Project Management Professional (PMP)® certification, as well as a Master of Professional Services in Leadership and Organizations with an emphasis in Strategic Innovation from the University of Denver. He is a career public servant, having served in the United States Marine Corps, and he has worked for the state of Colorado, the city of Boulder (Colorado), and with the Regional Transportation District (RTD) in the Denver/Metro area.

Brett brings a variety of experiences to this book, including project management work on several enterprise resource planning projects, web and e-commerce application implementation, and computer/network infrastructure management. Brett holds the following credentials: PMP®, Gamification, Lean IT Foundation, and ITIL Foundation v3. Brett earned a bachelor's degree in Business Administration with an emphasis in Computer Information Systems from Colorado Mesa University, and he holds a project management certificate from Colorado State University.

It is rare, but not unheard of, to have an extravert in the IT field. Brett would love for you to reach out to him, and you can reach him on LinkedIn: https://www.linkedin.com/in/brettfeddersen.

Contents

CompTIA.

Becoming a CompTIA Certified IT Professional is Easy

It's also the best way to reach greater professional opportunities and rewards.

Why Get CompTIA Certified?

Growing Demand

Project management is one of the business world's most in demand skill sets. Many employees need understand project management skills. While not every individual is a project leader, all individuals need to understand the fundamental concepts of project management.

Higher Salaries

Professionals with certifications on their resume command better jobs, earn higher salaries and have more doors open to new multi-industry opportunities.

Verified Strengths

91% of hiring managers indicate CompTIA certifications are valuable in validating expertise, making certification the best way to demonstrate your competency and knowledge to employers.**

Universal Skills

Professionals who would like to embark on a project management career path possess skills that can be used in virtually any industry – from information technology to consumer goods to business services. This career mobility ensures that project managers can readily find work in any industry.

 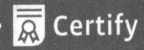 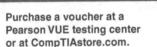

Learn more about what the exam covers by reviewing the following:

- Exam objectives for key study points.

- Sample questions for a general overview of what to expect on the exam and examples of question format.

- Visit online forums, like LinkedIn, to see what other IT professionals say about CompTIA exams.

Purchase a voucher at a Pearson VUE testing center or at CompTIAstore.com.

- Register for your exam at a Pearson VUE testing center:

- Visit pearsonvue.com/CompTIA to find the closest testing center to you.

- Schedule the exam online. You will be required to enter your voucher number or provide payment information at registration.

- Take your certification exam.

Congratulations on your CompTIA certification!

- Make sure to add your certification to your resume.

- Check out the CompTIA Certification Roadmap to plan your next career move.

Learn more: **Certification.CompTIA.org/projectplus**

* Source: CompTIA 9th Annual Information Security Trends study: 500 U.S. IT and Business Executives Responsible for Security
** Source: CompTIA Employer Perceptions of IT Training and Certification

Introduction

Welcome to *CompTIA Project+ Practice Tests*! Project management is a fast-growing field that seems to be in constant need of dependable, certified talent. Project managers are needed in just about every field, including, but not limited to, construction, engineering, government and civil initiatives, nonprofits, information technology, logistics, and transportation. Moreover, it can be mighty handy for those projects in your life such as moving, putting in a new kitchen, or helping to organize an event for your local parent-teacher organization. Heck, it was even surprisingly helpful in writing a book on practice questions for the CompTIA Project+ exam.

The Computing Technology Industry Association (CompTIA) promotes the Project+ exam for people interested in project management to earn certifications. The exam helps to validate the various skills, including business and communication skills, that an individual would need to lead projects confidently toward on-time and on-budget completion.

The purpose of this book is to help you pass the CompTIA Project+ Exam PK0-004. As you approach the final validation of your project management knowledge before taking this exam, this book will help prepare you for the types of questions and content that you might encounter on the exam itself. Remember, because of the broad range of knowledge and fields that use project management, this should not be the only resource you use to prepare for the exam. It will be important to use study guides and other exam resources in your studies. The more varied resources to which you expose yourself, the greater the probability of a successful result on the exam.

One such resource you should consider is the *CompTIA Project+ Study Guide: Exam PK0-004* by Kim Heldman (Sybex, 2017). It provides a great overview, reference, and additional review questions as you strive for certification in your project management career.

How This Book Is Organized

This book consists of four chapters, each based on one of the four domains in the CompTIA Project+ objectives for the PK0-004 exam. The book also has two chapters that are meant to simulate the exam based on a variety of the questions from all four domains. The chapters are organized as follows:

- Chapter 1, "Project Basics (Domain 1.0)," covers the basic concepts of project management, such as project properties, roles and responsibilities, project phases, cost control, organizational structures, project schedules, the Agile method of project management, and human resources and personnel management.

- Chapter 2, "Project Constraints (Domain 2.0)," focuses on the constraints and influences on a project, as well as risk strategies and activities.

- Chapter 3, "Communication and Change Management (Domain 3.0)," delves into communication method selection, influences on communication methods, communication triggers and adaptation to the target audience, change control processes, and types of organizational change.

- Chapter 4, "Project Tools and Documentation (Domain 4.0)," covers project management tools, project-centric documentation, and mutual binding documents and procurement methods.

- Chapter 5 and Chapter 6 consist of practice exams, roughly representing the mix of questions that you will see on the actual exam from each of the domains. They also carry a representative time limit so that you can simulate the testing experience as a part of your preparation.

Each chapter begins with a list of the Project+ objectives that are covered in that chapter. Remember, however, that each chapter does not cover the objectives in order, so do not be alarmed as you encounter each of the objectives in a randomized order.

WARNING   The questions included in this book are *not* derived from the actual Project+ exam questions. They serve to provide exposure to the underlying content and to deliver a comparable testing vehicle for you to prepare for the exam. It will not be a useful exercise to memorize the answers to these questions and assume that doing so will enable you to pass the exam. The underlying subject matter is the important focus of your studies so that you will be able to pass the exam.

Congratulations on investing in your career and your future as a project manager.

Project+ Exam Map

The following objective map will allow you to find the chapter in this book that covers each objective for the exam.

1.0 Project Basics

Exam Objective	Chapter
1.1 Summarize the properties of a project.	**1, 5, 6**
Temporary	1, 5, 6
Start and finish	1, 5, 6
Unique	1
Reason/purpose	1, 5

Exam Objective	Chapter
Project as part of a program	1
Project as part of a portfolio	1, 6
1.2 Classify project roles and responsibilities.	**2, 5, 6**
Sponsor/champion	2, 5, 6
Project manager	2, 5, 6
Project coordinator	2
Stakeholder	2, 5
Scheduler	2
Project team	2
Project Management Office (PMO)	2, 6
1.3 Compare and contrast standard project phases.	1, 2, 5, 6
Initiation	1, 5, 6
Planning	1, 5, 6
Execution	1, 5, 6
Monitor and control	1, 2, 5, 6
Closing	1, 5, 6
1.4 Identify the basics of project cost control.	1, 5, 6
Total project cost	1, 5, 6
Expenditure tracking	1, 5, 6
Expenditure reporting	1
Burn rate	1, 5, 6
Cost baseline/budget	1, 5, 6

Exam Objective	Chapter
1.5 Identify common project team organizational structures.	1, 2, 5, 6
Functional	1, 2, 5, 6
Matrix	1, 2, 5, 6
Projectized	1, 2, 5, 6
1.6 Given a scenario, execute and develop project schedules.	1, 2, 5, 6
Work breakdown structure	1, 2, 5, 6
Scheduling activities	1, 2, 5, 6
1.7 Identify the basic aspects of the Agile methodology.	1, 2, 5, 6
Readily adapt to new/changing requirements	1, 6
Iterative approach	1, 5
Continuous requirements gathering	1, 6
Establish a backlog	1, 2, 6
Burndown charts	1
Continuous feedback	1, 2
Sprint planning	1, 5, 6
Daily standup meetings/SCRUM meetings	1, 5
SCRUM retrospective	1, 2, 5, 6
Self-organized and self-directed teams	1
1.8 Explain the importance of human resource, physical resource, and personnel management.	1, 5, 6
Resource management concepts	1, 5, 6
Personnel management	1, 5, 6

2.0 Project Constraints

Exam Objective	Chapter
2.1 Given a scenario, predict the impact of various constraint variables and influences throughout the project.	**2, 5, 6**
Common constraints	2, 5, 6
Influences	2, 5, 6
2.2 Explain the importance of risk strategies and activities.	2, 5, 6
Strategies	2, 5, 6
Risk activities	2, 5, 6

3.0 Communication & Change Management

Exam Objective	Chapter
3.1 Given a scenario, use the appropriate communication method.	**3, 5, 6**
Meetings	3, 5, 6
Email	3, 6
Fax	3
Instant messaging	3
Video conferencing	3, 5
Voice conferencing	3, 5
Face-to-face	3, 5
Text message	3, 6
Distribution of printed media	3, 6
Social media	3, 5, 6

Exam Objective	Chapter
Business continuity response	3, 6
Incident response	3, 5
Resource changes	3
3.4 Given a scenario, use the following change control process within the context of a project.	**3, 5, 6**
Change control process	3, 5, 6
Types of common project changes	3, 5, 6
3.5 Recognize types of organizational change.	**3, 5, 6**
Business merger/acquisition	3, 5, 6
Business demerger/split	3, 5, 6
Business process change	3, 6
Internal reorganization	3, 5, 6
Relocation	3, 5
Outsourcing	3, 5, 6

4.0 Project Tools & Documentation

Exam Objective	Chapter
4.1 Compare and contrast various project management tools.	**2, 4, 5, 6**
Project scheduling software	4, 6
Charts	4, 5, 6
Dashboard/status report	4
Knowledge management tools	4, 5
Performance measurement tools	4, 6

Exam Objective	Chapter
SWOT analysis	2, 4, 5, 6
Responsible, Accountable, Consulted, Informed (RACI) Matrix	2, 4, 6
4.2 Given a scenario, analyze project centric documentation.	**4, 5, 6**
Project charter	4, 5
Project management plan	4, 6
Issues log	4
Organizational chart	4, 5, 6
Scope statement	4, 5
Communication plan	4, 5
Project schedule	4, 6
Status report	4, 5
Dashboard information	4, 6
Action items	4
Meeting agenda/meeting minutes	4, 5, 6
4.3 Identify common partner or vendor-centric documents and their purpose.	**2, 4, 5, 6**
Request for Information	2, 4, 5, 6
Request for Proposal	2, 4
Request for Quote	2, 4, 6
Mutually binding documents	2, 4, 5, 6

Chapter

1

Project Basics (Domain 1.0)

THE FOLLOWING COMPTIA PROJECT+ EXAM OBJECTIVES ARE COVERED IN THIS CHAPTER:

✓ **1.1 Summarize the properties of a project.**

- Temporary

- Start and finish

- Unique

- Reason/purpose

- Project as part of a program

- Project as part of a portfolio

✓ **1.2 Classify project roles and responsibilities.**

- Sponsor/champion

  - Approval authority

    - Funding

    - Project charter

    - Baseline

    - High-level requirements

  - Control

  - Marketing

  - Roadblocks

  - Business case/justification

- Project manager

  - Manage team, communication, scope, risk, budget, and time

  - Manage quality assurance

  - Responsible for artifacts

- Project coordinator
  - Support project manager
  - Cross-functional coordination
  - Documentation/administrative support
  - Time/resource scheduling
  - Check for quality
- Stakeholder
  - Vested interest
  - Provide input and requirements
  - Project steering
  - Expertise
- Scheduler
  - Develop and maintain project schedule
  - Communicate timeline and changes
  - Reporting schedule performance
  - Solicit task status from resources
- Project team
  - Contribute expertise to the project
  - Contribute deliverables according to schedule
  - Estimation of task duration
  - Estimation of costs and dependencies
- Project Management Office (PMO)
  - Sets standards and practices for organization
  - Sets deliverables
  - Provides governance
  - Key performance indicators and parameters
  - Provides tools
  - Outlines consequences of non-performance
  - Standard documentation/templates
  - Coordinate resources between projects

✓ **1.3 Compare and contrast standard project phases.**

- Initiation
    - Project charter
    - Business case
    - High-level scope definition
    - High-level risks
- Planning
    - Schedule
    - Work breakdown structure
    - Resources
    - Detailed risks
    - Requirements
    - Communication plan
    - Procurement plan
    - Change management plan
    - Budget
- Execution
    - Deliverables
- Monitor and control
    - Risks/issues log
    - Performance measuring and reporting
    - Quality assurance/governance
    - Change control
    - Budget
- Closing
    - Transition/integration plan
        - Training
    - Project sign off
    - Archive project documents
    - Lessons learned
    - Release resources
    - Close contracts

✓ **1.4 Identify the basics of project cost control.**

- Total project cost
- Expenditure tracking
- Expenditure reporting
- Burn rate
- Cost baseline/budget
  - Plan vs. actual

✓ **1.5 Identify common project team organizational structures.**

- Functional
  - Resources reporting to Functional Manager
  - Project Manager has limited or no authority
- Matrix
  - Authority is shared between Functional Managers and Project Managers
  - Resources assigned from Functional area to project
  - Project Manager authority ranges from weak to strong
- Projectized
  - Project Manager has full authority
  - Resources report to Project Manager
  - Ad hoc resources

✓ **1.6 Given a scenario, execute and develop project schedules.**

- Work breakdown structure
- Scheduling activities
  - Determine tasks
  - Determine task start/finish dates
  - Determine activity/task durations
  - Determine milestones
  - Set predecessors

- Set dependencies
- Sequence tasks
- Prioritize tasks
- Determine critical path
- Allocate resources
- Set baseline
- Set quality gates
- Set governance gates
  - Client sign off
  - Management approval
  - Legislative approval

✓ **1.7 Identify the basic aspects of the Agile methodology.**

- Readily adapt to new/changing requirements
- Iterative approach
- Continuous requirements gathering
- Establish a backlog
- Burndown charts
- Continuous feedback
- Sprint planning
- Daily standup meetings/SCRUM meetings
- SCRUM retrospective
- Self-organized and self-directed teams

✓ **1.8 Explain the importance of human resource, physical resource, and personnel management.**

- Resource management concepts
  - Shared resources
  - Dedicated resources
  - Resource allocation
  - Resource shortage
  - Resource overallocation
  - Low quality resources

- Benched resources
- Interproject dependencies
- Interproject resource contention
- Personnel management
  - Team building
  - Trust building
  - Team selection
  - Skill sets
  - Remote vs. in-house
  - Personnel removal/replacement
  - Communication issues
  - Conflict resolution
    - Smoothing
    - Forcing
    - Compromising
    - Confronting
    - Avoiding
    - Negotiating

1. What are the defining characteristics of a project? (Choose two.)
   - **A.** A group of related tasks
   - **B.** Temporary in nature
   - **C.** Operational activities
   - **D.** Reworking of an existing project
   - **E.** Creation of a unique product or service

2. The project team is responsible for all of the following EXCEPT
   - **A.** Providing governance on the project
   - **B.** Contributing to the deliverables according to the schedule
   - **C.** Contributing expertise to the project
   - **D.** Estimating costs and dependencies

3. What is a work breakdown structure?
   - **A.** A task-oriented decomposition of a project
   - **B.** A deliverable-oriented decomposition of a project
   - **C.** A graphic representation of tasks and their sequence
   - **D.** A high-level outline of milestones on a project

4. What elements are explained in a business case?
   - **A.** Justification by identifying the organizational benefits
   - **B.** Alternative solutions
   - **C.** Alignment to the strategic plan
   - **D.** All of the above
   - **E.** A and C

5. Of the following, which are considered key activities of the Monitor and Control phase?
   - **A.** Performance Measuring and Reporting
   - **B.** Develop the Quality Plan
   - **C.** Perform Quality Assurance
   - **D.** Monitor the Budget
   - **E.** Develop the Change Control Plan
   - **F.** Develop the Project Charter

6. What plan determines the information needs of the stakeholders, format of information delivery, delivery frequency, and the preparer?
   - **A.** Stakeholder Analysis Plan
   - **B.** Project Charter
   - **C.** Human Resources Plan
   - **D.** Communications Plan

7. Which type of cost estimating uses a mathematical model to compute costs?

    A. Top-down estimating

    B. Bottom-up estimating

    C. Parametric estimating

    D. Three-point estimating

8. A project has an earned value of $2,500 and an actual cost of $2,275. The cost variance for this project would be which of the following?

    A. $2,275

    B. $225

    C. $2,500

    D. $-225

9. During an Agile daily stand-up meeting, what are three questions that are asked and answered?

    A. What did I accomplish yesterday? What will I do today? What are the necessary next steps?

    B. What did I accomplish today? Who will I be working with today? What obstacles are preventing progress?

    C. What did I accomplish yesterday? Who will I be working with today? What obstacles are preventing progress?

    D. What did I accomplish yesterday? What will I do today? What obstacles are preventing progress?

10. Marcus works for Wigitcom, and he has been assigned to work on a project. Marcus's regular boss pulls him back to work on assignments and will conduct his performance review. What type of organizational structure is Wigitcom using?

    A. Agile

    B. Functional

    C. Matrix

    D. Projectized

11. A project has a key contributor who is absent from meetings, not meeting deadlines, and affecting the morale of other individuals on a team. There is no other person within the company with the expertise needed to perform the tasks assigned to this team member. Which of the following would be the appropriate action for the project manager?

    A. Bring the team member in for a counseling session.

    B. Leave the employee alone and distribute work to other team members.

    C. Remove the team member from the project and seek a replacement.

    D. Relocate the team member to a different facility.

12. The high-level scope definition describes which of the following?

    A. High-level deliverables of the project

    B. Objectives of the project

   C. Reason for the project

   D. All of the above

13. In what project phase are the majority of the processes and project documents created?

   A. Initiation

   B. Planning

   C. Execution

   D. Monitor and Control

   E. Closing

14. Which component of the project charter describes the characteristics of the product produced by the project?

   A. Project description

   B. Business case

   C. Deliverables

   D. Quality plan

15. What are the three types of estimates used in three-point estimates?

   A. Fastest Schedule, Least Resources, Most Desirable

   B. Most Likely, Optimistic, Pessimistic

   C. Most Likely, Least Resources, Fastest Schedule

   D. Fastest Schedule, Optimistic, Most Desirable

16. In what organizational structure does a project manager have the most limited authority?

   A. Weak-matrix

   B. Projectized

   C. Strong-matrix

   D. Functional

17. A building project requires the following steps: construction, purchasing the build site, blueprinting, and inspection. Purchasing the build site has what relationship to construction?

   A. It is a successor task.

   B. It is a mandatory task.

   C. It is a predecessor task.

   D. It is a discretionary task.

18. Which of the following is the form in which project schedules are typically displayed?

   A. PERT

   B. Calendar

   C. Gantt chart

   D. Pareto chart

19. In what project phase is the influence of stakeholders the least effective?

    A. Initiation

    B. Planning

    C. Execution

    D. Monitor and Control

20. When the project team is dependent on an entity outside the organization, like a product vendor delivering equipment, this is known as what type of dependency?

    A. Discretionary

    B. Mandatory

    C. External

    D. Financial

21. Which conflict resolution technique produces a win-lose result for the parties?

    A. Forcing

    B. Confronting

    C. Avoiding

    D. Attacking

22. A project has task A, which will take 2 days; task B, which will take 3 days, task C, which will take 2 days; task D, which will take 2 days; and task E, which will take 3 days. Task A is a predecessor for task B and for task C. Task C is a predecessor for task D. Both task B and task D are predecessors for task E.

What is the task sequence for the critical path?

    A. A => B => E

    B. A => B => C => D => E

    C. A => B => D => E

    D. A => C => D => E

23. All of the following are aspects of an Agile sprint, EXCEPT

    A. It is limited to a timeframe such as two weeks.

    B. A planning meeting is held to figure out what the team can accomplish.

    C. A small feature set is taken to completion.

    D. The team works at an incredible pace for the entire time.

24. April works for Wigitcom and has recently been assigned to a project. She was given assignments from both her functional manager and the project manager, but was directed to do the project work. When April requested leave, it was granted by her functional manager, but then denied by the project manager. What type of organizational structure is Wigitcom using?

    A. Projectized

    B. Strong-matrix

    C. Balanced-matrix

    D. Weak-matrix

25. During the Closing phase of the project, what two activities are conducted?

    A. Accept project deliverables and perform quality assurance.

    B. Finalize project work and close all vendor contracts.

    C. Manage stakeholder expectations and close all vendor contracts.

    D. Finalize project work and perform quality assurance.

26. In which project phase is the kickoff meeting typically held?

    A. Initiation

    B. Planning

    C. Execution

    D. Monitor and Control

    E. Closing

27. Chase is a project manager, and he has released all of the team members from the project, closed vendor contracts, and archived project documents. In what phase is the project?

    A. Initiation

    B. Planning

    C. Execution

    D. Monitor and Control

    E. Closing

28. What are governance gates?

    A. A checkpoint between project phases where approval is obtained to move forward

    B. A checkpoint where quality is checked against a previously established criterion

    C. Checkpoints at the beginning and end of the project only

    D. After a project governor is appointed, unplanned interruptions from this project sponsor

29. What are the defining characteristics of a project? (Choose two.)

    A. Has a definitive start and end date

    B. Is assigned to a portfolio

    C. Creates a unique product or service

    D. Is a part of ongoing operational activities

    E. Is part of an organization's strategic plan

30. Which of the following describes a portfolio?

    A. A collection of the sample work a project manager has done that should be brought to an interview

    B. A collection of programs, subportfolios, and projects that support strategic business goals or objectives

    C. A group of related projects that are managed together using shared resources and similar techniques

    D. A group of project investments that are maintained to help finance projects

31. The project charter is prepared and agreed to in which project phase?
    A. Planning
    B. Closing
    C. Execution
    D. Initiation

32. After the project charter is signed, what meeting is held to introduce the project team and stakeholders as well as outlining the goals for the project?
    A. Lessons learned meeting
    B. Project introductory meeting
    C. Kickoff meeting
    D. Team building lunch

33. Which soft skills are important for a project manager?
    A. Time management, earned value calculation, listening, critical path diagrams
    B. Leadership, time management, team building, listening
    C. Time management, earned value calculation, leadership, critical path diagrams
    D. Leadership, following, independence, listening

34. Work produced in the high-level risk assessment should be documented in which of the following?
    A. Work breakdown structure
    B. Project charter
    C. Risk register
    D. Quality control plan

35. A project schedule serves what function?
    A. Determines the project cost accounting codes
    B. Creates a deliverable-based decomposition of the project
    C. Lists the actions that should be resolved to fulfill deliverables
    D. Determines start and finish dates for project activities

36. Analogous estimating is where the cost-estimate is developed by which of the following?
    A. Using a mathematical model to compute costs for the project
    B. Calculating the cost of each activity in the work breakdown structure
    C. Using a similar, past project to develop a high-level estimate
    D. Averaging three different estimates of the project cost

37. All of the following are ways to determine whether a project is completed, EXCEPT
    A. When the project manager declares the project is complete
    B. When the project is canceled

    C.   When it has been determined that the goals and objectives of the project cannot be accomplished

    D.   When the objectives are accomplished and stakeholders are satisfied

38. Money actually spent for a specific timeframe for complete work is known as which of the following?

    A.   Cost variance

    B.   Planned value

    C.   Actual cost

    D.   Earned value

39. The creation of a peanut butter and jelly sandwich has the following steps:

Serve

Gather bread, peanut butter, and jelly

Place bread on a plate

Get a knife

Spread peanut butter on one slice of bread

Put both slices of bread together

Spread jelly on the other slice of bread

What is the correct sequence for this project?

    A.   Serve; put both slices of bread together; gather bread, peanut butter, and jelly; get a knife; spread peanut butter on one slice of bread; place bread on a plate; spread jelly on the other slice of bread.

    B.   Gather bread, peanut butter. and jelly; get a knife; spread peanut butter on one slice of bread; place bread on a plate; spread jelly on the other slice of bread; serve; put both slices of bread together.

    C.   Gather bread, peanut butter, and jelly; get a knife; place bread on a plate; spread peanut butter on one slice of bread; spread jelly on the other slice of bread; put both slices of bread together; serve.

    D.   Gather bread, peanut butter, and jelly; get a knife; place bread on a plate; spread peanut butter on one slice of bread; spread jelly on the other slice of bread; serve; put both slices of bread together.

40. Which of the following steps are important in the development of the project schedule? (Choose three.)

    A.   Determine tasks

    B.   Set the quality plan

    C.   Set the communication plan

    D.   Sequence the tasks

    E.   Construct a Pareto diagram

    F.   Identify the critical path

41. Not including time off, holidays, or nonproject work, the total time involved for an individual to complete a task is known as which of the following?

    A. Analogous estimating

    B. SWAG

    C. Work effort estimate

    D. SPI

42. Resource allocation, including assigned equipment, team members, and money to support a project, occurs in which project phase?

    A. Initiation

    B. Planning

    C. Execution

    D. Monitor and Control

    E. Closing

43. A project manager is having problems with one team member who is being insubordinate. The project manager approaches the team member to find out what is going on and determines that a change can be made now that the facts are known. This is an example of which of the following?

    A. Forcing

    B. Avoiding

    C. Confronting

    D. Smoothing

44. Which of the following are tools and techniques used for developing a project team? (Choose three.)

    A. Team-building activities

    B. Project requirements

    C. Recognition and rewards

    D. Lessons learned meetings

    E. Setting the ground rules

    F. Project kickoff meetings

45. In what stage of team development are teams the most productive and trust levels the highest among team members?

    A. Forming

    B. Storming

    C. Norming

    D. Performing

    E. Adjourning

46. Wigitcom has a project where quality is the most important consideration for the sponsor. Which personnel model would make the most sense for this project?

    A. Outsourcing

    B. Collocation

    C. Virtual teams

    D. Videoconferencing

47. A startup company is attempting to compete in an emerging product market. There are constant disruptive technology changes, and the market is shifting in their product tastes. This type of situation would be best served by which of the following?

    A. Agile approach

    B. Projectized environment

    C. Functional environment

    D. Traditional, or waterfall

48. Kayla works for Wigitcom, and she has been assigned to work on a project. Kayla's project manager gives her direction, and consistently prevents Kayla's regular supervisor from giving her any assignments. At the end of the project, the project manager will conduct Kayla's performance review. What type of organizational structure is Wigitcom using?

    A. Agile

    B. Functional

    C. Matrix

    D. Projectized

49. In an Agile methodology, what is a user story?

    A. Key information about stakeholders and their jobs

    B. Short stories about someone using the product or service

    C. Customer survey results after product release

    D. Visual representation of product burndown

50. A large, well-established organization that has been in business for many decades would likely have which organizational structures?

    A. Weak-matrix

    B. Projectized

    C. Strong-matrix

    D. Functional

51. What does PMP stand for?

    A. Preferred master project

    B. Preferred management plan

    C. Project management plan

    D. Project management practice

52. What is a list of all things to be completed, whether technical or user-centric in nature, which are in the form of user stories, known as?

    A. Requirements

    B. Backlog

    C. Risk register

    D. Stakeholders

53. What are the standard project phases?

    A. Discovery, Planning, Building, Quality Check, Closing

    B. Initiation, Preparing, Building, Monitor and Control, Wrap-up

    C. Initiation, Planning, Execution, Monitor and Control, Closing

    D. Discovery, Preparing, Execution, Quality Check, Wrap-up

54. What are milestones?

    A. A measure of the distance traveled on a project

    B. Characteristics of deliverables that must be met

    C. Checkpoints on a project to determine Go/No-Go decisions

    D. Major events in a project used to measure progress

55. Which type of cost estimating is done by assigning a cost estimate to each work package in the project?

    A. Top-down estimating

    B. Bottom-up estimating

    C. Parametric estimating

    D. Three-point estimating

56. Developing the project team involves all of the following, EXCEPT

    A. Developing a team that lasts longer than the project

    B. Creating a positive environment for team members

    C. Creating an effective, functioning, and coordinated group

    D. Increasing the team's competency levels

57. All of the following are types of dependencies, EXCEPT

    A. Mandatory

    B. Discretionary

    C. External

    D. Backlog

58. A stakeholder has asked to add a change to a project, but the request is rejected by the project manager. What is the likely reason the scope was rejected?

   A. There is interaction between constraints.

   B. Scope creep is occurring on the project.

   C. The request can be handled without the formality.

   D. The sponsor is on vacation.

59. The characteristics of the lower-level WBS include all of the following, EXCEPT

   A. WBS components are a further decomposition of project deliverables.

   B. WBS components should always happen concurrently with determining major deliverables.

   C. WBS components should be tangible and verifiable.

   D. WBS components should be organized in terms of project organization.

60. A project manager meets with upset team members to listen to their concerns. After hearing their concerns, the project manager makes some of the team members' recommendations in exchange for the team members accepting other rules. This is an example of which of the following?

   A. Forcing

   B. Compromising

   C. Confronting

   D. Smoothing

61. A company is expanding and has several projects underway. One project is building a new wing on the headquarters building, and the other is installing a new high-speed fiber network. The framing of the new building must begin before the installation of the new network can begin. This is an example of what type of logical relationship?

   A. Finish-to-finish

   B. Start-to-start

   C. Finish-to-start

   D. Start-to-finish

62. A project has task A, which will take 2 days; task B which will take 3 days; task C, which will take 2 days; task D, which will take 2 days; and task E, which will take 3 days. Task A is a predecessor for task B and for task C. Task C is a predecessor for task D. Both task B and task D are predecessors for task E.

   What is the duration of the critical path?

   A. 7 days

   B. 9 days

   C. 10 days

   D. 11 days

63. In what project artifact would you find information relating to the quality and availability of resources?

   A. Project schedule

   B. Organization chart

   C. Resource calendar

   D. Risk register

64. In which of the following situations would team-building efforts provide the most impact on a project? (Choose three.)

   A. Team discord

   B. Schedule changes

   C. Missed deliverables

   D. Project phase completion

   E. Lessons learned meeting

   F. Change in project manager

65. An organization needs to add vendor resources to a project, but they do not have the physical space to house the team. What approach should the organization use for their personnel management?

   A. Deploy projectized teams

   B. Deploy functional teams

   C. Use in-house teams

   D. Use remote teams

66. Nyssa works for Wigitcom and has been assigned to a project. She wants to take a week off for a family reunion, which conflicts with a project deadline. The project manager denied her leave request, but her functional manager lets her attend the family reunion. What type of organizational structure is Wigitcom using?

   A. Projectized

   B. Strong-matrix

   C. Balanced-matrix

   D. Weak-matrix

67. When is a project considered to be a success?

   A. Stakeholder expectations have been met.

   B. The phase completion has been approved.

   C. All project phases have been completed.

   D. The vendor has been released from the project.

68. Which of the following in an example of a deliverable?

   A. The date work on the project begins

   B. The design for a new product

C. Time and materials applied to the project

D. PMO

69. A project sponsor would be responsible for all of the following, EXCEPT

A. Developing high-level requirements for the project

B. Functioning as the approval authority and removing roadblocks

C. Marketing the project across the organization

D. Estimating the costs and dependencies of the project activities

E. Serving to help control the direction of the project

70. What elements are explained in a business case?

A. Justification by identifying the organizational benefits

B. Alternative solutions

C. Alignment to the strategic plan

D. All of the above

E. A and C

71. All projects are constrained by which three elements as they affect quality?

A. Time, budget, scope

B. Time, risks, budget

C. Cost, benefits, scope

D. Cost, risks, scope

72. What key milestone is triggered when the project charter is signed?

A. A project sponsor can now be chosen.

B. Key stakeholders are freed from project communication.

C. The project is authorized to begin.

D. Project resources are released from the project.

73. The Closing processes include all of the following, EXCEPT

A. Archiving of project documents

B. Release of project members

C. Review of lessons learned

D. Monitoring of the risks and issues log

74. All of the following are examples of project resources, EXCEPT

A. Team members

B. Equipment

C. WBS

D. Materials

75. Analogous estimating is also referred to as which of the following?

    A. Top-down estimating

    B. Bottom-up estimating

    C. Parametric estimating

    D. Three-point estimating

76. Earned value is an indication of which of the following?

    A. The actual cost of completing work in a specific timeframe

    B. The cost of work that has been authorized and budgeted

    C. The value of the work completed to date compared to the budgeted amount

    D. The total sum of sales earned at project completion

77. Fast-tracking a project is a technique involving which of the following?

    A. Performing two tasks in parallel that were previously scheduled to start sequentially

    B. Looking at cost and schedule trade-offs such as adding more resources

    C. Moving later deliverables to earlier phases to appease stakeholders

    D. Removing critical path activities that are unnecessary

78. Deliverables are an output of which of which phase?

    A. Initiation

    B. Planning

    C. Execution

    D. Monitor and Control

    E. Closing

79. What does a resource shortage mean?

    A. There is a shortage of things for team members to work on.

    B. Not enough resources are available for the task, leading to over allocation.

    C. There are too many resources, leading to under-allocation.

    D. There is an abundancy of things for team members to work on.

80. In what stage of team development do the members stop working with one another and return to their functional jobs?

    A. Forming

    B. Storming

    C. Norming

    D. Performing

    E. Adjourning

81. Wigitcom has a project where cost is the most important consideration for the sponsor. Which personnel model would make the most sense for the project?

    A. Premium team assignments

    B. Collocation

    C. Virtual teams

    D. Videoconferencing

82. Where would the following information be found: types of contracts the project will use, authority of the project team, and information on how multiple vendors will be managed?

    A. Budget

    B. Procurement plan

    C. WBS

    D. Detailed risks

83. An organization that has a fixed budget and offers a stable environment would be best suited for which type of project management approach?

    A. Traditional, or waterfall

    B. Projectized environment

    C. Agile approach

    D. Functional environment

84. All of the following are phases of a project, EXCEPT

    A. Planning

    B. Closing

    C. Development

    D. Execution

85. What does a change control board (CCB) do to support the project?

    A. Helps vet and manage changes to the scope

    B. Provides an accounting structure for tasks

    C. Sets the standards and templates for the project

    D. Sets the costs of quality for the project

86. Which project role is responsible for coordinating resources between projects?

    A. Project management office (PMO)

    B. Project coordinator

    C. Project manager

    D. Project scheduler

87. When does an item move from the risk register to the issue log?
    A. As soon as the risk as identified
    B. When the risk is triggered
    C. Never
    D. In the creation of the project plan

88. A team member is upset about having to stay late because he will miss a Scouts meeting with his son. He approaches the project manager, who lets him know that it is a one-time thing, and if they work that night they will not have to come in on the weekend. Though upset, the team member stays and finishes his work. This is an example of what type of conflict resolution?
    A. Smoothing
    B. Confronting
    C. Compromising
    D. Avoiding
    E. Forcing

89. When should employee performance expectations be set on a project?
    A. Lessons learned meeting
    B. Employee performance review
    C. Stakeholder identification meeting
    D. First meeting with a new team member

90. All of the following are used in an Agile approach to project management, EXCEPT
    A. Burndown charts
    B. WBS
    C. Continuous requirements gathering
    D. Sprint planning

91. A company decides to bring in a team from outside the organization to assist on the project, instead of using company employees. This is an example of which of the following?
    A. Insourcing
    B. Outsourcing
    C. Layoffs
    D. Collocation

92. Teams normally go through a similar development cycle. Which is the correct order of those stages?
    A. Norming, Forming, Storming, Adjourning, Performing
    B. Forming, Storming, Norming, Performing, Adjourning
    C. Forming, Norming, Performing, Storming, Adjourning
    D. Norming, Storming, Forming, Adjourning, Performing

93. In the development of project schedule, the need to set governance gates is important. All of the following are examples of governance gates, EXCEPT
   A. Daily standup meetings
   B. Client sign-off
   C. Management approval
   D. Legislative approval

94. Which project role outlines the consequences of nonperformance?
   A. Project manager
   B. Project coordinator
   C. Project scheduler
   D. Project management office

95. A building project requires the following steps: construction, purchasing the build site, blueprinting, and inspection. Construction has what relationship to blueprinting?
   A. It is a successor task.
   B. It is a mandatory task.
   C. It is a predecessor task.
   D. It is a discretionary task.

96. The types of organizational structures include which of the following? (Choose three.)
   A. Agile
   B. Functional
   C. Matrix
   D. Colocation
   E. Projectized

97. A construction company is in the middle of a project to build a guest room on a house. The EV value for the project is $7,000, and the actual cost for the project is $9,500. Select the CV for the project and its meaning.
   A. $2,500 and the project is under budget
   B. -$2,500 and the project is under budget
   C. $2,500 and the project is over budget
   D. -$2,500 and the project is over budget

98. The Closing phase of a project serves what critical purpose?
   A. Formal acceptance and turnover to ongoing maintenance and support
   B. Performing governance activities and turnover to ongoing maintenance and support
   C. Formal acceptance and producing deliverables
   D. Performing governance activities and producing deliverables

99. A project management office (PMO) has which of the following responsibilities? (Choose three.)

   A. Markets the project across the business

   B. Provides governance for projects

   C. Manages the team, communication, scope, risk, budget, and time of the project

   D. Maintains standard documentation and templates

   E. Establishes key performance indicators and parameters

   F. Develops and maintains the project schedule

100. Which project role helps to market the need and success of the project and provides a level of control for funding?

   A. Project sponsor or champion

   B. Project manager

   C. Project coordinator

   D. Project scheduler

101. In terms of project management, what is a program?

   A. A listing of all individuals involved in the project, including key stakeholders

   B. The software package used to enter and track project management aspects

   C. Related projects that are coordinated and managed with similar techniques

   D. A collection of projects and subportfolios that support the strategic goals of the business

102. This role supports the project manager, performs cross-functional coordination, conducts time and resource scheduling, and checks for quality. What role is it?

   A. Project sponsor or champion

   B. Project manager

   C. Project coordinator

   D. Project scheduler

103. Which of the following is the measure of the cost efficiency of budgeted resources, expressed as a ratio?

   A. AC

   B. EV

   C. CPI

   D. SPI

104. A government agency is working to launch a new service. Members of the project team are required to report to both the project manager and their functional manager, who share authority for the resources. What type of organizational structure is this?

   A. Projectized

   B. Strong-matrix

C. Balanced-matrix

D. Weak-matrix

105. When breaking down project deliverables, what is the lowest level that is recorded in a WBS?

A. Daily work schedules

B. High-level requirements

C. Work package

D. Major milestones

106. Which of the following are conflict resolution techniques? (Choose two.)

A. Threatening

B. Smoothing

C. Storming

D. Norming

E. Negotiating

107. In what stage of team development do team members begin to confront each other and vie for position and control?

A. Forming

B. Storming

C. Norming

D. Performing

E. Adjourning

108. A company is expanding and has several projects underway. One project is constructing a new wing on the headquarters building, and the other is installing a new high-speed fiber network. The framing of the new building must be completed before the installation of the new network can begin. This is an example of which of the following?

A. Interproject resource contention

B. Start-to-Finish relationship

C. Interproject resource dependencies

D. Dedicated resources

109. Robert is assigned to work on a project. One of his tasks is to reach out to resources and solicit task status on the progress of the project. Robert is most likely which of the following?

A. Project manager

B. Project team member

C. Project scheduler

D. Project coordinator

110. In an Agile approach to project management, what is a backlog?

    A. Delayed work that is cause by bottlenecks

    B. Customer prioritized functionality list that still needs to be added to the product

    C. Inventory not added to the project because of shipping delays

    D. A daily meeting focusing on three questions

111. What factors should be considered when scheduling a video or telephone conference?

    A. Ensure meeting room has sufficient seating.

    B. Check whether team members are introverted or extroverted.

    C. Recognize the different time zones/schedules being used.

    D. Make writing materials available in the room.

112. Nestor is a project manager assigned to build a new branch office for a bank. The branch office will be of a similar size and design as another branch office. He has been asked to create cost and schedule estimates and to follow the bank's best practices for projects. Whose responsibility is it to help Nestor with this effort?

    A. Project sponsor

    B. Project management office

    C. Project team

    D. Project scheduler

113. During the initiation phase, what are two activities that should be performed?

    A. Developing the project charter and project kickoff meeting

    B. Holding the project kickoff meeting and identifying the stakeholders

    C. Developing the project charter and stakeholder identification

    D. Creating the project plan and develop the project charter

114. Where would an organization document the results of their buy versus build analysis?

    A. WBS

    B. Budget

    C. Change management plan

    D. Procurement plan

115. All of the following techniques can be used to estimate the duration of an activity, except

    A. Expert judgment

    B. Three-point estimating

    C. Analogous estimating

    D. Pareto diagramming

116. Which role of the project is responsible for working to create the deliverables according to the project schedule?

    A. Project stakeholders

    B. Project team members

    C. Project scheduler

    D. Project coordinator

117. Which type of cost estimation uses a mathematical model to compute costs?

    A. Top-down estimating

    B. Bottom-up estimating

    C. Parametric estimating

    D. Three-point estimating

118. Which of the following project documents are created during the Execution phase? (Choose two.)

    A. Project charter

    B. Communication plan

    C. Issues log

    D. Lessons learned

    E. Action items

119. Project managers should spend how much of their time communicating?

    A. Up to 40%

    B. Up to 50%

    C. Up to 75%

    D. Up to 90%

120. A project stakeholder has which of the following responsibilities?

    A. Documentation and administrative support, estimation of task duration, soliciting task status from resources, expertise

    B. Vested interest, providing input and requirements, project steering, expertise

    C. Documentation and administrative support, providing input and requirements, project steering, expertise

    D. Vested interest, providing input and requirements, cross-functional coordination, expertise

121. Jenny works for a company undertaking a project. She will ultimately benefit from the service created and would like to share her thoughts and input on how it should be created. She is also a subject-matter expert in the product area. Jenny is most likely which of the following?

    A. Project stakeholder

    B. Project champion

    C. Project sponsor

    D. Member of the PMO

122. The following deliverables/activities all occur in the Initiation phase, EXCEPT

    A. Project sign-off

    B. Project charter

    C. Business case

    D. High-level risks

123. High-level risk identification is the responsibility of which of the following?

    A. Project sponsor

    B. Project manager

    C. Project coordinator

    D. Project team

124. Which of the following project documents are created during the Planning phase of a project? (Choose three.)

    A. Status reports

    B. Communication plan

    C. Organizational chart

    D. Lessons learned

    E. Project schedule

    F. Action items

125. Which project role is responsible for all project artifacts like project plans, meeting minutes, and project delivery?

    A. Project coordinator

    B. Scheduler

    C. Project team

    D. Project manager

126. What are project requirements?

    A. A measure of the distance traveled on a project

    B. Characteristics of deliverables that must be met

    C. Checkpoints on a project to determine Go/No-Go

    D. Major events in a project used to measure progress

127. What are critical elements that need to be included in the project schedule?

    A. Define activities, sequence activities, estimate resources, estimate duration

    B. Define activities, budget activities, estimate resources, estimate completion

    C. Budget activities, estimate resources, determine milestones, estimate completion

    D. Develop schedule, determine completion date, check stakeholder assumptions, conduct feasibility assessment

128. In which phase is the project kickoff meeting held?

    A. Initiation

    B. Planning

    C. Execution

    D. Monitor and Control

    E. Closing

129. Determining the burn rate and measuring costs to the baseline are elements of what activity?

   A. Expenditure tracking

   B. Spending plan

   C. Parametric estimating

   D. Cost accounting

130. Which of the following is the sprint planning meeting used to do?

   A. Get a head start on the work needed for the project

   B. Prepare the project charter and kickoff meeting

   C. Set a realistic backlog of items completed during this iteration

   D. Set the communication and quality plans for the project

131. What is the indication of how fast a project is spending its budget?

   A. Fast-tracking

   B. Expenditure tracking

   C. Crashing

   D. Burn rate

132. The project manager has the following responsibilities (choose two):

   A. Managing quality assurance

   B. Setting key performance indicators and parameters

   C. Estimating task duration

   D. Managing the team, communication, scope, risk, budget, and time

133. The high-level scope definition should be included in which project document?

   A. Communication plan

   B. Project schedule

   C. Project charter

   D. Lessons learned

134. Which of the following is the main activity of the Execution phase?

   A. Performance measuring and reporting

   B. Creating and verifying deliverables

   C. Key stakeholder identification

   D. Determining needed project resources

135. You would expect the WBS dictionary to contain all of the following information, EXCEPT

   A. Explanations of team member's roles and responsibilities

   B. Description of the work of the component

   C. Quality requirements

   D. Required resources

136. In what step would the make-or-buy decision occur?

    A. During the design of the product or service

    B. In the creation of the procurement plan

    C. In the execution of the project plan

    D. During the kickoff meeting

137. All of the following are cost-estimating techniques, EXCEPT

    A. Bottom-up estimating

    B. Program Evaluation and Review Technique (PERT)

    C. Parametric estimating

    D. Analogous estimating

138. The EV for a project is 900 and AC is 1100. The CPI for the project would be which of the following?

    A. .82

    B. 1.22

    C. −200

    D. 200

139. In what type of organizational structure would resources report solely to the project manager?

    A. Weak-matrix

    B. Projectized

    C. Strong-matrix

    D. Functional

140. Predecessor and successor tasks can have four possible logical relationships. Which of the following is not one of them?

    A. Finish-to-finish

    B. Start-to-deferred

    C. Finish-to-start

    D. Start-to-finish

141. What aspect of project management is shared with Agile and other approaches?

    A. Sprint planning

    B. Self-organized and self-directed teams

    C. Iterative approach

    D. Adaptive to new/changing requirements

142. A scope management plan contains which of the following elements? (Choose three.)

    A. Process for creating the schedule

    B. Process for creating the scope statement

    C. Definition of how the deliverables will be validated

    D. Process for creating, maintaining, and approving the WBS

    E. Process for creating the budget

143. A project team member is not meeting deadlines, and she is starting to be tardy in showing up for work. The project manager meets with her and inquires as to what is going on. The team member replies that she wants to do good work, but that she doesn't seem to have the skills needed for certain tasks. They agree to get the team member a mentor for those tasks. This is an example of what type of conflict resolution?

   A. Smoothing

   B. Forcing

   C. Compromising

   D. Confronting

   E. Avoiding

144. In terms of resource assignments, which best describes how resources are assigned in a projectized environment?

   A. Resources are assigned on an ad hoc basis.

   B. Resources are assigned from a functional area to the project.

   C. Resources must be outsourced.

   D. Resources must not be collocated.

145. A software company has a project team working to establish a new platform. What mechanism would the company use to protect their intellectual property?

   A. OBS

   B. NDA

   C. IMS

   D. COQ

146. When would an Adaptive method be preferable to a more rigid project management style?

   A. In a mature organization with defined processes

   B. When the scope can be easily and thoroughly defined

   C. Where small incremental improvements offer no value to stakeholders

   D. When an organization is dealing with a rapidly changing environment

147. When evaluating the project phases, in which phase will project costs be the highest?

   A. Initiation

   B. Planning

   C. Execution

   D. Monitor and Control

   E. Closing

148. As a project approaches a critical deadline, Ed contacts the project manager about taking a few days off. The project manager needs Ed's skills to meet the deadline but can see how exhausted Ed has become. They agree that Ed will work through the deadline, and then get a couple of days off after that. Ed accepts this plan and goes back to work. This is an example of what type of conflict resolution?

   A. Smoothing

   B. Confronting

   C. Compromising

   D. Avoiding

   E. Forcing

149. Adric was recently assigned to a project at Wigitcom. He received task assignments from both the project manager and his normal supervisor. He is notified that both the project manager and the supervisor will contribute to his performance review. What type of organizational structure is Wigitcom using?

   A. Projectized

   B. Strong-matrix

   C. Balanced-matrix

   D. Weak-matrix

150. Wigitcom has a mobile geolocation application that was released last year. They are now working on the latest quarterly release of the application, which has minor updates and bug fixes. Which of the following statements is true regarding the geolocation application effort? (Pick all of the answers that are true.)

   A. This is a project because there are minor changes to the application.

   B. This not a project because the regular releases are a continuing effort.

   C. This is a project because this effort is temporary in nature.

   D. This is not a project because the product being produced is not unique.

151. An iterative, incremental approach to managing the activities on a project in a highly flexible manner is referred to as

   A. Waterfall methodology

   B. Matrixed management

   C. Projectized

   D. Agile methodology

152. A project has a team member who is absent from meetings, is not meeting deadlines, and is affecting the morale of other individuals on a team. The appropriate action for the project manager would be which of the following?

   A. Bring the team member in for a counseling session.

   B. Leave the employee alone and distribute work to other team members.

   C. Remove the team member from the project and seek a replacement.

   D. Relocate the team member to a different facility.

153. The Widget Company has a project team located in various cities across the same continent. There is an urgent update that needs to be sent to the entire project team. What would be the most effective way to send the communication?

   A. Phone calls

   B. Memo

   C. Email

   D. Videoconferencing

154. In what stage of team development are team members brought together and introduced to each other?

A. Forming

B. Storming

C. Norming

D. Performing

E. Adjourning

155. A project manager listens to the concerns of two team members who are upset with each other. After asking questions, listening, and getting them to talk with each other, the project manager gains agreement on a vested interest for all parties and work resumes. The team members agree to start behaving accordingly. This is an example of which of the following?

A. Negotiating

B. Compromising

C. Confronting

D. Avoiding

156. Benched resources is when the project has which of the following issues?

A. Individuals who are finished with the project but haven't yet started a new assignment

B. Individuals who have too much work for them to be able to complete the project

C. A lack of talent in the industry, which leads to a shortage of qualified personnel on the project

D. Individuals ordered to the sidelines because of their performance

157. Tiffany is the only digital marketer assigned to the project, but only 60 percent of her time is available to the project. There is enough work for a person assigned 100 percent of the time to the project, so Tiffany is struggling to meet her deadlines. This is an example of which of the following?

A. Low-quality resources

B. Interdependencies

C. Dedicated resources

D. Resource overallocation

158. Amy has been assigned to a project and reports to Kim, the project manager. John, Amy's functional manager, also requires Amy to report to him. What type of resource is Amy?

A. Dedicated

B. Physical

C. Digital

D. Shared

159. Obtaining a sign-off on the design of a product would be an example of which type of dependency?

    A. Discretionary

    B. Mandatory

    C. External

    D. Financial

160. What part of a project request defines the reason for the project, the deliverables at a high level, and the project objectives?

    A. Work breakdown structure

    B. High-level risks

    C. Business case

    D. High-level scope definition

161. High-level risk assessment includes all of the following, EXCEPT

    A. Risk identification and rolled-up (or categorized) work-task groups

    B. Cost-benefit analysis weighing relative risks to potential gains

    C. High-level responses to mitigate impact

    D. Risk identification of all potential project alternatives

162. A project coordinator has which of the following responsibilities? (Choose two.)

    A. Approval authority for funding

    B. Support for the project manager

    C. Time and resource scheduling

    D. Contribution of expertise to the project

    E. Coordination of resources between projects

163. At the completion of a project sprint, the project team meets to examine what went well, what didn't go well, and what improvements could be made. This is an example of which of the following?

    A. Governance gates

    B. Product backlog

    C. Daily SCRUM

    D. SCRUM retrospective

164. The project team has completed all of the deliverables for the project. They have meetings scheduled to begin the handoff from the project team to the ongoing operations team. In what phase is the project at this point?

    A. Initiation

    B. Planning

    C. Execution

    D. Monitor and Control

    E. Closing

165. With an Agile methodology, all of the following are true with an adaptive life cycle, EXCEPT

    A. Requires a high degree of stakeholder involvement

    B. All requirements must be gathered up front

    C. Rapid iterations

    D. Fixed time and resources

166. Jessie does not like how the assignments are being delegated and confronts the project manager with his complaint. The project manager reinforces that this is the way it is done, and Jessie better start getting on board with the method because it isn't going to change. Jessie acknowledges the situation, goes back to work, and doesn't bring it up again. What type of conflict resolution is this?

    A. Negotiating

    B. Confronting

    C. Compromising

    D. Avoiding

    E. Forcing

167. Wigitcom has a group of projects all related to security widgets. They want to add a new product for security cameras and sell them to customers. The effort must be completed within the next three months to beat the competition to market. There is an established group of resources that work on security efforts. Which of the following is true about this effort? (Choose three.)

    A. This effort is not a project because security is already done.

    B. This effort is a project because the product being developed is unique.

    C. This effort is a project and will be a part of a program.

    D. There is no reason to make this effort because they already do security.

    E. This meets the requirements for a project because it creates a unique product and is temporary in nature.

168. What is a visual representation of how quickly requirements are being completed with each iteration called?

    A. Fishbone diagram

    B. Burndown chart

    C. Gantt chart

    D. Pareto diagram

169. A company is located in multiple cities across a continent, and the project will be staffed with team members from various cities. The decision is made to leave all of the team members in their home locations and use technology to aid in communication. This is an example of which of the following?

    A. Insourcing

    B. Outsourcing

    C. Virtual teams

    D. Collocation

170. The designer for your project is also assigned to several other projects. The other projects have similar targets for their milestones. What type of situation does this describe?

    A. Interproject resource contention

    B. Forcing

    C. Task sequencing

    D. Resource shortage

171. In what stage of team development do things begin to calm down because the team members become more comfortable with one another?

    A. Forming

    B. Storming

    C. Norming

    D. Performing

    E. Adjourning

172. A project manager is having problems with one team member who is being insubordinate. The project manager does not approach the team member and just tries to carry on as business as usual. This is an example of

    A. Forcing

    B. Avoiding

    C. Confronting

    D. Smoothing

173. Benched resources are

    A. Great for an organization since there is always staff to work on project

    B. Bad for an organization since there is always staff to work on a project

    C. Costly because individuals are being paid to sit around

    D. Inexpensive because individuals are not being paid when they sit around

174. As a project manager, a dedicated resource would be the ideal situation because

    A. The team member will continue to share time with his or her functional work.

    B. The project manager has full authority and controls time and tasks.

    C. The dedicated resource won't have to be paid overtime.

    D. Low-quality resources aren't assigned to a project.

175. When a dependency is directly related to the type of work on which it is being performed, it is what type of dependency?

    A. Discretionary

    B. Mandatory

    C. External

    D. Financial

176. The work breakdown structure is created during which project phase?

    A. Initiation

    B. Planning

    C. Execution

    D. Monitoring and Control

    E. Closing

177. Acceptance criteria reviews that are used across the project are known as which of the following?

    A. Critical to quality

    B. Quality gates

    C. Kanban boards

    D. Deliverables

178. Which of the following are ways to organize the WBS? (Choose three.)

    A. Critical path

    B. Subprojects

    C. Project phases

    D. Prioritized by risk

    E. Major deliverables

179. Duane is a senior resource assigned to the project, but he has begun to be short-tempered in meetings, rigid in his positions, and argumentative. The project manager approaches Duane, but an argument ensues and Duane walks out. The next day the project manager decides to give Duane space and not discuss his behavior or performance. This is an example of which of the following?

    A. Negotiating

    B. Confronting

    C. Compromising

    D. Avoiding

    E. Forcing

180. Wigitcom is faced with changes to scope and personnel on a project. What is the appropriate method to share this information with the stakeholders?

    A. Via social media and text messages

    B. Using memos and email

    C. Holding a meeting with the project team

    D. Following the communication plan

181. Marion is a project manager working on implementing a new asset management system for an agency. She has encountered problems when trying to get participation from other departments, and it is creating problems. Whose responsibility would it be to help clear the obstacle?

   A. Project coordinator

   B. PMO

   C. Stakeholders

   D. Project sponsor

182. A project manager is seeking to boost the morale of the team through a meeting that includes both social and business attributes. The project manager is engaged in what type of activity?

   A. Trust building

   B. Forming

   C. Team building

   D. Management skills

183. A company is located in multiple cities across a continent, and the project will be staffed with team members from various cities. The decision is made to bring the project team to single location. This is an example of

   A. Insourcing

   B. Outsourcing

   C. Layoffs

   D. Collocation

184. Amber is a new team member who has joined the project. An expectation-setting meeting has been held, and Amber is getting settled. The first deliverables that have been turned in by Amber have been a couple of days late. When should Amber be notified of a performance discrepancy?

   A. At the lessons-learned meeting at the end of the project or phase

   B. As soon as possible so a correction can occur or help can be provided

   C. During the first performance review meeting, even if it is months away

   D. The project manager should wait for someone else to correct Amber's behavior

185. Ashley is a program manager for the construction of several transit projects. She asks the bridge project manager for updated estimates on the bridge's construction. Who has the responsibility for the estimating task duration and costs?

   A. Project manager

   B. PMO

   C. Stakeholders

   D. Project team

186. What is rolling wave planning?

    A. Planning for areas of intense activity to allocate team members according to the resource plan

    B. The process of elaborating deliverables or project chases into differing levels of the WBS

    C. A design technique used to ensure the structural integrity for earthquake-proof buildings

    D. A quick-start technique of where to begin a project with little planning or sign-off to generate momentum

187. Level 1 of the WBS always represents which of the following?

    A. Critical path

    B. Prioritized tasks

    C. Project

    D. Sponsor

188. What is the mechanism used to communicate on the status of the project budget?

    A. Expenditure tracking

    B. Expenditure reporting

    C. Budget baseline

    D. Work breakdown structure

189. After establishing the product backlog, what tool would be used to determine the project's velocity?

    A. Pareto diagram

    B. Fishbone diagram

    C. Kanban board

    D. Burndown chart

190. Which of the following would be found in the WBS dictionary? (Choose three.)

    A. List of scheduled milestones

    B. Common acronyms used on the project

    C. Criteria for acceptance

    D. Description of work component

    E. Frequency of communications

    F. Staffing plan

191. The scope baseline allows project managers to perform all of the following activities, EXCEPT

    A. Set the approach to conflict resolution

    B. Document schedules

    C. Assign resources

    D. Monitor and control project work

192. In a situation where the end product is uncertain and/or the conditions for developing a product or service are in flux, what would be the best project management approach?

　　A. Traditional, or waterfall

　　B. Projectized environment

　　C. Agile approach

　　D. Functional environment

193. All of the following are characteristics of an Agile project management approach, EXCEPT

　　A. Strict adherence to a change control process

　　B. Uses a flexible approach to requirements

　　C. Team members work in short bursts, or sprints

　　D. Each release is tested against the customers' needs

194. A project assumption can best be described as which of the following?

　　A. Internal or external factors affecting the project team

　　B. Factors that restrict the project

　　C. Factors considered to be true for planning purposes

　　D. Factors considered to be true for control purposes

195. The sprint planning meeting is used to achieve which of the following?

　　A. Getting a head start on the work needed for the project

　　B. Preparing the project charter and kickoff meeting

　　C. Setting a realistic backlog of items completed during this iteration

　　D. Establishing the communication and quality plans for the project

196. Which of the following are characteristics of an Agile project management approach? (Choose three.)

　　A. Self-organized teams

　　B. Sprint planning

　　C. Upfront, comprehensive requirements gathering

　　D. Formally organized teams

　　E. Continuous requirements gathering

　　F. Feedback based primarily in lessons learned meetings

197. How does a high-level scope definition help the planning of a project?

　　A. It creates a shared understanding of what is included and excluded from the project.

　　B. It sets exactly what a product or service will do.

　　C. It is so high level that it ensures that multiple changes can be accommodated by the project.

　　D. It helps to shift the blame to the project sponsor if the project is unsuccessful.

198. What are three of the responsibilities of a project sponsor?

    A. Develops the business case and justification

    B. Functions as the approval authority for funding

    C. Sets the standards and practices a project

    D. Provides input and requirements

    E. Helps to control the project's direction

    F. Manages the risks of the project

199. A project manager meets with team members who are upset. They discuss areas where there is agreement with each other and the situation. Work then resumes on the project. This is an example of which of the following?

    A. Forcing

    B. Avoiding

    C. Confronting

    D. Smoothing

200. Crashing is a project management technique involving which of the following?

    A. Performing two tasks in parallel that were previously scheduled to start sequentially

    B. Looking at cost and schedule trade-offs such as adding more resources

    C. Moving later deliverables to earlier phases to appease stakeholders

    D. Removing critical path activities that are unnecessary

201. All of the following are created during the Planning phase of a project, EXCEPT

    A. Project schedule

    B. Communications plan

    C. Lessons learned

    D. Change management plan

202. A construction company is working on a new building. The CPI for the project is 1.25, which means:

    A. The project is over budget.

    B. The project is behind schedule.

    C. The project is under budget.

    D. The project is ahead of schedule.

203. Judy is a program manager and is monitoring the work done on several projects. On the telecom project, she needs more information on when certain activities and milestones will occur. Who on the telecom project should Judy reach out to for this information?

    A. Project scheduler

    B. Project coordinator

    C. PMO

    D. Project manager

204. A project team is assigned two individuals directly out of college with no experience working in advanced electronics. The two team members cannot be assigned work without a more senior team member working alongside them. This is an example of which one of the following?

A. Shared resources

B. Resource shortage

C. Low-quality resources

D. Benched resources

205. Mitch is a project manager working in the Planning phase of the project. After completing a skills matrix to understand what kind of talent the project will need, he is screening the résumés of talent already employed by the company. What activity is Mitch performing at this stage of the project?

A. Team building

B. Team selection

C. Conflict resolution

D. Trust building

Chapter

2

Project Constraints (Domain 2.0)

THE FOLLOWING COMPTIA PROJECT+ EXAM OBJECTIVES ARE COVERED IN THIS CHAPTER:

✓ **2.1 Given a scenario, predict the impact of various constraint variables and influences throughout the project.**

- Common constraints
    - Budget
    - Scope
    - Deliverables
    - Quality
    - Environment
    - Resources
    - Requirements
    - Scheduling
- Influences
    - Change request
    - Scope creep
    - Constraint reprioritization
    - Interaction between constraints
    - Stakeholders/sponsors/management
    - Other projects

✓ **2.2 Explain the importance of risk strategies and activities.**

- Strategies
  - Accept
  - Mitigate
  - Transfer
  - Avoid
  - Exploit
- Risk activities
  - Identification
  - Quantification
  - Planning
  - Review
  - Response
  - Register
  - Prioritization
  - Communication

1. "Factors that may impact the change of an existing constraint or may bring about a new constraint" is the definition of which one of the following?

   A. A dependency

   B. A predecessor

   C. An influence

   D. A constraint

2. The steering committee originally mandated that cost was the most important factor to the project, keeping the project team size lean. As the project drags on, the steering committee shifts and tells the project manager that schedule is the most important factor to the project. This is an example of which type of influence on a project?

   A. Change request

   B. Constraint reprioritization

   C. Scope creep

   D. Interactions between constraints

3. What does the acronym SWOT stand for?

   A. Situation, weaknesses, open source, threats

   B. Strengths, work, opportunities, traceability

   C. Strengths, weaknesses, opportunities, threats

   D. Situation, work, open source, traceability

4. A potential future event that can have either a negative or positive impact on a project is known as which one of the following?

   A. An issue

   B. A risk

   C. A hope

   D. A requirement

5. As you identify all of the potential risks that might impact a project, you should record them in which one of the following?

   A. RACI chart

   B. Risk register

   C. Risk probability matrix

   D. Issue log

6. The activity of selecting risks that have the greatest chance of occurring and the biggest impact on the project should they occur is called which one of the following?

   A. Three-point estimating

   B. Pareto diagraming

   C. Monitoring and Controlling

   D. Risk analysis

7. The consequence or opportunity the risk poses to the project is known as which one of the following?

   A. Risk response plan

   B. Risk impact

   C. Risk register

   D. Risk probability

8. What are the three common constraints found in projects? (Choose three.)

   A. Time

   B. Personnel

   C. Working space

   D. Budget

   E. Inventory

   F. Scope

9. A road construction project is going to require the company's road paver, a piece of equipment that lays asphalt on roadways, in the next two weeks. The road paver is in use until this Friday in a different city and will require five days to be relocated. This is an example of which type of constraint?

   A. Environment

   B. Scheduling

   C. Scope

   D. Quality

10. In the determination of the project scope, which of the following constraints need to be factored into the discussion? (Choose two.)

    A. Project manager

    B. Predefined budget

    C. Mandated finish date

    D. Competitive advantage

11. A project calls for six master craftspeople in a particular discipline, but the organization only has four on staff. The Human Resources department has attempted to hire more, but there is a limited number of these craftspeople looking for work. What type of constraint does this represent?

    A. Resources

    B. Scheduling

    C. Requirements

    D. Quality

12. Lisa is the project manager on a project and receives a change request to add more scope to her project while not changing the schedule or the budget. Which of the following options are true of the change request?

   A. It represents an influence on the project.

   B. It represents a constraint on the project.

   C. It represents an avoidance strategy.

   D. It represents an environmental constraint.

13. Which of the following roles should be included in the identification of risk on a project?

   A. Subject matter experts (SME)

   B. Core team members

   C. Stakeholders

   D. All of the above

   E. Both B and C

14. The steering committee for Wigit Construction monitors existing projects and approves new ones. The company just won a bid for a new project that must be completed in April, which is the same month that an underway project must also be completed. The stakeholders are doing which of the following?

   A. Reprioritizing constraints by shifting a previously unmovable constraint within a project

   B. Submitting a change request because the scope changed for the existing project

   C. Demonstrating scope creep for the existing project as there are more deliverables to accomplish

   D. Exerting influence by losing interest in the existing project as a new project begins

15. At a minimum, which of the following types of information would be recorded on a risk register? (Choose three.)

   A. Risk score

   B. Risk trigger scores

   C. Impact if the risk occurs

   D. Risk owners

   E. Description of risk

   F. Mitigation strategy

16. A company is working on a project to produce a smartphone that will have similar features to a competitor's product. After a marketing demo, the company receives correspondence from its rival demanding that sale of the smartphone be halted and not taken up again later, because it violates their intellectual property. This is an example of which one of the following?

   A. Memorandum of agreement

   B. Cease and desist letter

   C. Letter of intent

   D. Request for proposal

17. If a project team wanted to enhance a positive risk, what are they trying to accomplish?

    A. Assign the risk to a third party who is best able to bring about opportunity

    B. Increase the probability or impact of the risk event to ensure that benefits are realized

    C. Choose to accept the consequences of the risk

    D. Look for opportunities to take advantage of positive impacts

18. Just allowing the consequences of a negative risk to happen is which type of risk response strategy?

    A. Avoid

    B. Transfer

    C. Mitigate

    D. Accept

19. What is the process of examining the risk analysis and establishing the appropriate course of action should it occur called?

    A. Risk analysis

    B. Risk probability

    C. Risk response planning

    D. Risk trigger

20. Which of the following is defined as the likelihood that a risk will occur?

    A. Risk response plan

    B. Probability and impact matrix

    C. Risk register

    D. Risk probability

21. In a SWOT analysis, opportunities generally look at which one of the following?

    A. Positive news within the company that affects the project

    B. External conditions that contribute to positive risks

    C. Job openings on the project where hiring can occur

    D. Long-term forecast of inclement weather during the project

22. Which of the following statements is true regarding a SWOT analysis?

    A. Strengths/weaknesses are external to the organization; opportunities/threats are internal to the organization.

    B. Strengths/weaknesses/opportunities/threats are all external to the organization.

    C. Strengths/weaknesses are internal to the organization; opportunities/threats are external to the organization.

    D. Strengths/weaknesses/opportunities/threats are all internal to the organization.

23. Which of the following techniques could be used to create an initial list of risks on a project? (Choose three.)

    A. Parametric estimating

    B. Brainstorming

    C. Three-point estimating

    D. Interviews

    E. Fishbone diagrams

    F. Facilitated workshops

24. What does IMS stand for in the project management sense?

    A. Impulsive management system

    B. Innovative mission statement

    C. Iterative mapping system

    D. Integrated master schedule

25. All of the following are true regarding influencers, EXCEPT

    A. A change request is an influencer.

    B. Scope creep can influence schedule and budget.

    C. Environmental factors can dictate when a project occurs.

    D. Influences impact existing constraints or create new ones.

26. A customer submits to have a different requirement added to a project, and it follows the formal approval process to be added to the scope. This is what type of influence on a project?

    A. Change request

    B. Scope creep

    C. An iteration between constraints

    D. Resource scarcity

27. A project team has been working for months on a project and is in the Execution phase. The customer discovers that a competitor has added new functionality to their product, and they would like to add that functionality to this project. To keep the project on time and on budget, this change cannot be accepted because of what type of constraint?

    A. Environment

    B. Budget

    C. Scope

    D. Scheduling

28. A road construction project is going to build a road through the mountains, and there is a window of June through September to get the work done because of the risk of inclement weather. This is an example of what type of constraint?

    A. Environment

    B. Budget

    C. Scope

    D. Scheduling

29. Every project faces all of the following potential constraints, EXCEPT

    A. Quality

    B. Budget

    C. Scope

    D. Staffing

    E. Time

30. Cherie is working on a construction project where weather has the potential to disrupt operations. She determines there is a 0.25 percent probability of a wetter than normal season, which would have a high impact on the project. What activity is Cherie performing?

    A. Risk identification

    B. Risk analysis

    C. Risk response

    D. Constraint identification

31. Which of the following is true of project constraints?

    A. Project constraints will never change during a project.

    B. Project constraints limit the options of the project team.

    C. Project constraints are elements assumed to be true.

    D. Project constraints have no impact on project outcomes.

32. Walt works for Wigit Construction, and he has been assigned as a project manager to build a new bridge. The team has six months to build the project and a fixed budget, and the bridge must handle four lanes of traffic. This is an example of which one of the following?

    A. Three-point estimating

    B. Cost of quality

    C. Triple constraints

    D. Progressive elaboration

33. Which of the following is a tool or technique used in identifying risks to a project?
    A. RASI
    B. SWOT
    C. RACI
    D. COQ

34. Wigitcom's general counsel lets you know that it received a C&D, and there will need to be a meeting on the future of the project. In this context, what is a C&D?
    A. Consequences and demands
    B. Constraints and deliverables
    C. Cease and demands
    D. Cease and desist

35. What does it mean to share a positive risk?
    A. Assign the risk to a third party who is best able to bring about opportunity.
    B. Monitor the probability or impact of the risk event to ensure that benefits are realized.
    C. Choose to accept the consequences of the risk.
    D. Look for opportunities to take advantage of positive impacts.

36. The risk response strategy that focuses on shifting the liability for a negative risk to a third party is known as which one of the following?
    A. Avoidance
    B. Transference
    C. Mitigation
    D. Acceptance

37. When determining risk probability and impact, which tool typically offers the best results?
    A. Expert judgment
    B. Parametric estimating
    C. Environmental factors
    D. Project documentation

38. What tool would be used to prioritize and quantify risks so that the information is easy to understand and is visually informative?
    A. Probability and impact matrix
    B. Fishbone diagram
    C. Histogram
    D. Responsibility assignment matrix

39. What does the weaknesses portion analyze in a SWOT analysis?

    A.   The market share of the smallest competitor

    B.   Which elements are weakest for the company's competitor

    C.   Which elements are weak areas within the company

    D.   Portfolio elements that bring a negative return

40. All of these are common potential risks to a project, EXCEPT

    A.   Teams not attending status meetings

    B.   Insufficient budget assigned to the project

    C.   Scope changes after the project execution begins

    D.   Legal ramifications resulting from the project

41. Risk planning includes all of the following activities, EXCEPT

    A.   Measuring the SPI and CPI

    B.   Analyzing the potential impacts of each risk

    C.   Identifying all potential risks to the project

    D.   Creating a response to each risk

42. What is a MOU?

    A.   Memorandum of understatement

    B.   Memorandum of usability

    C.   Memorandum of understanding

    D.   Memorandum of unacceptability

43. What does the acronym RACI stand for?

    A.   Responsible, accountable, consulted, and informed

    B.   Responsibility, authority, consult, and inform

    C.   Responsible, authority, consulted, and inform

    D.   Responsibility, accountable, consult, and informed

44. How do stakeholders, sponsors, and management exert influence on a project? (Choose all that apply.)

    A.   Shift the priorities of the project as it progresses

    B.   Lose interest in this project as newer projects begin

    C.   Don't attend all meetings

    D.   Don't work on project deliverables

45. The project scope statement mandates that a new product will be developed along with administrative documentation and a user manual in three languages, including English, Spanish, and French. What type of constraint does this represent?

   A. Quality

   B. Deliverables

   C. Time

   D. Budget

46. The launch of a new flagship hotel is coming down to the wire. The customer wants to add an additional welcome area to the hotel prior to the grand opening. Which of the following impacts would be true?

   A. The scope of the project has changed but not the schedule, so costs will increase.

   B. The schedule of the project has changed but not the costs, so the scope will change.

   C. The costs of the project have changed but not the scope, so the schedule will change.

   D. This change will not have a project impact due to contingencies.

47. An aircraft engineering company is forced to cut the project budget after poor financial results in the previous quarter. How would this most likely impact the project?

   A. The project is postponed due to lack of financial resources.

   B. The project scope is cut back to operate within the new budget.

   C. The project will take longer because the number of resources is cut.

   D. The project team goes to the steering committee for more funds.

48. A project is underway, and the team has missed several deliverable dates. The steering committee would like the project to stay on track, and the project manager indicates that the team will need to work overtime to make the deadline. The increased cost is restricted by which type of constraint?

   A. Environment

   B. Budget

   C. Scope

   D. Scheduling

49. A simple spreadsheet that contains an identification number, risk name, risk description, risk owner, and other elements is known as which one of the following?

   A. Risk response plan

   B. Probability and impact matrix

   C. RACI chart

   D. Risk register

50. George is working on both positive and negative elements that might affect a project. For each element, he is trying to figure out the chances of the element occurring and how that element would disrupt or enhance the project. George is using which one of the following?

 A. Probability and impact matrix

 B. Risk management plan

 C. Risk register

 D. Risk response plan

51. Which of the following would you need in the calculation of the risk score? (Choose two.)

 A. SPI

 B. Risk impact

 C. CPI

 D. Risk probability

 E. Risk trigger scores

 F. EAC

52. The project manager is looking for a way to determine the shortest duration in which the project can be completed. The project manager tells the scheduler to use CPM. What is CPM?

 A. Cost production management

 B. Critical project management

 C. Critical path method

 D. Cost project method

53. What is the event that detects that a known risk's variable has changed and that it is time to move the item from the risk register to the issue log?

 A. Risk response plan

 B. Risk identification

 C. Risk trigger

 D. Probability and impact matrix

54. What does it mean to exploit a positive risk?

 A. Assign the risk to a third party who is best able to bring about opportunity

 B. Monitor the probability or impact of the risk event to ensure that benefits are realized

 C. Choose to accept the consequences of the risk

 D. Look for opportunities to take advantage of positive impacts, thereby ensuring it occurs

55. Attempting to ensure that a risk doesn't happen at all, or eliminating the cause of a negative risk, is what type of risk response strategy?

A. Transfer

B. Mitigate

C. Accept

D. Avoid

56. In a SWOT analysis, threats are which one of the following?

A. Situations where physical security is needed

B. Internal conditions that would lead to negative impacts

C. Arguments that get out of hand, leading to raised voices

D. External conditions that would lead to negative impacts

57. The Transportation Exchange held a kickoff meeting where they explained the project goals and high-level timeline and performed project introductions. What phase of the project are they in?

A. Initiation

B. Planning

C. Execution

D. Monitor and Control

E. Closing

58. What is the activity of determining and documenting any potential risks that might happen on a project?

A. Risk planning

B. Risk mitigation

C. Risk avoidance

D. Risk identification

59. In the project management sense, what does ISO stand for?

A. International Standards Organization

B. Isomorphic Standards of Operations

C. International Structure of Operations

D. Intentional Standards Operations

60. What does the acronym RASI stand for?

A. Responsible, authority, superior, and inform

B. Responsibly, accountable, support, and informed

C. Responsible, accountable, superior, and inform

D. Responsibility, authority, support, and inform

61. The scope of a project is expanded through the formal change control process, causing the schedule to be extended beyond the original due date. This is an example of which type of influence?

    A. Stakeholders, sponsors, and management

    B. Interaction between constraints

    C. Constraint reprioritization

    D. Environmental factors

62. Even though the project scope statement has been approved, the customer has routinely asked for more features to be added to the product, causing the due date and resources to be adjusted consistently. This is an example of which type of influence?

    A. Change request

    B. Constraint reprioritization

    C. Schedule constraint

    D. Scope creep

63. Which of the following are examples of influences? (Choose three.)

    A. Change request

    B. Scope statement

    C. Scope creep

    D. Constraint reprioritization

    E. Deliverables

    F. Requirements

64. Which of the following is defined as anything that restricts or forces the actions of the project team?

    A. A requirement

    B. An assumption

    C. A constraint

    D. An influence

65. A wedding planner receives notice that the big event needs to be moved forward two weeks due to the pending military deployment of a member of the bridal party. How would this impact the project?

    A. The wedding is called off because of the schedule change.

    B. The wedding is moved to an indoor facility.

    C. The wedding is moved to a different date in the future.

    D. The wedding costs will be increased as people are added to meet the deadline.

66. A project wants to build a concrete highway in a region that experiences frequent snow-storms during winter months. The snow mitigation plan the city uses calls for putting down magnesium chloride to keep the streets from freezing. The problem with magnesium chloride is that it will eat away at the rebar underneath the concrete, shortening the total life of the highway. What type of constraint does this present to the project?

A. Scope

B. Budget

C. Environment

D. Scheduling

67. Walter is an ace programmer with unique skills that are needed on the project. His time is in high demand, and he is working on several projects. To keep your project on track, Walter needs to complete his work by the end of next month, but he also has his other project commitments. This is an example of which type of constraint?

A. Environment

B. Budget

C. Scope

D. Scheduling

68. What is a MOA?

A. Memorandum of allowance

B. Memorandum of agreement

C. Memorandum of allegiance

D. Memorandum of activity

69. Asking questions such as "Does a task have multiple dependencies?" or "Does the task utilize new or unfamiliar technology?" is a step in which process?

A. Quality assurance

B. Risk identification

C. Building the project charter

D. Building the project schedule

70. There is a section of the project management plan that contains elements of risk, including the project methodology, roles and responsibilities, stakeholder tolerances, and categories. What is this called?

A. Risk register

B. Risk matrix

C. Risk response plan

D. Risk management plan

71. In the project management context, what does COQ stand for?
    A. Cost of quality
    B. Critical to quality
    C. Cost of quantities
    D. Critical of quantities

72. In which phase of a project would you keep an eye on risks to see if any immediate action should be taken?
    A. Initiation
    B. Planning
    C. Execution
    D. Monitor and Control
    E. Closing

73. All of the following are response strategies to positive risks, EXCEPT
    A. Mitigate
    B. Exploit
    C. Share
    D. Enhance

74. Nermit has been working on a chart that lists all the risks that have been identified on a project, along with a numerical score of the likelihood that the risk has of occurring and the score for how impactful the results of the risk occurring would be. What is Nermit creating?
    A. Risk response plan
    B. Risk register
    C. Probability and impact matrix
    D. RACI chart

75. All of the following are strategies to deal with negative risks, EXCEPT
    A. Register
    B. Avoid
    C. Mitigate
    D. Accept

76. What is resource smoothing?
    A. Accommodating resource availability within activity float times
    B. A schedule compression technique
    C. An attempt to balance assignments to prevent overload
    D. A method for loading heavy equipment

77. Wigitcom's project to build a new processor has operated with budget being the most important constraint. Having just learned that their competitor is going to release a product that is 25 percent faster than the one Wigitcom is building, the governance board mandates that their processor be 33 percent faster than the original design. This is an example of which one of the following?

    A. Budget constraint

    B. Schedule constraint

    C. Scope constraint

    D. Constraint reprioritization

78. What is the project artifact that breaks down resources by category and type?

    A. Resource breakdown structure

    B. Organizational breakdown structure

    C. Equipment breakdown structure

    D. Work breakdown structure

79. The marketing department has prepared a full marketing blitz to announce a new refrigerator that has been developed. Before they can go forward, they need photos of the finished unit and the ability to shoot some video. This is known as what type of dependency?

    A. Internal

    B. Discretionary

    C. External

    D. Mandatory

80. What are major accomplishments of the project or key events known as?

    A. Milestones

    B. Deliverables

    C. Requirements

    D. Risks

81. A road construction company has been asked to improve and widen a road along the coastline. Before taking on the project, they evaluate whether the stability and structure of the coastline could support the effort. What is this process known as?

    A. Using expert judgment

    B. Conducting a feasibility study

    C. Performing a cost-benefit analysis

    D. Using a weighted scoring model

82. With a forecast for a worse than average hurricane season, a construction company is aware that certain material costs could rise if a hurricane makes landfall. They begin daily monitoring of the National Weather Service, and start actively tracking any tropical storms as they form so they can quickly act to purchase materials in case a hurricane becomes a legitimate threat. What type of risk response strategy is this?

A. Mitigate

B. Transfer

C. Share

D. Enhance

83. In the creation of a work breakdown structure, the project managers ask to see the OBS as an input to creating the document. What is an OBS?

A. Office of business structure

B. Operational business support

C. Organizational breakdown structure

D. Office breakdown structure

84. A project manager is going to conduct a brainstorming exercise to get a list of potential risks on a project. She invites sponsors, core team members, stakeholders, and SMEs. What is an SME?

A. Service material extract

B. Service matter expert

C. Service material expert

D. Subject matter expert

85. What is the organization responsible for setting the best practices for project, program, and portfolio management?

A. CompTIA

B. PMI®

C. RACI

D. DoD

86. Katie is a project manager whose last performance review just barely met the core standards of the organization. Which of the following choices would most accurately express Katie's risk tolerance?

A. Risk avoider

B. Risk decider

C. Risk taker

D. Risk observer

87. What is an individual or organization's comfort level with how likely they are to accept or avoid risk?

   A. Risk register

   B. Risk avoider

   C. Risk taker

   D. Risk tolerance

88. While a project to build a new computer processor chip is underway, a key stakeholder approaches the project team to double the processing speed from that which was originally requested. This is an example of which one of the following?

   A. Schedule constraint

   B. Constraint reprioritization

   C. Scope creep

   D. Project requirements

89. What is a form of mathematical analysis used to shorten the project schedule duration while keeping the project scope the same?

   A. PERT analysis

   B. Schedule compression

   C. Resource smoothing

   D. Resource leveling

90. What is the critical chain method?

   A. Schedule network analysis technique

   B. Dependency model

   C. Signature path for project charter approval

   D. Earned value method

91. When estimating activity resources, a project manager looks to variations and other options to complete the work. What is this tool or technique called?

   A. Parametric estimating

   B. Bottom-up estimating

   C. Alternative analysis

   D. Fishbone diagraming

92. Process or procedure driven, or best practices techniques, are known as what type of dependency?

   A. Internal

   B. Discretionary

   C. External

   D. Mandatory

93. In preparation to begin a project, the project manager makes a list: (1) The customer will review delivery submissions within 48 hours, (2) the customer will make needed personnel available to the project, and (3) executive support will be given to the project. These are all examples of which one of the following?

A. Constraints

B. Objectives

C. Requirements

D. Assumptions

94. A project has fallen behind schedule, and the project manager has decided to run the next several activities in parallel instead of sequentially to help make up time. This is an example of which one of the following?

A. Crashing

B. Risk avoidance

C. Fast tracking

D. Critical path method

95. A software company is working on a revolutionary new mobile app when a new craze hits the market that utilizes geolocation services. The company has no internal expertise in this field, and it agrees to partner with another company where geolocation functionality is a core competency. What risk response strategy is being used?

A. Accept

B. Exploit

C. Share

D. Enhance

96. Ron in purchasing needs you to create an SOW prior to the releasing an RFP. What is does SOW stand for?

A. Service of workforce

B. Statement of work

C. Statement of workforce

D. Support of work

97. Beth has been charged with gathering information from suppliers to have them bid on specific products or services. What is the appropriate procurement vehicle for this activity?

A. RFI

B. Sole source

C. RFP

D. RFQ

98. What are vital system capabilities that must be satisfied in order for a system or project to meet its operational goals known as?

   A. KPIs

   B. RFPs

   C. MOUs

   D. KPPs

99. Karen is a superstar for a company who has had several stellar performance reviews in a row. Which choice would most accurately express Karen's risk tolerance?

   A. Risk avoider

   B. Risk observer

   C. Risk decider

   D. Risk taker

100. What are two types of discretionary fund allocations that a project may be granted?

   A. Top-down and bottom-up

   B. Contingency and discretionary

   C. Parametric and analogous

   D. Contingency and management

101. What is resource leveling?

   A. A storage technique for physical resources

   B. A schedule compression technique

   C. An attempt to balance assignments to prevent overload

   D. A method for loading heavy equipment

102. Chuck is the project manager for a project, and he needs a specialized piece of heavy equipment so that he can get work scheduled. Which project artifact should Chuck look to when checking availability?

   A. Project charter

   B. Resource calendar

   C. Project schedule

   D. Project calendar

103. The situation where the project team is stuck on the last piece of work, which prevents the project from completing, is known as which one of the following?

   A. Pareto diagram

   B. The 95 percent phenomenon

   C. IRR

   D. The 80/20 rule

104. Wigit Construction is organized by projects where the project managers have ultimate authority over resources like personnel and equipment. What type of organization is Wigit Construction?

    A. Projectized

    B. Matrix

    C. Functional

    D. Agile

105. A road construction company is working on a project to widen 100 miles of road over a six-month period. They are determined to meet the deadline. To do so, they must complete a little over 3.5 miles a week. They start tracking and reporting against this target. What is this an example of?

    A. COQ

    B. KPP

    C. ETC

    D. KPI

106. A contractor needs to ensure that the subcontractor on the project fulfills the expectations of the customer and wants to create SLAs with the subcontractor. What is an SLA?

    A. Service-level agreement

    B. Statement logistical alignment

    C. Support-level agreement

    D. Service-level assignment

107. What is the measure of how well a company or project is doing at achieving key business objects as gauged through a specific value?

    A. COQ

    B. KPP

    C. ETC

    D. KPI

108. Alex is a project sponsor for a startup company. The company is dependent on massive growth to remain competitive in its market. Which choice would most accurately express Alex's risk tolerance?

    A. Risk observer

    B. Risk avoider

    C. Risk taker

    D. Risk decider

109. When there are scarce resources to perform specific activities on a project, and the activities must be completed at certain times, which tool or technique would you use?

 A. Fast tracking

 B. Reverse resource allocation

 C. Resource smoothing

 D. Resource leveling

110. A software company is about to launch a revolutionary new technology. Before the product can launch, the company must wait for the approval of their patent to protect their intellectual property. This is an example of what type of dependency?

 A. Internal

 B. Discretionary

 C. External

 D. Mandatory

111. The project has been going for several months, and it is in the planning phase of the project. After another pass through the planning steps, the scope, risk register, and budget were just modified for the fourth time. This is an example of which type of dependency?

 A. Internal

 B. Discretionary

 C. External

 D. Mandatory

112. A project has fallen behind schedule, and the project manager has decided to have team members work ten hours of overtime each week instead of bringing in new team members. This is an example of which one of the following?

 A. Crashing

 B. Risk avoidance

 C. Fast tracking

 D. Critical path method

113. Francis is working on a project and has an established risk plan setting the importance of each item. Unexpectedly, there is a natural disaster putting a strain on material availability for the construction project. Which risk activity now comes into play?

 A. Identification

 B. Review

 C. Prioritization

 D. Communication

114. Richard works for a mature organization in a stable industry that is dependent on slow, steady growth. Which choice would most accurately express Richard's risk tolerance?

    A. Risk observer

    B. Risk avoider

    C. Risk taker

    D. Risk decider

115. What is the longest full path of any project known as?

    A. Critical path

    B. Total float

    C. Delphi technique

    D. Pareto analysis

116. The project has been going for several months, and it is in the planning phase. After another pass through the planning steps, the scope, risk register, and budget were modified for the fourth time. This is an example of which one of the following?

    A. Agile management

    B. Feasibility study

    C. Progressive elaboration

    D. Project sprints

117. Wigit Construction won a bid to widen a stretch of highway on one of the most heavily traveled roads in the country. The proposal calls for Wigit Construction to work around the clock for four months to limit the inconvenience to the public. The weather forecast for the next four months calls for seasonal monsoons, but Wigit Construction has made the decision to move forward as planned. Which risk response strategy are they using?

    A. Accept

    B. Exploit

    C. Share

    D. Enhance

118. Mark submits a purchase requisition to his company's procurement section. He must wait for a PO to be cut in order for the vendor to begin work. What is a PO?

    A. Planned objective

    B. Purchase office

    C. Purchase order

    D. Planned order

119. The practice of adding a percentage of time to a work package, or adding a percentage of money to a project for an emergency, is known as which one of the following?

A. Risk response plan

B. Delphi technique

C. Allowing risk strategy

D. Contingency reserves

120. Which of the following are risk response strategies? (Choose two.)

A. Avoidance

B. Assumptions

C. Acceptance

D. Analysis

E. Actual cost

121. A construction company has been monitoring tropical storms because of the impact a hurricane that might make landfall would have on the project. A tropical storm has just formed, and forecasters are calling for it to make landfall in a populated part of the country. The company begins to buy extra inventory in lumber and other materials. This is an example of which one of the following?

A. Risk register

B. Risk trigger

C. Risk taker

D. Risk tolerance

122. While working on a major software project, a company's competitor becomes available for sale. The competitor has a core competency in the new functionality being added, and the base company moves quickly to try to merge the two companies. What type of risk response strategy are they using?

A. Accept

B. Exploit

C. Share

D. Enhance

123. When a company is interested in procuring a commodity or service, they conduct a bidding process where suppliers submit business proposals. What is this process known as?

A. RFI

B. Sole source

C. RFP

D. RFQ

124. Donna is working on procuring services for a project, but she is uncertain about what is available and what the capabilities of various suppliers are to meet this demand. What is the procurement vehicle that she should use?

   A. RFI

   B. Sole source

   C. RFP

   D. RFQ

125. Alex is a project sponsor for a startup company. The company is dependent on massive growth to remain competitive in its market. Which choice would most accurately express Alex's risk tolerance?

   A. Risk observer

   B. Risk avoider

   C. Risk taker

   D. Risk decider

126. A project team is considering using a newly developed material on its project. There would be a considerable cost savings achieved by using this material, but the quality of the material is unknown. To prevent possible rework in the future, the project team chooses not to use this material. What risk response strategy is being used?

   A. Avoid

   B. Transfer

   C. Mitigate

   D. Accept

127. What is the approach of developing contingency reserves to deal with risks should they occur?

   A. Transfer

   B. Passive acceptance

   C. Active acceptance

   D. Exploit

128. The project team has done an in-depth root cause analysis as to why certain risks might happen. The impact of these risks would lead to positive outcomes. What type of strategy is this project employing?

   A. Accept, negative risk strategy

   B. Exploit, positive risk strategy

   C. Enhance, positive risk strategy

   D. Transfer, negative risk strategy

129. A project team has purchased materials from a third-party provider. To help ensure against defective material, they have entered into a contract ensuring a warranty for the durability of the goods. What type of risk strategy does this represent?

A. Avoid

B. Transfer

C. Mitigate

D. Accept

130. The process of determining what impact identified risks will have on project objectives and the probability that they will occur is called what?

A. Qualitative risk analysis

B. Identify risk

C. Quantitative risk analysis

D. Risk categorization

131. All of the following are information-gathering techniques used in project management, EXCEPT

A. Brainstorming

B. Delphi technique

C. Gantt chart

D. Root cause analysis

132. A highway construction company is responsible for building a bridge that will handle three million cars a year. What is the likely risk tolerance for the project?

A. Gambler

B. Risk taker

C. Moderate risk tolerance

D. Risk avoider

133. Which is the only risk response strategy that can be used for either a positive or negative risks?

A. Avoid

B. Transfer

C. Mitigate

D. Accept

134. What are the two forms of acceptance when considering risk response strategies?

A. Passive

B. Deliberate

C. Unintentional

D. Active

135. Wigit Construction has an opportunity to win additional work prior to the finish date of the current project. They decide to send their most experienced foreman and senior engineers to the current project to increase the likelihood that it will finish ahead of schedule, so the new project can be tackled. What type of risk strategy is this?

A. Accept, negative risk strategy

B. Exploit, positive risk strategy

C. Share, positive risk strategy

D. Transfer, negative risk strategy

136. What is the process of putting numerical probabilities to each risk and the impacts on project objectives?

A. Qualitative risk analysis

B. Identify risk

C. Quantitative risk analysis

D. Risk categorization

137. Who is responsible for high-level risk identification?

A. Project manager

B. Key stakeholders

C. Project team

D. Project champion

138. In which project phase would the brainstorming, evaluation, and impact of risk be assessed?

A. Initiation

B. Planning

C. Execution

D. Monitor and Control

E. Closing

139. A government agency sees the risk of public backlash to a new road-widening project through a part of the city. The project team elects to add activities for public comment and outreach to better educate the community on the project. What risk response strategy are they employing?

A. Transfer

B. Mitigate

C. Accept

D. Avoid

140. A construction company has its resources spread too thin across multiple projects. One project carries contractual penalties for not completing on time, but the burden is small enough so that it doesn't warrant hiring more staff. What type of risk response strategy is this?

A. Accept, negative risk strategy

B. Exploit, positive risk strategy

C. Share, positive risk strategy

D. Transfer, negative risk strategy

141. Wigitcom has launched a new website that collects personally identifiable information. Accounting for what could be increased liability, they purchase insurance in case of a data breach. This is what type of risk strategy?

A. Avoid

B. Transfer

C. Mitigate

D. Accept

142. What is the activity that determines how soon potential risks might occur and determines responses for those risks?

A. Risk urgency assessment

B. Risk categorization

C. Risk data quality assessment

D. Impact and probability matrix

143. All of the following are examples of categories that might be included in a resource breakdown structure, EXCEPT

A. External

B. Project management

C. Organizational

D. Probability and impact

144. In which project phase would a risk response plan be activated?

A. Initiation

B. Planning

C. Execution

D. Monitor and Control

E. Closing

145. A project is faced with a risk that the project team is unable to eliminate. It has a low probability of occurring and will not impact the project, so no additional action is taken. This is known as which one of the following?

A. Transfer

B. Passive acceptance

C. Active acceptance

D. Exploit

146. A government agency has hired a firm to perform work on its sewer system. As a part of the RFP, the agency requires the successful vendor to carry insurance for errors and omissions. What type of risk strategy is this?

A. Accept, negative risk strategy

B. Exploit, positive risk strategy

C. Share, positive risk strategy

D. Transfer, negative risk strategy

147. All of the following would be updates to the risk register following a qualitative risk analysis, EXCEPT

A. Causes of risks

B. Watch list of low-priority risks

C. Risks requiring near-term responses

D. Numerical evaluation of each risk

148. What is the activity that involves determining the usefulness of data gathered to evaluate risk?

A. Risk urgency assessment

B. Risk categorization

C. Risk data quality assessment

D. Impact and probability matrix

149. A startup in the technology industry would most likely have what type of risk tolerance?

A. Gambler

B. Risk taker

C. Moderate risk tolerance

D. Risk avoider

150. Progressively elaborating deliverables into differing levels of a WBS is known as which one of the following?

A. Producing a backlog

B. Progressive iteration

C. Rolling wave planning

D. Prioritizing tasks

151. Patrick works for a company and has been assigned to a project. It is clear that Patrick's regular boss will be giving him his performance review, and she is routinely pulling him back to work on regular assignments. What type of structure is this project operating under?

    A. Weak-matrix

    B. Projectized

    C. Strong-matrix

    D. Functional

152. Wigitcom has just completed the prototype for a new application and has received user acceptance of the design. This is an example of which one of the following?

    A. Gate check

    B. Milestone

    C. Deliverable

    D. Lessons learned

153. Trevor is the project manager over a civil engineering project, and one of the risks of the project was the potential for a sinkhole in the area where a road is supposed to be built. The project team reports that a sinkhole did in fact form in this area. Which two items are true about this event? (Choose two.)

    A. The risk has now become an issue.

    B. The project team accepted this risk.

    C. The risk trigger has happened, calling for a response.

    D. This needs to go through the change control process.

154. In which project phase would an issues log generally be developed?

    A. Initiation

    B. Planning

    C. Execution

    D. Monitor and Control

    E. Closing

155. Gerry is a new project manager in a company, and he has been told that this project must go through checkpoints between phases of the project with a steering committee. What is the name for these checkpoints?

    A. Lessons learned

    B. SCRUM introspective

    C. Governance gates

    D. Kickoff meetings

156. All of the following are types of organizational structures, EXCEPT

    A. Agile

    B. Functional

    C. Matrix

    D. Projectized

157. At the conclusion of a defined work period, Yolanda got the project team together to figure out what went well, what didn't go well, and what improvements could be made. What type of meeting was this?

    A. SCRUM introspective

    B. Product backlog

    C. Daily SCRUM

    D. Kickoff meeting

158. The Transportation Exchange project team is assembled and introductions are being performed. What stage of team development is this?

    A. Storming

    B. Norming

    C. Performing

    D. Forming

159. A meeting has just been conducted on a project where the expectations, goals, and objectives of the project have been explained, including the milestones and timelines of the project. Project sign-off is also likely to occur during this meeting. What type of meeting was this?

    A. Lessons learned

    B. Gate check

    C. Status meeting

    D. Kickoff meeting

160. Gayle, the project sponsor, has said that the transit project needs to have four working bus lines operating 18 hours a day when the project is complete. Gayle has given which one of the following?

    A. Criteria for approval

    B. Gate check

    C. Deliverable

    D. Lessons learned

161. Wigit Construction has been asked to erect a building that has two bathrooms, a conference room, and an open space for cubicles. Which of the following do the bathrooms, conference room, and open space all represent?

 A. Deliverables

 B. Constraints

 C. Assumptions

 D. Requirements

162. Lisa is a contract project manager assisting a government agency that is implementing companywide software. Lisa is operating the project with the belief that executive sponsorship will be strong on the project, and that all project team members will be free of other responsibilities. This is an example of which one of the following?

 A. Deliverables

 B. Constraints

 C. Assumptions

 D. Requirements

163. A government agency has invited bids on a project that must be completed by the end of year, have a mobile application to interface the information, and be credit card compliant. These are all examples of which one of the following?

 A. Deliverables

 B. Constraints

 C. Assumptions

 D. Requirements

164. In which project phase would an action items list generally be developed?

 A. Initiation

 B. Planning

 C. Execution

 D. Monitor and Control

 E. Closing

165. Sarah works for an agency and has recently been assigned to a project. She has been given assignments from both her functional manager and the project manager, but was directed to do the project work. What type of organizational structure is this agency using?

 A. Balanced-matrix

 B. Weak-matrix

 C. Projectized

 D. Strong-matrix

166. Only two senior engineers are available to work on a project, and one of them is already committed to work on another project until the middle of the next quarter. This is an example of which one of the following?

    A. Deliverables

    B. Constraints

    C. Assumptions

    D. Requirements

167. Assessing the status of the budget, reviewing risks/issues logs, and measuring performance occurs in what project phase?

    A. Initiation

    B. Planning

    C. Execution

    D. Monitor and Control

    E. Closing

168. Kim is a project manager for a generational construction company. What type of project management methodology would be the best choice for Kim to use?

    A. Agile

    B. Waterfall

    C. Informal

    D. Adaptive

169. Stephanie is a project manager and has worked with the key stakeholders to get agreement on the project charter. At the kickoff meeting, she makes sure that all key stakeholders and sponsors sign the project charter. This is an example of which one of the following?

    A. Formal approval

    B. CYA

    C. Gate check

    D. Lessons learned

170. A project team has agreed that limited rework is an element of success, and it targets the product to be 99 percent defect-free by the end of the project. This is an example of which one of the following?

    A. KPP

    B. MOU

    C. KPI

    D. RFP

171. Wigit Construction did not pass the customer's inspection of a building, and the project team needs to tear out a wall and rebuild it. This is an example of which one of the following?

A. Risk response plan

B. Cost of quality

C. Memorandum of understanding

D. Scope creep

172. Joey has been assigned a project where the deadline must be done before the start of the youth activities season, and there is a limited budget for the project. This is an example of what type of influence?

A. Scope creep

B. Interaction between constraints

C. Constraint reprioritization

D. Stakeholders opinions on the project

173. After risks have been identified, analyzed, and prioritized, and a response has been planned, what is the last risk activity to account for?

A. Quantification

B. Review

C. Response

D. Communication

174. What is the risk response strategy that attempts to minimize the impact or the probability of a negative risk?

A. Avoid

B. Transfer

C. Mitigate

D. Accept

175. Which parts of a SWOT analysis are focused on issues internal to the organization?

A. Strengths and threats

B. Opportunities and weaknesses

C. Opportunities and threats

D. Strengths and weaknesses

176. While working on a project, Valdene has been assigned to identify potential risks, assess the impact of these risks, and work on responses should those risks occur. On what activity is Valdene working?

A. Risk planning

B. Risk register

C. Risk identification

D. SWOT analysis

177. Measuring the spending to date, determining the burn rate, and accounting for purchases is known as which one of the following?

A. Expenditure reporting

B. Expenditure tracking

C. Cost accounting

D. ETC

178. A government agency has certain bureaucratic steps it must meet before it can move forward with payment to a vendor. What kind of dependency does this represent?

A. Discretionary

B. External

C. Internal

D. Optional

179. The project team on which Jenny is working has a detailed set of requirements the project must meet, but the company has limited resources to work on the project. What is the likely result of these two constraints?

A. The scope must be reduced.

B. The company must find more resources.

C. The scope and resources must be adjusted.

D. The time will expand to deal with scope and cost.

180. The Wigitcom project team is trying to determine what to do with certain negative risks that they have identified on the project. All of the following are strategies to deal with negative risks, EXCEPT

A. Exploit

B. Avoid

C. Transfer

D. Mitigate

181. Fred works for a bank where the industry generally protects the investments and life savings of its customers. The likely risk tolerance for the bank is which one of the following?

    A. Very high

    B. High

    C. Low

    D. Very low

182. What is a list of risks that includes the identification number, name, description, owner, and response plan?

    A. Risk response plan

    B. Issues list

    C. Risk register

    D. Activity log

183. Wigit Construction has completed the risk assessment and cost estimating activities. For certain risks, they have set aside money to cover the costs resulting from possible adverse effects on the project. What are these funds referred to as?

    A. Contingency reserve

    B. Ready reserve

    C. Resource reserve

    D. Management reserve

184. Two parties would like to enter into a non-legally binding agreement that outlines the good faith actions each will take. What type of vehicle is this?

    A. MOA

    B. C&D

    C. MOU

    D. RFP

185. Scott and his team of network engineers have been working through of list of risks and developing counter actions should those risks appear during the course of a project. They are working on which one of the following?

    A. Risk register

    B. Risk response plan

    C. Probability and impact matrix

    D. RACI chart

186. Which of the following best describes progressive elaboration?

    A. An Agile technique where work sprints are used

    B. The continuous modification and detailing of the project plan

    C. Creating better, more detailed explanations for senior management

    D. A phrase referring to the over-complication of a project

187. Wigitcom's management team authorized and funded a project. In addition to the funds requested after the cost estimation, they set aside funds to handle any unforeseen circumstances should they arise. What are these funds known as?

    A. Contingency reserve

    B. Ready reserve

    C. Resource reserve

    D. Management reserve

188. Before a construction company can begin building a road over a mountain pass, they must wait for the spring thaw to occur so that they can get heavy machinery into the work location. This is known as what type of dependency?

    A. Internal

    B. Discretionary

    C. External

    D. Mandatory

189. In a briefing to the CEO, the project team explains that there is a risk that the company's two biggest competitors might merge. The CEO asks about the likelihood that this will happen. What exactly is she asking for?

    A. A probability and impact matrix

    B. The risk impact

    C. The risk probability

    D. The risk register

190. Harry works for a research and development firm trying to create a revolutionary new product. The likely risk tolerance for the company is which one of the following?

    A. Very high

    B. High

    C. Low

    D. Very low

191. A project team failed to identify all of the stakeholders for a project, and a new stakeholder pointed out several requirements that are needed for the project to be useful. This is an example of which one of the following?

    A. Influencer

    B. Constraints

    C. SCRUM introspective

    D. Risk trigger

192. Which parts of a SWOT analysis are focused on issues external to the organization?

    A. Strengths and threats

    B. Opportunities and weaknesses

    C. Opportunities and threats

    D. Strengths and weaknesses

193. Management for Wigit Construction is concerned with understanding what the negative or positive impacts potential future events might have on a project. What is the management team asking about?

    A. Contingency planning

    B. MOU

    C. Risk

    D. Issues

194. What is the creation of documents that details how money on the project has been spent, graphical representations of spend rate, and money remaining?

    A. Expenditure reporting

    B. Expenditure tracking

    C. Cost accounting

    D. ETC

195. What does the strengths portion analyze in a SWOT analysis?

    A. What your customers/stakeholders view as your positive attributes

    B. What you view as your competitor's positive attributes

    C. The combined skill sets of the project team

    D. The market share the organization has with the product

196. When a project team is assigned to work solely on a project, it is an example of what type of resource?

    A. Dedicated

    B. Physical

    C. Shared

    D. Collocated

197. Tony is a project manager, and he gets the team together for a brainstorming activity. At the end of the meeting, they have a list of all of the items that need to be completed during the next work period. What type of meeting just occurred?

    A. SCRUM introspective

    B. Daily SCRUM

    C. Product backlog

    D. Delphi technique

198. The Transportation Exchange is a new ride-sharing service trying to break into the marketplace. Which of the following benefits would make sense for them to use an adaptive method of project management?

  A. There is no value with small incremental improvements.

  B. Processes are thoroughly defined.

  C. The environment is rapidly changing.

  D. Scope is easily identified and designed.

199. Fernando is a project employee whose employment will terminate at the end of the software development project. What vehicle would the company use to protect their intellectual property?

  A. C&D

  B. RFP

  C. KPI

  D. NDA

200. In the development of a project idea, a stakeholder writes down the purpose of the project, what it might cost, and what business value or benefits will be achieved. What is the document being created?

  A. Project description

  B. Business case

  C. Deliverables

  D. Project charter

201. A project manager has been asked to report on all expenditures to date on a project. What has the project manager been asked to provide?

  A. Actual cost

  B. Planned value

  C. Earned value

  D. Cost variance

202. All of the following are examples of deliverables, EXCEPT

  A. Blueprints

  B. Sign-off on the project charter

  C. User documentation

  D. The finished product

203. A software development company is considering using an Agile approach on a new project. They would use all of the following, EXCEPT

  A. Gate checks

  B. Burndown charts

  C. Sprint planning

  D. Continuous requirements gathering

204. To achieve a successful result on the project, Wigit Construction partners with another company to add project staff. This is an example of which one of the following?

    A. Collocation

    B. Outsourcing

    C. Layoffs

    D. Insourcing

205. A project manager is having problems with one team member who is being insubordinate. The project manager approaches the team member and spells out how the behavior is inappropriate and how the team member will behave from now on. This is an example of which one of the following?

    A. Forcing

    B. Avoiding

    C. Confronting

    D. Smoothing

Chapter

3

Communication and Change Management (Domain 3.0)

THE FOLLOWING COMPTIA PROJECT+ EXAM OBJECTIVES ARE COVERED IN THIS CHAPTER:

✓ **3.1 Given a scenario, use the appropriate communication method.**

- Meetings
  - Kick-off meetings
  - Virtual vs. in-person meetings
  - Scheduled vs. impromptu meetings
  - Closure meetings
- Email
- Fax
- Instant messaging
- Video conferencing
- Voice conferencing
- Face-to-face
- Text message
- Distribution of printed media
- Social media

✓ **3.2 Compare and contrast factors influencing communication methods.**

- Language barriers
- Time zones/geographical factors

- Technological factors
- Cultural differences
- Interorganizational differences
- Intraorganizational differences
- Personal preferences
- Rapport building/relationship building
- Tailor method based on content of message
- Criticality factors
- Specific stakeholder communication requirements
  - Frequency
  - Level of report detail
  - Types of communication
  - Confidentiality constraints
  - Tailor communication style

✓ **3.3 Explain common communication triggers and determine the target audience and rationale.**

- Audits
- Project planning
- Project change
- Risk register updates
- Milestones
- Schedule changes
- Task initiation/completion
- Stakeholder changes
- Gate reviews
- Business continuity response
- Incident response
- Resource changes

✓ **3.4 Given a scenario, use the following change control process within the context of a project.**

- Change control process
  - Identify and document
  - Evaluate impact and justification
    - Regression plan (Reverse changes)
  - Identify approval authority
  - Obtain approval
  - Implement change
  - Validate change/quality check
  - Update documents/audit documents/version control
  - Communicate throughout as needed
- Types of common project changes
  - Timeline change
  - Funding change
  - Risk event
  - Requirements change
  - Quality change
  - Resource change
  - Scope change

✓ **3.5 Recognize types of organizational change.**

- Business merger/acquisition
- Business demerger/split
- Business process change
- Internal reorganization
- Relocation
- Outsourcing

1. To help save costs and attract and retain employees, a technology company decides to allow individuals to work from home three days a week. This is an example of what types of organizational change? (Choose two.)

   A. Outsourcing

   B. Internal reorganization

   C. Relocation

   D. Business process change

2. All of the following are reasons to update the project plan after an approved change, EXCEPT

   A. Ensuring that the project staff has things they can work on

   B. Capturing changes as they happen so that they are not forgotten

   C. Creating an accurate record of the project

   D. Creating artifacts to be used during lessons-learned sessions

3. After a subject matter expert (SME) evaluates the impacts of a change, they should analyze the following specific elements of the change, EXCEPT

   A. Additional equipment needs

   B. Costs

   C. Approving or rejecting the change

   D. Resource hours needed

4. Once a change request is submitted, where should it be recorded and assigned an identification number for tracking purposes?

   A. Risk register

   B. Issue log

   C. Business process repository

   D. Change request log

5. After a project change is identified, evaluated, and approved, what is the next step in the change control process?

   A. Updating documents

   B. Validating the change and doing a quality check

   C. Obtaining approval

   D. Implementing the change

6. Wigit Construction has been using a steamroller to repave a road. A different project finishes early with its paving machine and sends it to the first project to complete the work faster. What type of project change does this represent?

   A. Resource change

   B. Timeline change

   C. Requirements change

   D. Quality change

7. When the schedule slips on a project because the work is taking longer than planned, what type of common project change does this represent?

   A. Risk event

   B. Requirements change

   C. Funding change

   D. Timeline change

8. Due to an election, the leadership of a government agency is changed and the project sponsor role shifts to a new individual. This is an example of what type of communication trigger?

   A. Stakeholder changes

   B. Resource changes

   C. Project change

   D. Business continuity response

9. All of the following are common communication triggers, EXCEPT

   A. Project planning

   B. Schedule changes

   C. Milestones

   D. Distribution of printed media

10. The cybersecurity team has discovered that hackers have compromised the newly launched web application and turned the server into a gambling website. The team recommends that the server be shut down and a root cause analysis conducted. What type of communication trigger is this?

   A. Audit

   B. Incident response

   C. Schedule change

   D. Project chance

11. The communication plan calls for weekly status email updates, monthly status meetings, and semiannual printed newsletters. This plan is laying out which one of the following?

   A. Criticality factors

   B. Types of communication

   C. Level of report detail

   D. Tailor communication style

12. Pete is a human resources (HR) manager who needs to communicate to Ashley a complaint issued against her. How would the content of this message dictate what type of communication is used with Ashley?

   A. It is of a confidential nature, so Pete should meet with her face-to-face.

   B. Personal preferences suggest using social media.

   C. Pete should use voice conferencing to avoid personal threat.

   D. Pete should use instant messaging to allow time for Ashley to digest the information slowly.

13. Two companies are considering a merger, and they are looking to hold a meeting between the key stakeholders of both companies. One company is transparent with their employees in everything they do, whereas the second company holds key information at the senior executive level. What factors would influence the communication of this meeting?

    A. Tailoring the method based on content of message

    B. Interorganizational differences

    C. Cultural differences

    D. Language barriers

14. Nancy swings by Michael's office to find out about his upcoming trip as a Scout Master. Michael fills her in on where they are going, when he would return, and the plans for the weekend. This is an example of which one of the following?

    A. Intraorganizational differences

    B. Language barriers

    C. Criticality factors

    D. Relationship building

15. A project team is based in four different locations of a large metropolitan city. What factors would influence the scheduling of impromptu meetings?

    A. Intraorganizational differences

    B. Interorganizational differences

    C. Personal preferences

    D. Geographical factors

16. A company needs to communicate with the general public regarding a project on which they are working. Which of the following would be appropriate methods to use? (Choose two.)

    A. Fax

    B. Instant message

    C. Social media

    D. Text messaging

    E. Distribution of printed media

17. The project team is located in multiple cities across a continent. The customer requires the signing of a nondisclosure agreement by each team member and would like them all by the end of the next business day. What is the best communication method to use to collect these documents?

    A. Video conferencing

    B. Impromptu meeting

    C. Instant messaging

    D. Fax

18. Wigitcom has just been hacked, and millions of records containing personal information of their customers have been stolen. The CEO is in a meeting for the rest of the day. What is the best communication method to let the boss know of the situation?

    A. Social media

    B. Impromptu meeting

    C. Text messaging

    D. Distribution of printed media

19. Mickey is in a project meeting where a risk trigger was identified that will need resolution. Mickey's boss is in another meeting for the rest of the day, but Mickey wants to give his boss a brief update as quickly as possible. What would be the best method for Mickey to communicate with his boss?

    A. Social media

    B. Video conferencing

    C. Text messaging

    D. Distribution of printed media

20. Amber works for a staffing firm and is a project manager brought in to help with a spike in projects for a company. When the projects are complete, Amber no longer does work for the company. This is an example of which one of the following?

    A. Relocation

    B. Risk response

    C. Outsourcing

    D. Business process change

21. An organization decides to stop using paper applications for its hiring processes and instead implements an electronic application through the company's website. What type of change does this represent?

    A. Business split

    B. Business acquisition

    C. Business process change

    D. Business merger

22. Which of the following are types of organizational change? (Choose three.)

    A. Organic shifts

    B. Business process change

    C. Technological shifts

    D. Outsourcing

    E. Internal reorganization

    F. Staff turnover

23. When regular project status meetings begin, what element of the change process should be regularly reviewed?

    A. Change request log

    B. Risk register

    C. Issue log

    D. Social media

24. Wigitcom is working on a cutover to a new phone system for an agency with a security component. During the planned outage, a problem is discovered that cannot be solved immediately. What should the project team do?

    A. Continue to implement the change.

    B. Implement the regression plan and reverse the changes.

    C. Evaluate the impact and justification of an extended outage.

    D. Identify and document the change.

25. After a change request has been recorded in the change request log, what is the next step that should be performed?

    A. Submit it to the CCB to be accepted or rejected.

    B. Defer until there is a break in the project schedule.

    C. Implement the change.

    D. Analyze the impact of the change.

26. Madeline is a project manager whose team has just implemented a change to the project, and they have completed the step of updating project documentation. What is the next step that Madeline should make sure is completed?

    A. Prioritizing the change to the bottom of the work list

    B. Communicating the change according to the communication plan

    C. Validating the change

    D. Seeking approval from the CCB

27. Who can submit a change request?

    A. Project manager

    B. Most people working on or associated with the project

    C. Project sponsor

    D. Change control board

28. The project management plan originally called for no fewer than 5 percent defects on project work. After a steering committee meeting, this number is reduced to 2 percent to maintain the quality brand of the company. What type of common project change is this?

    A. Funding change

    B. Risk event

    C. Quality change

    D. Scope change

29. During a merger, the new company has decided to expand their headquarters building, which was a project currently under construction. They have allocated an additional $300,000 to the project to make this happen. Which common project changes does this represent? (Choose two.)

   A. Requirements change

   B. Scoping change

   C. Timeline change

   D. Funding change

30. All of the following are common types of project changes, EXCEPT

   A. Organizational changes

   B. Timeline changes

   C. Scope changes

   D. Requirement changes

31. Wigitcom has a key programmer who must leave the project due to a family emergency. The project manager has been able to find another individual who has the experience and skills to take over, and that person is added to the project. This type of communication trigger is known as which one of the following?

   A. Project planning

   B. Resource changes

   C. Incident response

   D. Stakeholder changes

32. Among the following, who would be the target audience that should be notified that a milestone has been completed? (Choose three.)

   A. Project sponsor

   B. Auditors

   C. Project team

   D. Product end users

   E. Steering committee

   F. Shareholders

33. The cybersecurity team has been reviewing the security logs and has discovered a potential vulnerability in the software that a project team is developing. The team suggests remediation. What type of communication trigger is this?

   A. Audit

   B. Gate review

   C. Schedule change

   D. Business continuity response

34. MaryAnn is a deputy executive director, and she has asked not be disturbed until noon, as she is working on a time-sensitive assignment. The field team reported that they have completed the setup of a new drill in the field. The team does not interrupt MaryAnn to give her the news. This is an example of which one of the following?

    A. Personal preferences

    B. Criticality factors

    C. Level of report detail

    D. Interorganizational differences

35. Wigit Construction has an operations division and an administrative division. The administrative division honors a standard 8–5 Monday through Friday schedule, whereas the operations division routinely has to work around the clock. This is an example of which one of the following?

    A. Intraorganizational differences

    B. Interorganizational differences

    C. Technology factors

    D. Personal preferences

36. An offshore team has issued a holiday schedule to the project manager that differs from the company's established holiday schedule. This is an example of which one of the following?

    A. Language barriers

    B. Time zones

    C. Cultural differences

    D. Criticality factors

37. A large organization has a human resources project that will impact the pay and benefits for everyone in the company. It sets up a listserv that emails project updates and allows recipients to set the frequency to daily, weekly, or monthly. This is an example of which one of the following?

    A. Cultural differences

    B. Personal preferences

    C. Criticality factors

    D. Rapport building

38. Murthy is a project manager working on an international software project. Which of the following is a factor influencing the communication methods on the project?

    A. Language barriers

    B. Fax

    C. Risk identification

    D. Scope creep

39. An independent auditor has just completed a project evaluating the practices of an organization. What would be the best communication method to disclose the findings?

    A. Virtual meeting

    B. In-person meeting

    C. Kickoff meeting

    D. Closure meeting

40. Sasha is in a project meeting where a major risk was revealed to be impacting the project. Sasha's boss is in another meeting for the rest of the day, but she needs to provide a detailed update to her boss as quickly as possible. What would be the best method to communicate with Sasha's boss?

    A. Email

    B. Distribution of printed media

    C. Instant messaging

    D. Text message

41. Wigit Construction is about to begin a project phase replacing a bridge over a major highway. The work will require the highway to be closed at night for several weeks. What is the most appropriate communication method to share these outages with the general public?

    A. Social media

    B. Impromptu meeting

    C. Instant messaging

    D. Email

42. Phil and Fernando are technicians working on a project out in the field. Power was supposed to be turned off at 5 p.m. so that work can begin, but there is going to be a delay. What is the best way to communicate this change?

    A. Email

    B. Phone call

    C. Text message

    D. Scheduled meeting

43. A project is spread across a large city, and a technical problem has developed on the project. There are team members in the field, some located at the headquarters building, and a vendor in a different city. What is the appropriate communication method for this situation?

    A. Kickoff meeting

    B. In-person meeting

    C. Instant messaging

    D. Virtual meeting

44. A government agency has determined that they are best at providing their mandated function, and that they are not in the business of information technology. They hire a firm to take over all of the IT needs of the organization. This is an example of which one of the following?

A. Relocation

B. Internal reorganization

C. Business demerger/split

D. Outsourcing

45. Wigitcom decides to spin off its mobile gaming business unit into a completely separate business unit. This is known as which one of the following?

A. Business split

B. Business acquisition

C. Business process change

D. Business merger

46. All of the following are forms of organizational change, EXCEPT

A. Business merger

B. Organic shifts

C. Business demerger

D. Relocation

47. A key stakeholder is submitting change requests at a record level, and the project manager needs to communicate to the stakeholder the impact that this is having on the project. What type of impact does a change request have on the project team?

A. There is an opportunity cost of working on the project when a change request needs to be analyzed.

B. The interruptions are affecting morale as the stakeholder is being annoying.

C. The stakeholder should not be confronted because of their rank within the organization.

D. Change requests have no impact on a project team.

48. The project team has completed the implementation of an approved change. What should the project team do next?

A. Validate the change.

B. Update the project plan.

C. Communicate the change.

D. Seek CCB approval.

49. What kind of document will ensure that all of the needed information is captured in a change request for proper consideration?

    A. Email

    B. Template

    C. Project charter

    D. Meeting minutes

50. A project has a team member who routinely is not showing up to meetings or completing assignments. The appropriate place to capture this would be where?

    A. Change request log

    B. Issue log

    C. Risk register

    D. WBS

51. Which of the following are communication triggers? (Choose three.)

    A. Milestones

    B. Task initiation or completion

    C. Resource changes

    D. Technological factors

    E. Time zones

    F. Interorganizational differences

52. A change control template should include all of the following, EXCEPT

    A. The change that is requested

    B. The reason for the change

    C. The executive sponsor of the change

    D. What will happen if the change is not made

53. Wigitcom and Wigit Construction have agreed to partner on building a state-of-the-art facility for a customer. Wigit Construction has a strict rule that all project meetings start on time, and everyone comes prepared. Wigitcom has a more laid-back approach, and team members routinely show up five minutes late to meetings. This is an example of which one of the following?

    A. Cultural differences

    B. Rapport building

    C. Interorganizational differences

    D. Language barriers

54. The executive team has decided that it would like to be updated on the project in a meeting that occurs no more frequently than once every other month. What type of factor is this in terms of communication methods?

    A. Criticality factors

    B. Tailoring the method based on the content of the message

    C. Personal preferences

    D. Interorganizational differences

55. Nora is a project manager implementing an enterprise software package, and she is being assigned an onshore and offshore team. What are factors that will influence communication methods on the project? (Choose three.)

    A. Time zones

    B. Cultural differences

    C. Level of report detail

    D. Criticality factors

    E. Language barriers

    F. Technological factors

56. A government agency is holding a public hearing about a controversial new project where the facts are becoming skewed. During the meeting, what is the best communication method to get the facts and answers to common questions to the general public?

    A. Text message

    B. Distribution of printed media

    C. Instant messaging

    D. Email

57. Brad is a junior software developer who is having problems remembering where the source code is for a certain routine. He needs to contact Bridget, the senior developer on the project. What would be the ideal way to contact her?

    A. Email

    B. Impromptu meeting

    C. Instant messaging

    D. Fax

58. A project manager is managing a team located in multiple cities of the same continent. There is an interpersonal problem developing between the customer and a project team member in a different city. Choose the appropriate communication method to work on resolving the problem.

    A. Virtual meeting

    B. In-person meeting

    C. Closure meeting

    D. Kickoff meeting

59. When two businesses come together to operate as one, the single entity is known as which of the following?

    A. Business split

    B. Business acquisition

    C. Business process change

    D. Business merger

60. A team is not going to finish a project by the assigned date, and it has asked that three more members be assigned to the work so that the date can be achieved. This is an example of which one of the following?

    A. Issue

    B. Risk

    C. Change

    D. Milestone

61. When a change is being considered, the change control board wants to know how the changes can be reversed if needed. What is this called?

    A. Requirements change

    B. Validation

    C. Version control

    D. Regression plan

62. Avinash is a senior database administrator assigned to a project. After two months, he hands off the work to Allyson, who is a journey-level database administrator. This represents what type of common project change?

    A. Timeline change

    B. Requirements change

    C. Quality change

    D. Resource change

63. Which of the following are used to conduct virtual meetings? (Choose two.)

    A. Face-to-face

    B. Impromptu visits

    C. Videoconferencing

    D. Voice conferencing

64. All of the following would be communicated in a risk register update, EXCEPT

    A. Project manager

    B. PMO

    C. Project sponsor

    D. Project team

65. Mo is a project manager working on an assignment, and she has asked not to be disturbed until noon. The project team reported that the helicopter that was doing routine scouting of a project site hit a power line and crash landed. Should the project team interrupt Mo and give her an update?

   A. No, the personal preferences of the stakeholder should be honored.

   B. No, the criticality factors do not warrant an interruption.

   C. Yes, this is an opportunity for rapport building for that big raise.

   D. Yes, the criticality factors mandate that an interruption take place.

66. Wigitcom is an international software company with offices in Ireland, India, and the United States. The practices in each office for developing software are based on the same model, but the implementation of the practices are different in each country. This is an example of which one of the following?

   A. Cultural differences

   B. Interorganizational differences

   C. Intraorganizational differences

   D. Personal preferences

67. A pharmaceutical company is working on a new drug. A member of the project team is getting lunch in the cafeteria, and a friend from a different part of the company asks how she has been and what's she been working on. Which factor would influence her answer?

   A. Criticality factors

   B. Confidentiality constraints

   C. Rapport building

   D. Cultural differences

68. A project manager is trying to get a safety update to project team members out in the field. What are appropriate methods to communicate the update to the team? (Choose two.)

   A. Fax

   B. Text message

   C. Social media

   D. Voice conferencing

   E. Distribution of social media

69. Wigitcom is starting a marketing company to build interest in a new mobile device. To help promote the product's "coolness," they have created a series of funny videos about the product. What would be the best method to communicate these videos?

   A. Social media

   B. Impromptu meeting

   C. Instant messaging

   D. Email

70. A project manager wants to hold a meeting with an offshore team. She is excited because the company just installed a new video conference room, but she isn't sure that the project team has one in their location. What factor is influencing the communication method?

    A. Technological factors

    B. Cultural differences

    C. Time zones

    D. Language barriers

71. Gus is working in an oilfield assigned to a project in a remote area. The trailer he works out of has a telephone line, but Internet connectivity and mobile phone coverage is spotty. What would be the best method to send Gus instructions for the next day?

    A. Email

    B. Impromptu meeting

    C. Instant messaging

    D. Fax

72. A project manager is managing a team located in multiple cities on the same continent. The communication plan calls for a weekly status meeting. What is the appropriate method for this communication?

    A. Virtual meeting

    B. In-person meeting

    C. Instant messaging

    D. Kickoff meeting

73. A government agency has two different business units that have a fleet of trash trucks to pick up garbage. To help save money, the agency decides to move the garbage collection function to a single agency and sell the trash trucks of the other agency. What type of business change is this?

    A. Business process change

    B. Outsourcing

    C. Internal reorganization

    D. Staff turnover

74. The published schedule for a project has a filename of `ProjectSchedule_v1`. The project manager makes an update to the file, and it now is called `ProjectSchedule_v2`. This is an example of which one of the following?

    A. Version control

    B. Communicating changes

    C. Change request logs

    D. Risk register

75. Wigit Construction has obtained approval to add improved landscaping to an off-ramp project within a certain city. What is the next step the project team should tackle?

    A. Update documentation

    B. Communicate throughout as needed

    C. Implement the change

    D. Enact the regression plan

76. What is the appropriate method for a change request to be submitted?

    A. In writing

    B. Verbally

    C. Via video conference

    D. Executive session of the change control board (CCB)

77. A key stakeholder, Don, is very detail-oriented and likes to do deep dives on the status of projects. He has asked for a highly detailed status report to be emailed to him weekly so that he can stay informed about the project. Which of the following specific stakeholder communication requirements is he asking for? (Choose two.)

    A. Frequency

    B. Level of report detail

    C. Confidentially constraints

    D. Criticality factors

78. A construction site suffered a setback when a crane fell over, blocking the entrance to a major highway. What factors would influence the communication method?

    A. Criticality factors

    B. Time zones

    C. Language barriers

    D. Relationship building

79. The project manager has been gathering a batch of routine organizational messages, project updates, and status reports. What would be the best communication method to share this information?

    A. Video conference

    B. Impromptu meeting

    C. Social media

    D. Scheduled meeting

80. Cheryl is a technical lead on a project that is wrapping up remote work at a customer site. What is the best method to communicate the work efforts and next steps with the customer?

    A. Virtual meeting

    B. In-person meeting

    C. Closure meeting

    D. Kickoff meeting

81. A project is entering the Execution phase, the project planning is complete, and it is time to introduce the project team. What is the appropriate form of communication for the next step?

    A. Video conference

    B. Impromptu meeting

    C. Email

    D. Kickoff meeting

82. Wigit Construction has put in a bid to buy Wallocot Steel, one of its primary suppliers. What type of organizational change does this represent?

    A. Business split

    B. Business acquisition

    C. Business process change

    D. Business merger

83. A construction project had anticipated a drop in oil prices as oil production was predicted to increase globally. The prices start to drop after a few months, and the project is able to buy all of the oil needed for the remainder of the project at a lower rate than stated in the budget. What type of common project change does this represent?

    A. Timeline change

    B. Funding change

    C. Risk event

    D. Quality change

84. Wigitcom is going to experience a delay in a project because a key programmer is going to be out on emergency leave. What type of communication trigger does this represent?

    A. Incident response

    B. Business continuity response

    C. Schedule change

    D. Gate review

85. Joyce is an executive who is not a big user of technology, and she has asked to receive all updates verbally rather than through email. This stakeholder's communication requirement is which one of the following?

    A. Frequency

    B. Level of report detail

    C. Confidentiality constraints

    D. Types of communication

86. A project team is located in three different cities on the same continent. Which of the following would be the biggest factor in scheduling recurring status meetings?

    A. Language barriers

    B. Time zones

    C. Cultural differences

    D. Intraorganizational differences

87. Greg is working in an oilfield assigned to a project in a remote area. The trailer he works out of has a telephone line, but Internet connectivity is limited, and mobile phone coverage is spotty. What would be the best method for Greg to participate in a status meeting?

    A. Email

    B. Voice conferencing

    C. Video conferencing

    D. In-person meetings

88. A rapidly growing company has decided to build a new facility in a different city that will have enough room to house the entire company with room to spare. What type of organizational change does this represent?

    A. Relocation

    B. Outsourcing

    C. Internal organization

    D. Business merger

89. Mandy is a project manager for a team located at three locations around the globe. She just received an update from the customer of an urgent nature. What type of communication method should Mandy use to get this information out to the team?

    A. Email

    B. Impromptu meeting

    C. Virtual meeting

    D. Scheduled meeting

90. Which steps in the change control process are most often skipped or overlooked? (Choose two.)

    A. Validating the change

    B. Seeking CCB approval

    C. Requesting the change

    D. Updating the project plan

91. Wigit Construction's customer has changed their mind on the color of the exterior, and has decided that the bathrooms in a building all need to be accessible to those with disabilities. This is an example of what type of project change?

    A. Resource change

    B. Requirements change

    C. Funding change

    D. Scope change

92. Andy is a project manager for a collocated team, and he just received a mandate from Human Resources (HR) about a lack of compliance from the project team. HR informs Andy that the compliance is important to meet federal law. What type of communication method should Andy use to get this information out to the team?

   A. Video conference

   B. Impromptu meeting

   C. Email

   D. Scheduled meeting

93. The practice of documenting who updated a document when and with what information is known as which one of the following?

   A. Progressive elaboration

   B. Validation

   C. Documentation

   D. Version control

94. Wigitcom's customer has asked for a reporting engine to be added to their software, which was not originally part of the project scope. Which common project changes does this represent? (Choose two.)

   A. Scoping change

   B. Funding change

   C. Quality change

   D. Timeline change

95. Alice is a project manager for a collocated team, and she just received an update from the customer of an urgent nature. What type of communication method should Alice use to get this information out to the team?

   A. Email

   B. Impromptu meeting

   C. Closure meeting

   D. Scheduled meeting

96. A project team had identified a potential event on a project and now needs to take action. What is the appropriate method to deal with this event?

   A. Submit a change request.

   B. Add it to the issue log.

   C. Ignore the new event.

   D. Look to the risk response plan.

97. Jane is the CEO of a company, and there is an update of a security breach at a customer site. She needs to be notified immediately. What is the best method to notify her of the problem?

    A. Social media

    B. Face-to-face conversation

    C. Fax

    D. Text message

98. A project manager for a distributed project team has been gathering a batch of routine organizational messages, project updates, and status reports. What would be the best communication method with which to share this information?

    A. Videoconference

    B. Impromptu meeting

    C. Email

    D. Scheduled meeting

99. When considering a change, who should analyze the schedule, budget, and resource allocations to determine what impacts will occur due to the change?

    A. Project manager

    B. Subject matter expert

    C. Project sponsor

    D. Change control board

100. A project to restore a 75-year-old building and give it historical status is in need of funding and support. The building is located in an area that is nationally known for being a retirement community. What would be the best way to get project information to the community?

    A. Distribution of printed media

    B. Text message

    C. Instant messaging

    D. Email

101. What is the entity that reviews change requests, evaluates impacts, and ultimately approves, denies, or defers the request?

    A. CAB

    B. CCB

    C. NDA

    D. MOU

102. Wallace is the project manager on a team that just crossed a major project milestone. He takes the team to have pizza and a drink on Friday afternoon. This is an example of which one of the following?

    A. Confidentiality constraints

    B. Types of communication

    C. Relationship building

    D. Intraorganizational differences

103. A project team based in Europe needs to conduct a job interview with a candidate in India. What is the best communication method to conduct the interview?

    A. Virtual meeting

    B. In-person meeting

    C. Email

    D. Social media

104. When considering a basic communication model, what are the basic elements that are needed? (Choose three.)

    A. Receiver

    B. Transmission

    C. Inbox

    D. Nonverbal communication

    E. Sender

    F. Message

    G. Decoder

105. The architectural design team has completed the blueprints for a new building and communicates this to the project manager. What type of communication trigger is this?

    A. Task completion

    B. Task initiation

    C. Incident response

    D. Resource changes

106. Who is the target audience and what is the rationale behind conducting a gate review?

    A. Project manager, to ensure resource availability

    B. Project sponsor, to see if they picked a good project

    C. Project team, to find out what they are doing wrong

    D. Project governance, to ensure accountability and objective alignment

107. Functional testing of a fire alarm system has been underway in a new building. The test completed successfully, and the project manager informs all of the occupants and workers in the building of the progress. What is the trigger for this communication?

A. Milestone

B. Task completion

C. Schedule changes

D. Project planning

108. A project to build a wing on a new building has been delayed due to an unseasonably snowy winter. The project manager tells the sponsor, steering committee, and project team. What was the trigger for this communication?

A. Task initiation

B. Milestones

C. Schedule change

D. Task completion

109. DewDrops's project manager has assembled the project team together to review the proposed project schedule and receive feedback on the feasibility of the schedule. What was the trigger for this communication?

A. Risk register updates

B. Project change

C. Project planning

D. Schedule changes

110. A government transportation agency has a group within their organization that examines, validates, and makes recommendations regarding projects and their success in meeting their objectives. What type of communication trigger does this represent?

A. Change request

B. Audit

C. Risk response

D. Business continuity response

111. The convoy carrying materials and equipment to a construction project site has been caught in a major traffic jam due to an accident. This will delay work on the project site for a couple of hours. The project manager sends a text message to the work foreman about the situation. What influenced the use of this communication method?

A. Tailoring the method based on the content of the message

B. Interorganizational differences

C. Personal preferences

D. Confidentiality constraints

112. The IT department normally works the core hours designated by the organization but responds to calls 24×7. The procurement team is all working a flex schedule of four 10-hour shifts. making the scheduling of meetings on Friday problematic. This is an example of which one of the following?

   A. Intraorganizational differences

   B. Personal preferences

   C. Criticality factors

   D. Interorganizational differences

113. Andrew is a project coordinator on a project, and he receives instruction from the company's CEO that she only wants to receive communication on a weekly basis with summary data included. Andrew is addressing the CEO's

   A. Intraorganizational differences.

   B. Interorganizational differences.

   C. Criticality factors.

   D. Personal preferences.

114. The customer site for a project is located in a rural part of a region, whereas the project headquarters is located in a metropolitan hub. What would be the biggest impediment to face-to-face communication?

   A. Technological factors

   B. Times zones

   C. Geographical factors

   D. Intraorganizational differences

115. New, complex instructions need to be communicated to a project team. What is the best communication method with which to distribute this information?

   A. Distribution of printed media

   B. Email

   C. Text message

   D. Social media

116. DewDrops has wrapped up project work, and they are looking to hand off the project to the customer and revisit how the project went for everyone. What is the appropriate communication method with which to conduct these activities?

   A. Kickoff meeting

   B. Virtual meeting

   C. Email

   D. Closure meeting

117. To help celebrate the completion of a major project milestone, the project sponsor wants to hold a barbeque on Friday afternoon to celebrate. What is the best communication method to share this information with the team?

A. Email

B. Impromptu meeting

C. Scheduled meeting

D. Fax

118. What type of communication method would make sense for routine status meetings on a project where the team is spread out over different cities on the same continent?

A. In-person meetings

B. Virtual meetings

C. Closure meetings

D. Kickoff meetings

119. During a project to replace a telephone switch, the project team discovers that one piece of equipment is faulty and a new router will need to be configured. The project manager prepares an email to the organization saying the outage will be extended by an hour to deal with the faulty equipment. What was the trigger for this communication?

A. Task initiation

B. Task completion

C. Project change

D. Schedule change

120. A key stakeholder has considered a project and discovered a new risk that was not previously identified. The project manager shares this information with the appropriate stakeholders, including the project team. What was the trigger for this communication?

A. Project change

B. Risk register update

C. Milestone

D. Task completion

121. When a project manager is working on the creation of artifacts like the scope, budget, and schedule of a project, what type of communication trigger does this represent?

A. Audit

B. Project planning

C. Project change

D. Milestones

122. A systematic and independent examination of project procedures, documentation, spending, statutory compliance, and reporting is known as which one of the following?

   A. Project change

   B. SCRUM retrospective

   C. Gate review

   D. Audit

123. Wigitcom is working on a revolutionary new technology that will potentially alter the entire industry. At an industry conference, a project team member is asked what the team is working on. The employee doesn't share any project details. What is most likely the cause of the employee refusing to share information?

   A. Criticality factors

   B. Cultural differences

   C. Confidentiality constraints

   D. Intraorganizational differences

124. The project team in the field is called in to give a status report that everything is going as planned and that work is going smoothly. Why would the project manager not send a communication to all stakeholders on this update?

   A. Criticality factors

   B. Intraorganizational differences

   C. Technological factors

   D. Personal preferences

125. SmartDrill is an environmentally conscientious energy company operating in a barren, rural part of a country. Mobile phone coverage is poor in this region, and the project team needs to drive for an hour to reach a location where reliable mobile phone coverage and Internet access is available. What factors influence communication with the project team? (Choose two.)

   A. Technological factors

   B. Intraorganizational differences

   C. Geographical factors

   D. Criticality factors

126. Which of the following factors will present challenges to using an offshore team on a project? (Choose three.)

   A. Level of report detail

   B. Language barriers

   C. Time zones

   D. Technological factors

   E. Criticality factors

   F. Cultural differences

127. DewDrops's customer has completed their legal review, and they are returning signed copies of an executed contract. While they have sent the originals in the mail, DewDrops asks them to transmit a copy soon so that contract routing can begin. What is the best communication method to comply with this request?

    A. Fax

    B. Instant messaging

    C. Social media

    D. Distribution of printed materials

128. Allen is a project manager, and he has discovered that two different teams are proceeding in different directions on a work package. What is the appropriate method of communication to get everyone back on track?

    A. Email

    B. Scheduled meeting

    C. Videoconference

    D. Impromptu meeting

129. Which of the following is true regarding a kickoff meeting?

    A. It is the first time that the project team is introduced to each other.

    B. It happens in the Initiation phase.

    C. It occurs when project planning is complete.

    D. All of the above

    E. A and C

130. The project team is assembled and ready to begin work on replacing a telephone switch for an organization. The project manager sends an email to the entire organization to let them know of a three-hour outage. What was the trigger for this communication?

    A. Task completion

    B. Task initiation

    C. Schedule change

    D. Milestone

131. Beau is a project manager who schedules a meeting with subject matter experts to work on activity identification and duration estimation. What triggered this communication?

    A. Milestones

    B. Audit

    C. SCRUM retrospective

    D. Project planning

132. The project team drilling for water in a remote area has had a series of complicated circumstances, causing slow progress on the well. The project manager chooses to write a lengthy email explaining the reasons and the response for the project team. What factors influenced why the project manager chose this method?

   A. Criticality factors

   B. Tailoring the method based on the content of the message

   C. Personal preferences

   D. Rapport building

133. Molly is a key stakeholder on a project. She wants a weekly summary every Friday on the project's progress. An urgent issue comes up on Tuesday that could significantly delay the entire project unless a decision is made quickly. What two factors are in conflict with each other in this scenario?

   A. Intraorganizational differences

   B. Criticality factors

   C. Tailoring the method based on the content of the message

   D. Personal preferences

134. DewDrops has established an offshore project team in another English-speaking country. Several stakeholders are irritated because of the difficulty in understanding the offshore team due to their accents. This is an example of what kind of communication factor?

   A. Cultural differences

   B. Language barriers

   C. Interorganizational differences

   D. Personal preferences

135. Heather is an audience member at a board meeting scheduled to give details on a project. To help answer questions quickly, she has asked several project team members to stand by to provide information that she doesn't know. What form of communication would they use to share information?

   A. Face-to-face meetings

   B. Fax

   C. Email

   D. Instant messaging

136. Even if a project team is located within the same city, but in different parts of the city, what would be the appropriate communication method to conduct an impromptu meeting?

   A. Voice conferencing

   B. Instant messaging

   C. Daily stand-up meetings

   D. Face-to-face meeting

137. A construction project just passed all of the electrical inspections for their permits, and the team can now begin to drywall. The project manager shares this information with the work team. What was the trigger for this communication?

    A. Task completion

    B. Milestone

    C. Risk register update

    D. Gate reviews

138. Who would be the target audience of a project audit?

    A. Auditors

    B. Steering committee

    C. Key stakeholders

    D. Project team members

    E. All of the above

    F. B, C, and D

139. A government agency in charge of a construction project has completed emergency project work three days early. What is the best method to communicate this success to the general public?

    A. Fax

    B. Impromptu media

    C. Distribution of printed media

    D. Social media

140. DewDrops is working on building the project team, and it is attempting to conduct interviews with company employees located in a different city. They attempted to conduct video interviews, but they could not maintain a connection between the two locations. They decide to hold the interviews over the phone instead. What factors influenced this change in direction?

    A. Rapport building

    B. Intraorganizational differences

    C. Technological factors

    D. Language barriers

141. The headquarters for a project is located in California, whereas the customer site is in Florida. What will be the biggest factor affecting the scheduling of meetings, especially impromptu meetings?

    A. Cultural differences

    B. Language barriers

    C. Technological factors

    D. Time zones

142. With a major storm approaching, a construction project still has work teams out in the field. The weather service has indicated that everyone should take precautions immediately. What is the best communication method to let the teams in the field know? (Choose two.)

    A. Impromptu meeting

    B. Text messaging

    C. Scheduled meeting

    D. Phone call

143. Interpersonal conflicts are starting to develop on a project. What is the best communication method to use when confronting the problem?

    A. Instant messaging

    B. Video conferencing

    C. Face-to-face meetings

    D. Email

144. The project sponsor has called the project manager into his office. He lets her know that some additional funding has been secured to allow more resources to be hired onto the project. What was the trigger for this communication?

    A. Project change

    B. Risk register updates

    C. Milestones

    D. Schedule changes

145. At the completion of a project to implement enterprise software at an organization, the software manufacturer asks the project team to run certain programs that will inspect the number of licenses in use. This is an example of which one of the following?

    A. Project change

    B. Audit

    C. Gate review

    D. SCRUM retrospective

146. Cynthia, a member of an executive team, has a visual impairment and requires special software to help enlarge the font on her screen, or to read the screen to her. This is an example of what type of factor influencing communication?

    A. Interorganizational differences

    B. Technological factors

    C. Criticality factors

    D. Personal preferences

147. DewDrops is a struggling global startup with a project team located on three different continents. The customer of the project just radically altered one of the triple constraints. What is the best communication method to share this information with the project team?

   A. Impromptu meetings

   B. Virtual meeting

   C. Email

   D. Instant messaging

148. Michael has assembled the project team to determine what new requirements approved by the CCB can be incorporated into the plan. What was the trigger for this meeting?

   A. Schedule change

   B. Project planning

   C. Task initiation

   D. Project change

149. One project team member has been placed on a performance improvement plan while assigned to a project. The rest of the project team is upset because they do not see management correcting any of this team member's behaviors. What is causing this misunderstanding?

   A. Cultural difference

   B. Confidentiality constraints

   C. Rapport building

   D. Criticality factors

150. Local city government is beginning a project to add more parks to the available open areas, and they are going to hold a series of meetings to begin public comment hearings. What is the best method to communicate with the general public of these meetings? (Choose two.)

   A. Social media

   B. Phone calls

   C. Distribution of printed materials

   D. Impromptu meetings

151. After cost overruns begin to occur on a project to build a new hospital, a firm is brought in to examine the original budget, expenditures, and the contracts on the project. This is known as which one of the following?

   A. An audit

   B. A gate review

   C. A SCRUM retrospective

   D. A project change

152. The project sponsor is out on a two-week vacation and has designated someone to act in her place while she is gone. During the vacation, the budget for the project is suspended by the board of directors with a request to cancel the project. What factors would influence whether the project manager interrupts the sponsor's vacation?

   A. Tailoring the method based on the content of the message

   B. Intraorganizational differences

   C. Personal preferences

   D. Criticality factors

153. Local city government has a project to repave a street that residents must use to park their vehicles. Residents will be required to park their vehicles in a new locale for one week. What is the best communication method the project should use?

   A. Email

   B. Instant messaging

   C. Distribution of printed material

   D. Face-to-face meetings

154. After a productive week, a project team in the field has lots of detailed updates to share with the project manager back at headquarters. The work lead spends an hour writing up all of the accomplishments, problems, and next steps for the field team. What factors are influencing this communication?

   A. Tailoring the method based on the content of the message

   B. Intraorganizational differences

   C. Personal preferences

   D. Criticality factors

155. Members of a project team are dealing with the implementation of a new time reporting system and changed requirements from HR. Which of the following is the type of organizational change causing disruption on the team's project?

   A. Business merger

   B. Business acquisition

   C. Business process change

   D. Relocation

156. A country has just increased the tax burden on certain corporations operating within their borders. What type of organizational change might this bring about? (Choose two.)

   A. Internal reorganization

   B. Relocation

   C. Outsourcing

   D. Business merger

157. Wigitcom has an underperforming business unit that the company is losing interest in funding. What kind of organizational change should Wigitcom consider?

   A. Internal reorganization

   B. Relocation

   C. Outsourcing

   D. Business split

158. A company is struggling with inconsistent results in budgeting and finance using a model where each department has a budget manager. What type of organizational change could help this problem?

   A. Outsourcing

   B. Relocation

   C. Business process change

   D. Business split

159. In light of new tax incentives, a tech company incorporates in a different state and moves their headquarters. What type of organizational change does this represent?

   A. Demerger

   B. Relocation

   C. Internal reorganization

   D. Outsourcing

160. DewDrops is struggling with hiring in the different technical specialties (IT, engineering, marketing, and finance) with a centralized HR department. They move the responsibilities for hiring to the individual departments and give them each a staff member to assist with the process. This type of organizational change is known as which one of the following?

   A. Internal reorganization

   B. Business split

   C. Business process change

   D. Outsourcing

161. When a company decides to spin off, or sell off, one of its business units, what type of organizational change has occurred?

   A. Business acquisition

   B. Business merger

   C. Business split

   D. Internal reorganization

162. Wigit Construction's customer is concerned about children's safety in a new stairwell and asks the project team to add improved handrails. What type of project change does this represent?

A. Quality

B. Requirements

C. Funding

D. Timeline

163. Devdan received a file from the project manager to review. When he is finished, he saves the document with his initials at the end of the filename and emails it back to the project manager. Adding his initials at the end is a form of which one of the following?

A. Change requests

B. Risk response plan

C. Progressive elaboration

D. Version control

164. Richard is a constant morale problem, and he is under performing on a project. The project manager dismisses him from the project and seeks a replacement. This should trigger what kind of communication?

A. Resource change

B. Risk register updates

C. Milestones

D. Task completion

165. An earthquake suddenly strikes a city where a company's headquarters is located. The project team refers to documentation to determine where they should report in the event of disaster. This is an example of which one of the following?

A. Incident response

B. Gate review

C. Business continuity response

D. Resource changes

166. The project team receives an email that the owner of a functional area on an enterprise resource planning (ERP) project will be gone for several months on maternity leave. One of her leads, who is also assigned to the project, will serve as the acting functional area owner while she is out. What triggered this communication?

A. Audit

B. Business continuity response

C. Stakeholder changes

D. Resource changes

167. A nonprofit is attempting to get residents in a neighborhood to come out to help clean parks in the area. They go house to house placing flyers on the doors. What communication method is being used?

   A. Social media

   B. Email

   C. Distribution of printed media

   D. Fax

168. Struggling to compete in the competitive construction market, Wigit Construction agrees to be sold to a larger corporation. What type of organizational change occurred for the larger corporation?

   A. Business merger

   B. Business acquisition

   C. Business process change

   D. Relocation

169. A startup company in the high-tech industry is in need of custodial services for its new building. Which type of organizational change should the startup company consider?

   A. Internal reorganization

   B. Relocation

   C. Outsourcing

   D. Business split

170. Wigit Construction is starting to build a growing market in the southern part of the country, whereas sales have dropped dramatically in their current location. What type of organizational change would help this situation?

   A. Internal reorganization

   B. Relocation

   C. Outsourcing

   D. Business split

171. After an accident at a worksite, Wigit Construction adds new procedures and checklists to end-of-day inspections. This is an example of what type of organizational change?

   A. Risk register changes

   B. Internal reorganization

   C. Business process change

   D. SCRUM introspective

172. DewDrops presents their plan to the CEO where they can decrease defects by 25 percent. The CEO wants to see if they can decrease defects by 75 percent and asks the project team to reanalyze the project. What project variable is the CEO asking them to change?

    A. Quality

    B. Funding

    C. Scope

    D. Risk

173. The documentation strategy for a project calls for each change to be reflected in a log at the beginning of each document. This is known as which one of the following?

    A. Change request logs

    B. SCRUM retrospective

    C. Version control

    D. Risk register

174. An anticipated event of water damage in a construction project is confirmed. The project manager notifies appropriate stakeholders that they will need to bring in a team to perform mold mitigation. What type of communication trigger initiated this communication?

    A. Risk register updates

    B. Business continuity response

    C. Schedule change

    D. Resource change

175. Wigit Construction experienced a flood at the project site that caused several palettes of cement to go bad and is causing water damage to the new building. The project team is instructed to repair the damage and then resupply the project site. This type of communication trigger is known as which one of the following?

    A. Risk register updates

    B. Incident response

    C. Milestones

    D. Project change

176. A catastrophic blizzard has descended on a city, knocking out power in some areas and snowing people in for days. Dewdrops contacts its staff to let them know of a shift to operate on a skeleton crew and suspend project work until it is safe to return to work. What triggered this communication?

    A. Incident response

    B. Business continuity response

    C. Gate reviews

    D. Resource changes

177. The development of an architectural design took twice the amount of time that was projected. What type of project change would this represent?

    A. Scoping change

    B. Timeline change

    C. Quality change

    D. Funding change

178. Members of a project team are dealing with new processes and leadership changes, which resulted from their company joining forces with another company. What type of organizational change disrupted this project?

    A. Business merger

    B. Business acquisition

    C. Business process change

    D. Relocation

179. A government agency just received grant funding to grow its services for a temporary period of time. What is the correct organizational change this agency should consider?

    A. Internal reorganization

    B. Relocation

    C. Outsourcing

    D. Business split

180. Company A and Company B come together to do business as a new company, the originally named Company AB. What type of organizational change is this?

    A. Business merger

    B. Business acquisition

    C. Business process change

    D. Relocation

181. Wigit Construction wants to get out of building commercial properties and focus on residential ones. They sell the commercial part of their practice including staff, equipment, and materials to another company. What type of organizational change has happened?

    A. Business acquisition

    B. Demerger

    C. Business process change

    D. Internal organization

182. DewDrops is adding project staff to complete a project within the required timeline. What type of common project change does this represent?

    A. Timeline change

    B. Risk event

    C. Scope change

    D. Resource change

183. As a hurricane approaches a coastal city, a company sends instructions to the project team to return to their functional departments so that crews can work around the clock on restoring service and cleaning up. This is an example of which one of the following?

A. Business continuity response

B. Stakeholder changes

C. Task completion

D. Risk register updates

184. A retail company is starting to experience longer lines and an increase in customer complaints. The company responds by eliminating the need to sign credit card receipts for transactions under $50. What type of organizational change does this represent?

A. Business process change

B. Internal reorganization

C. Business demerger/split

D. Outsourcing

185. Members of a project team were recently transferred to a company office in a different state, and they can no longer work on the project. What type of organizational change disrupted this project?

A. Internal reorganization

B. Business split

C. Outsourcing

D. Relocation

186. A company is struggling with inconsistent results in budgeting and finance using a decentralized model. What type of organizational change could help this problem?

A. Internal reorganization

B. Relocation

C. Outsourcing

D. Business split

187. Wigit Construction wants to add residential, seaside building to their portfolio. To help gain expertise, they purchase a small business with experienced foremen. What type of organizational change is this?

A. Outsourcing

B. Business merger

C. Internal reorganization

D. Business acquisition

188. A government agency decides to consolidate the purchasing function into a single department for greater reporting and cost controls. What type of organizational change is this?

   A. Demerger

   B. Business acquisition

   C. Business process change

   D. Internal reorganization

189. The implementation of a new timekeeping system will affect every employee in a company, and they will have to log into a computer each pay period to get paid. What kind of organizational change does this represent?

   A. Outsourcing

   B. Risk response

   C. Internal reorganization

   D. Business process change

190. DewDrops has fallen on tough times, and they are looking to cut project costs to help make ends meet. They decide to outsource certain functions and cut back on the number of hours employees are working. What type of communication should this trigger? (Choose two.)

   A. Risk register updates

   B. Project change

   C. Incident response

   D. Resource change

191. In a stunning turn of events, the sponsor of a project was just selected to lead a new European branch of a company. Her replacement will take over as the sponsor of the project, and the project manager sent a memorandum to all stakeholders on the project about this change. Which communication trigger prompted the memorandum to be sent?

   A. Schedule changes

   B. Gate reviews

   C. Stakeholder changes

   D. Resource changes

192. A company has discovered losses due to embezzlement in the Accounting department. An audit is conducted, and a separation of duties is mandated for certain types of transactions. What type of organizational change does this represent?

   A. Relocation

   B. Risk response

   C. Outsourcing

   D. Business process change

193. An international firm has approached DewDrops to see if they are interested in uniting their strengths to compete on a global scale. What kind of organizational change would make sense for DewDrops?

    A.   Outsourcing

    B.   Business process change

    C.   Merger

    D.   Relocation

194. A government agency has a key department located in two different parts of the same city, affecting production, morale, and organizational identity. What type of organizational change would help this situation?

    A.   Internal reorganization

    B.   Merger

    C.   Business process change

    D.   Relocation

195. The steering committee sent an announcement to the project team letting them know that only changes to time, money, and scope will require executive review from now on. All other approvals can now be granted by the project manager. What has type of organizational change was made?

    A.   Project plan

    B.   Business process

    C.   Risk register

    D.   CCB

196. A construction company assigned to a project accidentally cuts the fiber-optic cables to the project site, disrupting communication. The team requests technicians to help repair the damage. What is the trigger for this communication?

    A.   Business continuity response

    B.   Task initiation

    C.   Risk register updates

    D.   Incident response

197. The wife of ace programmer Gary Ventura just had a baby and Gary is going to take a month off to be with his family. The company brings in a consulting resource of the same caliber as Gary to complete his assignments. What type of communication should this trigger?

    A.   Project change

    B.   Resource change

    C.   Schedule change

    D.   Risk register updates

198. DewDrops is impressed by a current business trend, and it decides to eliminate a layer of management in favor of more team members who produce. Select the type of organizational change this represents.

A. Internal reorganization

B. Relocation

C. Outsourcing

D. Business split

199. A country's tax code just regulated more stringent reporting for the banking industry. What kind of organizational change would that cause for a company within that business sector?

A. Internal reorganization

B. Merger

C. Business process change

D. Business split

200. A business is spending too much time trying to hire new staff for the different technical divisions. This has resulted in project teams not completing their project assignments, so the business hires a company to handle interviews, vetting, and hiring of new staff. This type of organizational change is known as which one of the following?

A. Internal reorganization

B. Outsourcing

C. Business acquisition

D. Staff turnover

201. The original project plan for the construction of a building called the facility to be 95 percent defect free by the end of the project. The customer wants few hassles after taking ownership of the building, and this changes to 98 percent defect free. What type of project change does this represent?

A. Scope

B. Risk

C. Timeline

D. Quality

202. A government agency lives by their interoffice mail system to route paper copies for signature all across the organization. A new software program will allow for electronic routing and signature capabilities. What kind of organizational change would implementing this functionality represent?

A. Business process change

B. Internal reorganization

C. Business merger

D. Business acquisition

203. The construction of a new data network originally asked for the network to be available 99.999 percent of time. Upon reflection, it was deemed that the new facility only needed 99.9 percent availability, dramatically decreasing the costs. What type of common project change was this?

A. Timeline change

B. Quality change

C. Risk event

D. Resource change

204. DewDrops has liquid assets as an organization but doesn't have adequate business expertise in a key market area. What type of organizational change should they consider?

A. Internal reorganization

B. Acquisition

C. Business process change

D. Relocation

205. The project manager just completed a meeting with the steering committee and announces to the team that the project can move forward. Which of the following initiated the communication?

A. Gate reviews

B. Resource changes

C. Business continuity response

D. Milestones

Chapter

4

Project Tools and Documentation (Domain 4.0)

THE FOLLOWING COMPTIA PROJECT+ EXAM OBJECTIVES ARE COVERED IN THIS CHAPTER:

✓ **4.1 Compare and contrast various project management tools.**

- Project scheduling software
- Charts
  - Process diagram
  - Histogram
  - Fishbone
  - Pareto chart
  - Run chart
  - Scatter chart
  - Gantt chart
- Dashboard/status report
- Knowledge management tools
  - Intranet sites
  - Internet sites
  - Wiki pages
  - Vendor knowledge bases
  - Collaboration tools
- Performance measurement tools
  - Key performance indicators
  - Key performance parameters
  - Balanced score card

- SWOT analysis
- Responsible, Accountable, Consulted, Informed (RACI) Matrix

✓ **4.2 Given a scenario, analyze project-centric documentation.**

- Project charter
- Project management plan
- Issues log
- Organizational chart
- Scope statement
- Communication plan
- Project schedule
- Status report
- Dashboard information
- Action items
- Meeting agenda/meeting minutes

✓ **4.3 Identify common partner or vendor-centric documents and their purpose.**

- Request for Information
- Request for Proposal
- Request for Quote
- Mutually binding documents
  - Agreements/contract
  - Non-disclosure agreement
  - Cease and Desist letter
  - Letters of Intent
  - Statement of Work
  - Memorandum of Understanding
  - Service Level Agreement
  - Purchase Order
  - Warranty

1. Ralph is the project manager for the opening of a new ice cream parlor. The owner is always asking for status updates from Ralph and pushes Ralph to finish with a quality store that is on-time and on-budget. Which role in a RACI matrix would Ralph hold for the entire project?

   A.   Responsible

   B.   Accountable

   C.   Consulted

   D.   Informed

2. Which knowledge management tool would be used for a team to communicate instantly, share information on task ownership and status, and see events for an entire workgroup?

   A.   Wiki pages

   B.   Intranet sites

   C.   Vendor knowledge bases

   D.   Collaboration tools

3. During a weekly project meeting, a list is kept of any assignments that are handed out during the meeting. What type of project document is this?

   A.   Issues log

   B.   Action items

   C.   Meeting minutes

   D.   Communication plan

4. The project's sponsor is reviewing a communication for the project manager. In the document, she reads that the project is on budget, but there was a delay in getting materials from a supplier since the last communication. Which project document is she reading?

   A.   Status report

   B.   Scope statement

   C.   Risk register

   D.   SCRUM retrospective

5. What type of project management tool is depicted here?

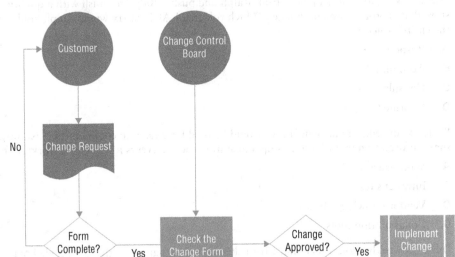

   A. Process diagram

   B. Histogram

   C. Pareto chart

   D. Gantt chart

6. The project schedule contains all of the following elements, EXCEPT

   A. Activity start and finish dates

   B. Activity duration

   C. Activity assignments to resources

   D. Authorization for the project to begin

7. Nathan is a software game developer assigned to a project to create a revolutionary new virtual reality game. He receives notice that he is to attend a meeting and give a presentation for 45 minutes on the capabilities of the technology that they will be using. Which document did Nathan receive that communicated this requirement?

   A. Meeting agenda

   B. Meeting minutes

   C. Action items

   D. Wiki pages

8. Which of the following are a means of communicating the current conditions of a project? (Choose three.)
   A. Dashboard information
   B. Status report
   C. Meeting minutes
   D. Meeting agenda
   E. Communication plan
   F. Project charter

9. Which of the following tools is used for entering data to generate a Gantt chart, WBS, or activity sequence automatically?
   A. Process diagram
   B. SCRUM retrospective
   C. Collaboration tools
   D. Project scheduling software

10. Which knowledge management tool is used to communicate only with internal employees for an entire organization?
    A. Wiki pages
    B. Intranet sites
    C. Internet sites
    D. Collaboration tools

11. What is a RACI matrix used for?
    A. Determining key performance indicators
    B. Identifying roles and responsibilities
    C. Analyzing risk at a moment in time
    D. Presenting status via a dashboard

12. A subject-matter expert who is not directly working on a project receives a phone call to get her opinion on two options facing the team. Which role in a RACI matrix has this stakeholder been assigned?
    A. Responsible
    B. Accountable
    C. Consulted
    D. Informed

13. Carl is the president of a binding company that won the job to bind the books for a new young adult novel. The publishing company needs 100,000 books delivered in 12 days. At the end of each day, Carl asks for the completed number of books to make sure that it is at 8,333 or higher. What does this number represent?

A. MOU

B. AC

C. SPI

D. KPI

14. To which project-centric document would you refer to get a description of the project, find out the key deliverables, and gain an understanding of the success and acceptance criteria for the project?

A. Project charter

B. Scope statement

C. Project schedule

D. Meeting minutes

15. During a regular meeting, the team creates a list that has next steps to be taken, who owns the task, and when it is due. What kind of project documentation does this list represent?

A. Action items

B. Issues log

C. Status report

D. Communication plan

16. In which of the following documents would you find information regarding the high-level budget and milestones for the project?

A. Request for information

B. Scope statement

C. Project charter

D. Action items

17. Meghan is a project manager. A team member reported to her an inappropriate and unprofessional interaction with a project team member on a different team. Meghan is not sure to whom this other team member reports. Which project document would help her find the correct person to whom to escalate this issue?

A. RACI matrix

B. Request for proposal

C. Organizational chart

D. Issues log

18. A construction project has just completed the demolition and grading of a worksite. The project manager needs to update the status of this task and see what the next task is that needs to start. Which project-centric document would the project manager look to for guidance?

    A. Project charter

    B. Project schedule

    C. Action items

    D. Dashboard information

19. During a project meeting, a key stakeholder looks at a report and sees that the schedule now has a yellow setting when last week it was set at green. What kind of data is the stakeholder viewing?

    A. Dashboard information

    B. Fishbone diagram

    C. Project management plan

    D. Risk register

20. What type of project management tool is depicted here?

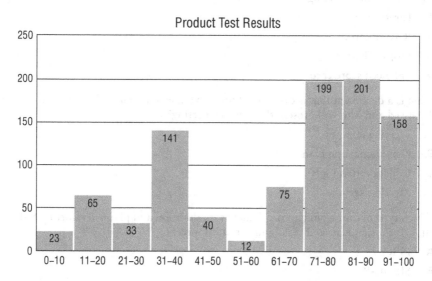

    A. Process diagram

    B. Histogram

    C. Pareto Chart

    D. Gantt Chart

21. The communication plan contains all of the following components, EXCEPT
    A. Stakeholder information needs
    B. When information should be distributed
    C. Report on status of deliverables and schedule
    D. How information will be delivered

22. Working on a project as a part of college class, Hannah takes notes on what occurs during a meeting, types up the information including action items, and disseminates the final version to the team. What project document did Hannah create?
    A. Meeting agenda
    B. Meeting minutes
    C. Status report
    D. Action items

23. Bert is a project manager assigned to the development of a new piece of hospital equipment. He is looking for the information that spells out who the stakeholders are, what the high-level scope is, assumptions, constraints, and the authorization to proceed. Which document is Bert looking for?
    A. Pareto chart
    B. RACI matrix
    C. Project charter
    D. Balanced score card

24. What is a document that is distributed prior to a meeting that spells out the topics to be discussed and who will present them at the meeting?
    A. Meeting minutes
    B. Communication plan
    C. Collaboration tools
    D. Meeting agenda

25. Which type of tool would auto-calculate task duration and planned effort by task and allow for assignment and reassignment of resources?
    A. PERT
    B. SIPOC-R
    C. Project scheduling software
    D. Histograms

26. When creating a RACI matrix, how many different positions can/must have the role of accountable?
    A. Zero
    B. One
    C. Two
    D. Three

27. The field team sends an update to the project manager letting him know that there were 12 employees at the project site, there were no accidents this week and no issues to report, and that the team is tracking toward on-time completion of their work. The project manager adds this information in a box on a report. What would you call this data provided to the project manager's report?

   A. Action items

   B. Dashboard information

   C. Organization chart

   D. Project management plan

28. Monty can't remember what the key performance indicators are to help measure success on the product the project team is creating. Where can Monty find this information?

   A. Issues log

   B. Scope statement

   C. Communications plan

   D. Action items

29. Which project plan sets how information will be shared on the project, what the frequency level is with which it will be shared, and with whom it will be shared?

   A. Meeting agenda

   B. Action items

   C. Project charter

   D. Communication plan

30. What is a set of quantifiable measures that an organization uses to gauge progress toward project goals?

   A. RACI

   B. SWOT

   C. KPI

   D. NDA

31. Susan is working on a project, and she is the lone specialist assigned to complete a deliverable on a task. She will do the work to complete the assignment, and she is the person who must answer for the correct and thorough completion of the deliverable. Which two participation types of a RACI matrix has she been assigned? (Choose two.)

   A. Responsible

   B. Accountable

   C. Consulted

   D. Informed

32. What is an inventory of project actions that should be resolved in order to fulfill deliverables?

    A. Histogram

    B. Wiki pages

    C. Action items

    D. Issues log

33. The project organizational chart would contain all of the following components, EXCEPT

    A. Project authorization

    B. Team member organization

    C. Reporting structures

    D. Visual representation of data elements

34. Scott is a board director for a nonprofit, and he is looking for an update on the financial aspects of a new project that the organization is attempting. Which document would help bring Scott up to speed on current conditions of the project?

    A. Issues log

    B. Project management plan

    C. SWOT analysis

    D. Status report

35. There is a question about a project decision that was made at a gathering earlier in a project. Where should the project manager look to help recall the decision and the circumstances that were discussed?

    A. Meeting agenda

    B. Project charter

    C. Action items list

    D. Meeting minutes

36. Which tool provides a visual representation of all of the steps required in a process?

    A. Process diagram

    B. Histogram

    C. Pareto chart

    D. Project scheduling software

37. When a RACI matrix is being created, what person or group of people are assign an "R" for responsible?

    A. The one who is ultimately answerable for the correct and thorough completion of the assignment

    B. Those whose opinions are needed before work or a decision is undertaken

    C. Those who do the work needed to complete the task or deliverable

    D. Those who are kept up-to-date when work or a decision is completed

38. To which document would a project manager refer in order to review the high-level scope, high-level risks, assumptions, and constraints, and to find out who are the key stakeholders?

    A. Scope statement

    B. Project charter

    C. Project management plan

    D. Meeting agenda

39. What type of project management tool is depicted here?

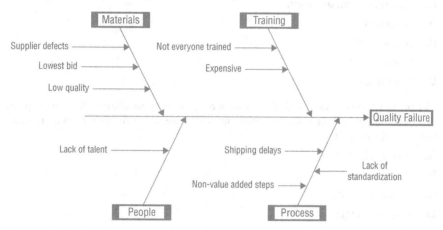

    A. Process diagram

    B. Histogram

    C. Pareto chart

    D. Fishbone diagram

40. During a meeting, the team reports that Brad is sorely underperforming. The project manager needs either to replace or reassign Brad. Where would this task get captured?

    A. Meeting agenda

    B. Lessons learned

    C. Issues log

    D. Action items

41. Which is a special form of a bar chart that visually displays the central tendency, dispersion, and distribution for statistical data?

    A. Kanban board

    B. Histogram

    C. Pareto chart

    D. SIPOC-R

42. Which knowledge management tools allow users to freely create and edit web page content using a web browser?

    A. Intranet sites

    B. Wiki pages

    C. Collaboration tools

    D. Internet sites

43. Troy, Tony, and Hannah are assigned to a project with several activities where their efforts will produce a deliverable. In a RACI matrix context, what role have these project team members been assigned?

    A. Responsible

    B. Accountable

    C. Consulted

    D. Informed

44. The project sponsor has decided to make a project manager change. Which project-centric document should the incumbent project manager use to get the new project manager up to speed on the project?

    A. Project charter

    B. Action items

    C. Project schedule

    D. Project management plan

45. Which document provides formal authorization to begin the project and allows the project manager to begin assigning resources to the project?

    A. Project charter

    B. Scope statement

    C. Project management plan

    D. Request for proposal

46. A project team tasked with creating a new software application has discovered that the programming needed is twice as complex as they thought it would be, and they have informed the project manager that they will need more resources or will need to push the due date out by two months. Where would this topic get recorded in project documentation?

    A. Project charter

    B. Issues log

    C. Action items

    D. Risk register

47. What type of project management tool is depicted here?

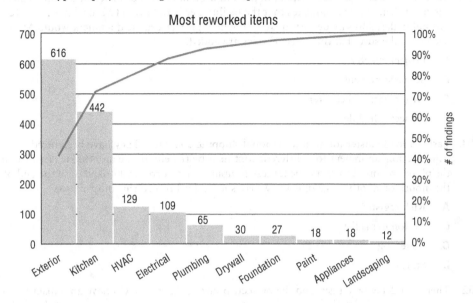

Most reworked items

A. Process diagram

B. Histogram

C. Pareto chart

D. Gantt chart

48. Which of the following is an electronic reporting tool where users can choose elements of the project to monitor project health and status?

A. Kanban board

B. Project scheduling software

C. Vendor knowledge bases

D. Dashboard information

49. A status report would contain all of the following information, EXCEPT

A. Recap of meeting discussion

B. Tracking toward deliverables

C. Condition of the project compared to the schedule

D. Updates on risks and issues

50. Molly is an expert planner helping to get a new bank branch designed and built to meet customer demand. She indicates that the facility needs to have ATM machines, a drive-through teller, and safe deposit boxes. To which project-centric document would Molly need to make sure that these deliverables are added?

A. Project charter

B. Scope statement

C. Organizational charter

D. Project schedule

51. Earl is a load master for an international shipping company. They have been hired to move construction equipment to a different continent by the end of the month. He is aware that the planes required to carry the largest equipment are currently booked until the end of the month on another assignment. Where should Earl record this information?

A. Risk register

B. Action items list

C. Issues log

D. Status report

52. There is a delay on a task, and the project sponsor asks if this will have an impact on the entire project. Which document would the project manager reference to see if this task is on the critical path?

A. Project charter

B. Issues log

C. Scope statement

D. Project schedule

53. Which type of chart or diagram is used to represent visually the cause and effect of potential problems to help identify their root causes?

A. Pareto chart

B. Histogram

C. Process diagram

D. Fishbone diagram

54. A project stakeholder receives a regular status update for various activities and milestones after they are completed. What role in a RACI matrix has this stakeholder been assigned?

A. Responsible

B. Accountable

C. Consulted

D. Informed

55. Andy is doing a review of a list that contains active problems on the project, their status, owner, and a due date to get resolution. Which project-centric document is Andy looking at?

   A. Issues log

   B. Organizational chart

   C. Action items

   D. Status report

56. At the completion of a meeting, the person who was designated as a scribe types up his notes along with any decisions that were made and any assignments that were handed out. What type of project-centric document is this?

   A. Action items

   B. Meeting agenda

   C. Status report

   D. Meeting minutes

57. What is the comprehensive collection of documents that spells out communication, risk management, project schedule, and scope management?

   A. Scope statement

   B. Request for proposal

   C. Project management plan

   D. Dashboard information

58. Emily has logged into the project website and is looking at various elements of the project health and status. What kind of project-centric documentation is Emily looking at?

   A. Meeting minutes

   B. Project management plan

   C. Action items

   D. Dashboard information

59. When dealing with a RACI chart, which of the following are true? (Choose three.)

   A. RACI is an acronym for responsible, accountable, consulted, and informed.

   B. RACI is a hierarchical and seniority-based matrix.

   C. RACI is an acronym for reasonable, accountable, conflicted, and informed.

   D. A RACI is matrix-based chart.

   E. A RACI is a form of a SWOT analysis for risk identification.

   F. A RACI is used to identify roles and responsibilities on a project.

60. What type of project management tool is depicted here?

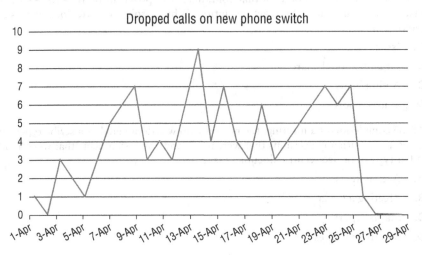

A. Run chart

B. Histogram

C. Pareto chart

D. Fishbone diagram

61. The scope statement contains all of the following components, EXCEPT

A. Product description

B. Key deliverables

C. Activity start and finish dates

D. Acceptance criteria

62. Nick is a subject-matter expert assigned to a project to host a major soccer tournament. He is providing input on the amount of time each activity of the project will take and in what order they should be attempted. To which document is Nick contributing?

A. Project schedule

B. Scope statement

C. Meeting agenda

D. Lessons learned

63. Before an upcoming meeting, Judy sends a document letting everyone know what needs to be discussed, how much time will be allowed to talk about each item, and who needs to be prepared to speak. What type of project-centric document does this represent?

A. Action items

B. Meeting agenda

C. Issues log

D. Meeting minutes

64. Which tool would be used to help find the distribution of issues (or other variables) from highest to lowest as bars on a chart?

A. Scatter chart

B. Histogram

C. Pareto chart

D. Run chart

65. Which knowledge management tool allows contractors or users of a company's products to find information about a particular issue or to find a work instruction on how to use a product?

A. Collaboration tools

B. Social media

C. Vendor knowledge bases

D. Intranet sites

66. The project management plan consists of all of the following components EXCEPT. (Choose two.)

A. Project schedule

B. Scope plan

C. Action items

D. Communication plan

E. Request for proposal

67. Simon is a high school intern assigned to help get the word out on a project. He is tasked with creating written reports, sending emails, and creating agendas. Which document would tell Simon what tasks need to be created and at what interval?

A. Communication plan

B. Lessons learned

C. Meeting minutes

D. Project schedule

68. In each meeting, a project team member is identified as the scribe to take notes on the topics, action items, and other issues identified in the meeting. What document is the scribe assigned with creating?

A. Meeting minutes

B. Status report

C. Dashboard information

D. Issues log

69. Which tool would be used to display observed data in a time sequence?

    A. Run chart

    B. Histogram

    C. Pareto chart

    D. Scatter diagram

70. A software development team lets the project manager know that they will need five more days to complete their assigned task. The project manager makes reference to a document and concludes that this will cause a delay of the entire project if nothing else changes. Which document was the project manager using to make this analysis?

    A. Status report

    B. Communication plan

    C. Project schedule

    D. Scope statement

71. The project team is required to attend a daily stand-up meeting to discuss the project's activities and roadblocks. Which document lets the project team know they need to attend this meeting?

    A. Project schedule

    B. Communication plan

    C. Project charter

    D. Scope statement

72. Pattie is a project manager for a firm that performs accreditations for higher education institutions. They have been asked to perform a review of a university system of three schools, so she starts to create a communication plan, scope plan, and project schedule. Into which project-centric document would this information get added?

    A. Project management plan

    B. Business case

    C. Project charter

    D. Lessons learned

73. What type of project management tool is depicted here?

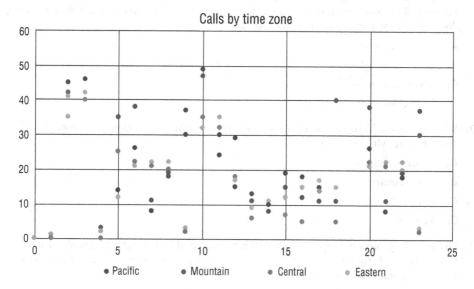

Calls by time zone

● Pacific   ● Mountain   ● Central   ● Eastern

A. Process diagram

B. Histogram

C. Pareto chart

D. Scatter chart

74. A new theater production for Halloween is underway. Josh is the director, Vanessa is in charge of costuming, Ren is in charge of set construction, and Seth is in charge of marketing and business operations. Where would this information be captured?

A. Project charter

B. Communications plan

C. Organizational chart

D. Balanced score card

75. Which tool would you use to create a regression line to forecast how the change in an independent variable will change a dependent variable?

A. Process diagram

B. Histogram

C. Pareto chart

D. Scatter chart

76. The project manager is reviewing a plan that contains the communication plan, risk management plan, schedule, quality management plan, and scope statement. Which planning document is the project manager looking at?

    A. Project charter

    B. Dashboard information

    C. Meeting agenda

    D. Project management plan

77. Which tool would you use to create a visual representation of timelines, start dates, durations, and activity sequences?

    A. Process diagram

    B. Pareto chart

    C. Gantt chart

    D. Histogram

78. Shane is the project manager assigned to a project, and he is creating a graphic that shows the project leads for each subject area along with the resources assigned to them. What type of document is Shane creating?

    A. Communication plan

    B. Pareto diagram

    C. Fishbone diagram

    D. Organizational chart

79. The project manager is responsible for the creation, updating, and completion of this collection of documents, spelling out intentions for budget, schedule, scope, communication, and risk. What is this collection of documents called?

    A. Communication plan

    B. Project schedule

    C. Memorandum of understanding

    D. Project management plan

80. The issues log would capture all the following data components, EXCEPT

    A. Issue description

    B. Owner

    C. Mitigation

    D. Due date

81. In the project meeting minutes, there is a section that contains work that was identified in the meeting to be completed along with the name of the person to perform the work and a due date. What does this section of the meeting minutes represent?

    A. Dashboard information

    B. Kanban board

    C. SIPOC-R

    D. Action items

82. Which knowledge management tool would an organization use to provide information to the general public, customers, and partners?

    A. Social media

    B. Intranet sites

    C. Internet sites

    D. Vendor knowledge bases

83. Jean is looking at a visual representation of the reporting structures that describe the project team member organization. What project-centric document is she looking at?

    A. Project charter

    B. Project schedule

    C. Organizational chart

    D. Communication plan

84. The project charter accomplishes all of the following project components, EXCEPT

    A. Sets high-level scope, budget, and milestones

    B. Sets the hierarchical reporting structure for the project

    C. Authorizes the project to begin

    D. Authorizes resources to begin to be applied to the project

85. Amelia is struggling to get a meeting with a key subject matter expert to gather project requirements within the planned timeframe. Where should this information be recorded?

    A. Communication plan

    B. Issues log

    C. Project schedule

    D. Action items

86. During a regular check-in meeting with stakeholders, the project manager presents information on all task areas. Each task area has a column for time, cost, resources, risks, issues, and changes, and each item shows a red, yellow, or green indication representing the condition of each task in each area. What project-centric document is being presented?

    A. Process diagram

    B. Gantt chart

    C. Dashboard information

    D. Run chart

87. The project sponsor has asked that the stakeholders be brought up to speed on project deliverables, schedule, risks, and issues. What is the project sponsor asking for?

    A. Meeting agenda

    B. Status report

    C. Action items

    D. Meeting minutes

88. A large, global project to create a new movie has over a thousand individuals assigned to the project. The project manager needs to find out which individuals are working with the second production unit. Which project-centric document would help give her this information?

   A. Organizational chart

   B. RACI matrix

   C. Fishbone diagram

   D. Project charter

89. The project manager is working with the project team on a weekly document explaining to stakeholders what tasks have been completed, how much budget has been spent, what issues exist, and any risks that are affecting the project. What document are they working on?

   A. Issues log

   B. Action items

   C. Status report

   D. Project management plan

90. A new team member is added to a project and asks a question about what work needs to get done and how the team will know that they are successful. Which document would help answer the questions that this team member is asking?

   A. Project charter

   B. Project schedule

   C. Action items

   D. Scope statement

91. The project coordinator has been instructed to send a weekly status update, by email, to an identified group of stakeholders. Which document would instruct the project coordinator to perform this activity?

   A. Project charter

   B. Project schedule

   C. RACI matrix

   D. Communication plan

92. A project team member learns from an email that she will need to give a brief presentation at the next meeting to outline the problem facing her team's tasks on the project along with possible solutions. Which project-centric document is this team member looking at?

   A. Meeting agenda

   B. Meeting minutes

   C. Status report

   D. Project schedule

93. DewDrops is wondering about the timeliness of their checkout process. Danielle has been tasked with creating a tool to track and display this observed data. What output should she create?

    A. Pareto chart

    B. Histogram

    C. Run chart

    D. Scatter diagram

94. What is the only role in a RACI matrix that can only be assigned once per task?

    A. Responsible

    B. Accountable

    C. Consulted

    D. Informed

95. Wigit Construction has reviewed an RFP response and has reached an agreement with the seller. How should they communicate the quantity of goods and services they need and the price that will be paid?

    A. Time and materials

    B. Purchase order

    C. Cost-reimbursable contract

    D. Fixed-price contract

96. *We are here for you!* is a temporary staffing firm that has sent two administrative assistants to a project to help keep up with demand. What is the best contract vehicle for them to use to deliver this service?

    A. Cost-reimbursable contract

    B. Purchase order

    C. Fixed-price contract

    D. Time and materials

97. Two government agencies have agreed to work with each other on a major project. They spend some time creating a memorandum of understanding (MOU) that both parties sign. What best describes what the MOU represents?

    A. Mutually binding document

    B. Non-mutually binding document

    C. An announcement of each agency's intentions

    D. Procurement method to gain more information

98. DewDrops has just completed a document with a customer. The document describes the services DewDrops will provide to the customer, what amount they will be paid, and what penalties DewDrops will face if they fail to deliver. What type of document is this?

A. Request for proposal

B. Warranty

C. Nondisclosure agreement

D. Contract

99. Hugh has been asked to investigate a new line of medical equipment for a hospital that an executive saw at a trade show. The hospital has no idea who supplies this equipment or how much it might cost. What is the appropriate procurement method Hugh should pursue?

A. SOW

B. RFI

C. RFP

D. RFQ

100. What is a SOW?

A. A procurement method intended to obtain more information about goods and services

B. A procurement method designed to invite bids, review, select, and purchase goods or services

C. A procurement document that details the goods and services to be procured from outside the organization

D. A meeting with prospective vendors prior to completing a proposal

101. Wigitcom is looking for a new storage solution to handle its increasing data needs. They are unclear exactly what kind of solution they might need, or even what vendors could sell them a solution. What is the best procurement method they should use?

A. Request for proposal (RFP)

B. Request for quotation (RFQ)

C. Request for information (RFI)

D. Statement of work (SOW)

102. Erik has been doing an analysis to compare any correlation between an independent and dependent variable. He has created a regression line chart to forecast the changes. What has Erik created?

A. Process diagram

B. Histogram

C. Pareto chart

D. Scatter chart

103. Why would a buyer issue a purchase order?

    A. To denote that the situation requires more flexibility and simplicity than a contract

    B. To outline the intent or actions of both parties before entering into a contract

    C. To describe the quantity of goods and services needed and what price will be paid

    D. To stop another company from using their intellectual property and to inform them not to do it again

104. DewDrops is looking to solicit bids for the creation of a new manufacturing facility and delivery dock. Which vendor solicitation method should DewDrops use?

    A. Statement of work (SOW)

    B. Request for quotation (RFQ)

    C. Request for proposal (RFP)

    D. Request for information (RFI)

105. What does a warranty specify to the buyer of a product or service?

    A. It specifies the quantity of goods and services needed and what price will be paid.

    B. It provides a guarantee that the product or service will meet expectations and perform as stated.

    C. It outlines the intent or actions of both parties before entering a contract.

    D. It assures that sensitive or trade secret information is not shared outside the partnership.

106. The process of submitting a SOW, receiving bids from vendors and suppliers, evaluating responses, and making a selection is known as which one of the following?

    A. C&D

    B. RFP

    C. SCRUM introspective

    D. RFQ

107. A legal document that describes the goods or services that will be provided, their cost, and any penalties for noncompliance is known as which one of the following?

    A. Request for proposal

    B. Nondisclosure agreement

    C. Contract

    D. Warranty

108. Vital characteristics, functions, requirements or design basis, which if changed, would have a major impact on product or service performance, scope, schedule, cost, and/or risk. What is this a definition for?

    A. Key performance indicator

    B. Memorandum of agreement

    C. Key performance parameter

    D. Dashboard information

109. Kim and Bill are co-project managers for a large complex project. They need to calculate and keep track of tasks and due dates, and they must produce reports quickly and accurately. What should they use for this purpose?

A. Kanban board

B. Daily SCRUM

C. Project scheduling software

D. Vendor knowledge bases

110. Wigit Construction has won a bid to build a new headquarters for a government agency that issued an RFP. The government agency is concerned that Wigit Construction will not agree to their terms and conditions, and they want assurances that there will not be a long, drawn-out contract negotiation. What document could Wigit Construction use to allow negotiations to begin?

A. Letter of intent

B. Warranty

C. Nondisclosure agreement

D. Cease and desist letter

111. What best describes an RFI?

A. Procurement method to obtain more information about goods and services

B. Procurement method to invite bids, and review, select, and purchase goods or services

C. Procurement document that details the goods and services to be procured from outside the organization

D. A meeting with prospective vendors prior to completing a proposal

112. DewDrops is the parent company for SunRays, Inc. and DaisyChains, Inc. SunRays and DaisyChains agree to provide services to each other and outline specific performance expectations, with any incentives or penalties spelled out should they not be followed. What is the best method to memorialize the arrangement?

A. MOU

B. SLA

C. NDA

D. RFP

113. *We are here for you!* has done work for DewDrops in the past, and it has begun to advertise and market that DewDrops is a client without DewDrops' consent. What document should be sent to *We are here for you!* to correct this behavior?

A. Nondisclosure agreement

B. Service-level agreement

C. Cease and desist letter

D. Warranty

114. Wigit Construction has completed a project. They submit an invoice to recover the money spent on special marble that they used in the creation of a dining room floor, which the contract allows them to do. What type of contract is Wigit Construction using?

    A. Time and materials

    B. Statement of work

    C. Cost-reimbursable contract

    D. Fixed-price contract

115. Why would two parties create service-level agreements?

    A. To assure that sensitive or trade secret information is not shared outside the partnership

    B. To outline the intent or actions of both parties before entering into a contract

    C. To outline the performance levels expected between the two organizations

    D. To stop another company from using their intellectual property and to inform them not to do it again

116. Jeff has completed the creation of a statement of work and submits it to his company's procurement section in order to solicit bids from vendors. The procurement team lets him know that he will need to evaluate responses from vendors and help make a selection. Which procurement method is described in this scenario?

    A. SOW

    B. RFI

    C. RFP

    D. RFQ

117. Which vendor solicitation method is best to use when more data is required about the goods and services that need to be procured?

    A. Request for information (RFI)

    B. Request for quotation (RFQ)

    C. Request for proposal (RFP)

    D. Statement of work (SOW)

118. Why would a technology company send a cease and desist letter to another company?

    A. To outline the service levels expected between the two organizations

    B. To outline the intent or actions of both parties before entering a contract

    C. To assure that sensitive or trade secret information is not shared outside the partnership

    D. To stop another company from using their intellectual property and to inform them not to do it again

119. A software development team is sharing their knowledge and progress by using a web browser to edit a common page. Which knowledge management tool are they using?

    A. Wiki pages

    B. Intranet sites

    C. Internet sites

    D. Collaboration tools

120. Trevor and Harry are working on creating the software code for a project. What RACI category have they been assigned for this task?

    A. Responsible

    B. Accountable

    C. Consulted

    D. Informed

121. DewDrops has issued a document allowing a seller to begin work on a project. The document spells out what the seller will be paid and what the exact deliverables are that need to be provided on the project. What document has DewDrops issued to the seller?

    A. Purchase order

    B. Cost-reimbursable contract

    C. Fixed-price contract

    D. Time and materials

122. Primarily used by the federal government and utility industry, what are performance attributes of a system considered critical or essential to the development of an effective capability?

    A. Key performance parameter

    B. Intergovernmental agreement

    C. Service-level agreement

    D. Letter of intent

123. What document provides the guarantee that a product or service will meet expectations and perform as stated?

    A. Warranty

    B. Service-level agreement

    C. Purchase order

    D. Memorandum of understanding

124. Which vendor solicitation method would be used to invite suppliers into a bidding process to bid on specific products or services?

    A. Request for information (RFI)

    B. Request for quotation (RFQ)

    C. Request for proposal (RFP)

    D. Statement of work (SOW)

125. What best describes an RFQ?

    A. A meeting with prospective vendors prior to completing a proposal

    B. Procurement document that details the goods and services to be procured from outside the organization

    C. Procurement method to invite bids, review, select, and purchase goods or services

    D. Procurement method to obtain more information about goods and services

126. All of the following are procurement methods, EXCEPT

    A. RFQ

    B. RACI

    C. RFI

    D. RFP

127. Vanina has taken over as the project manager for a large complex project. She has worked with the project team to get updated status and start dates on tasks. What tool would she use to turn this information into updated reports?

    A. Kanban board

    B. Project scheduling software

    C. Intranet sites

    D. Vendor knowledge bases

128. DewDrops is the parent company for SunRays, Inc. and DaisyChains, Inc. SunRays and DaisyChains are agreeing to provide service to each other and outline specific criteria each must follow. What is the best method to memorialize the arrangement?

    A. SLA

    B. MOU

    C. NDA

    D. RFP

129. Wigitcom has a patent for a mobile device technology that another company is using without their permission and without compensation. What should be Wigitcom's next step?

    A. Issue a purchase order

    B. Issue a letter of intent

    C. Issue a cease and desist letter

    D. Enter into a nondisclosure agreement

130. Why would two parties create and share a letter of intent?

    A. To assure that sensitive or trade secret information is not shared outside the partnership

    B. To outline the intent or actions of both parties before entering a contract

    C. To outline the service levels expected between the two organizations

    D. To stop another company from using their intellectual property and to inform them not to do it again

131. What vendor-centric document would be used to ensure that sensitive or trade secret information is not shared outside of the organization?

    A. MOU

    B. SLA

    C. NDA

    D. RFP

132. When an organization is ready to procure products or services so that work can begin, which procurement method should be used?

    A. Request for information (RFI)

    B. Request for quotation (RFQ)

    C. Request for proposal (RFP)

    D. Statement of work (SOW)

133. What is a bidder's conference?

    A. A daily meeting to ask three questions on project progress and hurdles

    B. A meeting with all prospective vendors to answer questions and clarify issues within an RFP

    C. An auction to help find the lowest cost bid for a product or service

    D. A document that spells out the good or service an organization is looking to procure from outside the organization

134. Wigitcom and DewDrops have entered into a partnership to complete a project. Wigitcom wants to ensure that their trade secrets are not revealed or used by DewDrops. What type of agreement should the two organizations use?

    A. RFP

    B. NDA

    C. SLA

    D. MOU

135. DewDrops has issued an RFP, but their statement of work is undeveloped because they are not sure what they want the finished product to do. Which type of contract would make sense in this situation?

    A. Cost-reimbursable contract

    B. Purchase order

    C. Fixed-price contract

    D. Time and materials

136. Wigit Construction is responding to an RFP where the work needed is well defined, clear, and concise. What is the best type of contract to use if they win the work?

    A. Fixed-price contract

    B. Service-level agreement

    C. Cost-reimbursable contract

    D. Time and materials

137. Which type of contract is riskiest for the buyer?

    A. Time and materials

    B. SCRUM methodology

    C. Cost-reimbursable contract

    D. Fixed-price contract

138. A government agency is looking for a new constituent management system. Though they are unclear about what options are available, they need to be able to make a decision quickly and move forward to procure a solution. What is the best procurement method for them to use?

    A. SOW

    B. RFI

    C. RFP

    D. RFQ

139. Which of the following are types of mutually binding documents? (Choose three.)

    A. Agreements/contract

    B. Memorandum of understanding

    C. SCRUM retrospective

    D. Issues log

    E. Purchase order

    F. Histogram

140. Wigitcom is developing a new product, and it needs a specific skills set to help accomplish the project. They find a staffing firm that can provide them with a resource, but Wigitcom is unsure what the specific deliverables of the engagement will be. Which contract vehicle will provide them with the most flexibility?

    A. Time and materials

    B. Purchase order

    C. Cost-reimbursable contract

    D. Fixed-price contract

141. DewDrops has issued an RFP, but their statement of work is undeveloped. They decide to use a cost-reimbursable contract with the seller. What best describes the risk condition to DewDrops in this scenario?

    A. Risk doesn't occur until the project is started and doesn't matter at the contract phase.

    B. Risk is evenly divided between buyer and seller.

    C. This is the riskiest type of contract because the buyer won't know the final cost until the project is completed.

    D. This is the least risky type of contract because the seller assumes the risk of unknown costs.

142. Noreen has been working on a document that outlines several pieces of equipment her company needs as well as the professional services required to install the equipment. What document has Noreen created?

   A. Request for information (RFI)

   B. Request for quotation (RFQ)

   C. Request for proposal (RFP)

   D. Statement of work (SOW)

143. A government agency has issued a request for quotation for a new computer solution to help their constituents. What other procurement method is comparable to an RFQ?

   A. SOW

   B. NDA

   C. RFP

   D. RFI

144. Why would two parties create a memorandum of understanding agreement? (Choose two.)

   A. The situation requires more flexibility and simplicity than a contract.

   B. The safety of information or trade secrets needs to be protected.

   C. The two parties are unable to enter into a contractual agreement.

   D. To inform another party to stop their actions and not to take them back up again.

145. Which type of contract would work best when the product or service needed is well defined?

   A. Time and materials

   B. SCRUM methodology

   C. Cost-reimbursable contract

   D. Fixed-price contract

146. Wigit Construction is responding to an RFP where the customer wants to use a fixed-price contract. Which of the following statements represents the risk to Wigit Construction should they win the work?

   A. Least risky because the buyer assumes the risk of unknown costs

   B. Riskiest because problems on the project will increase their costs

   C. Risk is evenly divided between buyer and seller

   D. Risk doesn't occur until the project is started and doesn't matter at the contract phase

147. DewDrops has issued an RFP for the purchase of a new enterprise software system. They host a phone call to answer any questions about the RFP and to clarify any issues. This call is an example of which one of the following?

   A. SCRUM retrospective

   B. Meeting minutes

   C. Bidder conference

   D. Fixed-price contract

148. Which two procurement methods serve a similar purpose of scanning the vendor landscape for number of vendors and to gain a cost estimate? (Choose two.)

A. RFQ

B. NDA

C. RFP

D. RFI

149. Which type of contract allows the seller to recover all allowable expenses associated with providing the goods or services?

A. Cost-reimbursable contract

B. Time and materials

C. Statement of work

D. Fixed-price contract

150. Wigit Construction has been considering the purchase of a new fleet of dump trucks. Upon receiving funding approval from their board of directors, senior leadership, or other appropriate managing body, they are ready to begin procurement. Which procurement method should they use?

A. Request for proposal (RFP)

B. Request for quotation (RFQ)

C. Statement of work (SOW)

D. Request for information (RFI)

151. What best describes an RFP?

A. Procurement method used to invite bids, review, select, and purchase goods or services

B. Procurement method used to obtain more information about goods and services

C. A meeting with prospective vendors prior to completing a proposal

D. Procurement document that details the goods and services to be procured from outside the organization

152. What document would be created by a buyer that describes the specifications and quantities of goods or services to be acquired and at what price?

A. Request for proposal

B. Purchase order

C. Request for information

D. Action items

153. Which document describes the goods or services an organization is interested in procuring from outside the organization?

A. SOW

B. RFI

C. RFP

D. RFQ

154. What document would be created to define performance expectations among two or more parties?

    A. MOU

    B. NDA

    C. SLA

    D. RFP

155. Which type of contract is riskiest for the seller?

    A. Cost-reimbursable contract

    B. Purchase order

    C. Fixed-price contract

    D. Time and materials

156. What document would be created to outline specific performance criteria or other actions between two parties?

    A. MOU

    B. SLA

    C. NDA

    D. RFP

157. A team that is geographically dispersed has the need to work on documents together and to have more tools than phone calls by which they can communicate. What is a good option for them to consider using?

    A. Wiki pages

    B. Intranet sites

    C. Vendor knowledge bases

    D. Collaboration tools

158. A long meeting is taking place to document all of the steps that have been taken to build a house in order to try to find improvement opportunities. What type of deliverable will be created?

    A. Gantt chart

    B. Histogram

    C. Process diagram

    D. Pareto chart

159. The project charter should contain all of the following information, EXCEPT

    A. High-level requirements

    B. High-level budget

    C. High-level action items

    D. Assumptions and constraints

160. A vendor is very strict in applying formal change control on a project for a customer, and few changes are actually getting approved. Which contract vehicle would cause a vendor to behave this way?

   A. Cost-reimbursable

   B. Fixed-price

   C. Time and materials

   D. Request for proposal

161. Alex is using a SWOT analysis to determine the internal strengths and weakness facing the project. What else would this analysis give him?

   A. The external opportunities and threats

   B. The internal opportunities and threats

   C. The external strengths and weaknesses

   D. There are no other contributions from the SWOT analysis

162. Which type of contract would be used in a staff augmentation situation?

   A. Time and materials

   B. Purchase order

   C. Cost-reimbursable contract

   D. Fixed-price contract

163. The project sponsor receives a phone call letting her know that a major task has been completed successfully and there were no safety issues to report. Which role has the project sponsor been assigned on this task?

   A. Responsible

   B. Accountable

   C. Consulted

   D. Informed

164. DewDrops is helping a customer implement a new business practice, and they are stuck on a problem that is holding up the project. The DewDrops consultant checks the company database to see if other clients have had this problem and what they did about it. Which knowledge management tool is this consultant using?

   A. Vendor knowledge bases

   B. Wiki pages

   C. Collaboration tools

   D. Internet sites

165. At a gate check meeting, the committee is presented with a report that shows health in different areas of a project: Schedule = Green, Budget = Yellow, Scope = Green, Risk = Yellow, and Publicity = Red. What type of tool is the committee looking at?

- **A.** Collaboration tool
- **B.** Scatter chart
- **C.** Pareto chart
- **D.** Balanced score card

166. Jack, Jill, and Harry are three shift managers who help a project work around the clock. What kind of tool would help them keep a log to allow for easy shift change?

- **A.** Social media
- **B.** Internet sites
- **C.** Wiki pages
- **D.** Vendor knowledge bases

167. After a change in leadership, the new project manager wants to get a sense of the structure and reporting relationships of the project. Which document would give them this information?

- **A.** Organizational chart
- **B.** Project chart
- **C.** Meeting minutes
- **D.** Lessons learned

168. Which type of document would be given to a committee during a gate check?

- **A.** Status report
- **B.** Communications plan
- **C.** Pareto chart
- **D.** Project scheduling software

169. At the completion of a government project requiring security clearance, what document would a vendor likely be asked to sign?

- **A.** Service-level agreement
- **B.** Warranty
- **C.** Request for proposal
- **D.** Nondisclosure agreement

170. The project adds a consultant to help determine all the steps needed in the invoice payment process for a company. Which tool would the consultant most likely use?

- **A.** Process diagram
- **B.** Pareto chart
- **C.** Project scheduling software
- **D.** Project charter

171. The project sponsor considers the project to be a failure because the budget continues to climb. What tool can the project manager use to help confirm or deny the project sponsor's suspicion?

A. Balanced score card

B. RACI matrix

C. Gantt chart

D. Project management plan

172. Which type of contract offers the greatest flexibility to change scope on a project?

A. Cost-reimbursable contract

B. Purchase order

C. Fixed-price contract

D. Time and materials

173. The project team is a ready to move forward with a cut over to the new system. Prior to beginning the task, they call Karen, who is a subject matter expert, to make sure that everything is ready. What role in an RACI chart is Karen assigned for this task?

A. Responsible

B. Accountable

C. Consulted

D. Informed

174. What type of project management tool is depicted here?

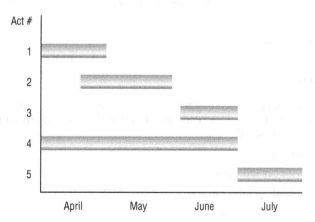

A. Process diagram

B. Gantt chart

C. Pareto chart

D. Scatter chart

175. What is the best tool for sharing information across an entire organization but that shields that information from those outside the organization?

   A. Intranet sites

   B. Wiki pages

   C. Collaboration tools

   D. Internet sites

176. How should a project team memorialize what was said and agreed to during project gatherings?

   A. Create a business case

   B. Create a project management plan

   C. Create a scope statement

   D. Create meeting minutes

177. A company has received a cease and desist letter regarding the building of a wall on a property line. What is this letter telling the company to do?

   A. Only bill them for time and materials for the wall's construction

   B. Reveal no information about the secrets of the wall

   C. Set the service-level expectations for care of the wall

   D. Stop building the wall, and do not resume this activity

178. Dean has been working on a project for six months, though he is not a permanent employee of the company—he is a contract employee provided by a vendor. Which contract vehicle makes the most sense to use in this case?

   A. Cost-reimbursable

   B. Fixed-price contract

   C. Time and materials

   D. Request for proposal

179. A project team member is spending time typing task information into a computer application that includes tasks, start and end date, and duration. Which project management tool is this team member using?

   A. Collaboration tools

   B. Key performance indicators

   C. Project scheduling software

   D. Project management plan

180. Wigit Construction needs to complete the replacement of six bridges as a part of a road-widening project. They need to complete one bridge every ten weeks for the project to be finished on time. What does the completion of a bridge every ten weeks represent?

A. COQ

B. KPI

C. ETC

D. KPP

181. Why would an organization and vendor enter into a nondisclosure agreement?

A. To inform one party to stop doing an activity and to not do that activity again

B. To ensure that sensitive or trade secret information is not shared outside the organization

C. To announce the intent or actions of both parties before entering a contractual agreement

D. To define the service-level performance expectations between the parties

182. An electronic board has six areas that contain information from different parts of a project. What is this screen displaying?

A. Wiki pages

B. Dashboard information

C. Internet sites

D. Collaboration tools

183. The project manager is reviewing a document with the team, and together they are determining the critical path for the project. What part of the project are they analyzing?

A. Scope statement

B. Project schedule

C. Budget variance

D. Kanban board

184. JoAnn has been tasked with tracking the production data for a prototype product for the first three months in order to ensure that it meets the forecast for quality. Which tool should she use for this analysis?

A. Pareto chart

B. Run chart

C. Fishbone diagram

D. Wiki pages

185. The project sponsor is looking for an environmental scan to determine if the project is well placed to be a success, especially when comparing their company to the competition. What is the best tool to complete this scan?

   A.   Process diagram

   B.   Histogram

   C.   Vendor knowledge bases

   D.   SWOT analysis

186. *We are here for you!* is a startup company offering staff augmentations for certain project implementations. What kind of tool would they use for customers to gain knowledge about their business?

   A.   Intranet sites

   B.   Wiki pages

   C.   Collaboration tools

   D.   Internet sites

187. What document would be used to outline the intent or actions of different parties prior to entering into a contract or other mutually binding agreement?

   A.   Cease and desist letter

   B.   Service level agreement

   C.   Nondisclosure agreement

   D.   Letter of intent

188. The project team is testing the prototype product they have built and trying to see how many times it can be used before it fails. What tool would they use to do analysis?

   A.   Scatter chart

   B.   Histogram

   C.   Pareto chart

   D.   Run chart

189. The list of items that need to be monitored and/or escalated to minimize the impact on the project team is called which one of the following?

   A.   Issues log

   B.   Action items

   C.   Risk register

   D.   Budget report

190. Valentine has been asked to determine the root cause of communication problems on a global project. Which tool should she use to help her with this analysis?

   A.   Pareto chart

   B.   Run chart

   C.   Wiki pages

   D.   Fishbone diagram

191. The project manager has been closely monitoring staff hours on a certain phase of the project. This phase has a potential risk that could cause both a schedule and budget over-run on the project. What do staff hours represent in this scenario?

    A. SWOT analysis

    B. Wiki pages

    C. Key performance indicator

    D. Risk register

192. What document would be used to force another party to quit doing a certain activity and let them know not to begin that activity again?

    A. Cease and desist letter

    B. Service level agreement

    C. Nondisclosure agreement

    D. Warranty

193. The project manager is given a bar chart representing the statistical distribution of traffic on a stretch of road that needs work. What tool has the project manager been handed?

    A. Pareto chart

    B. Histogram

    C. Process diagram

    D. Fishbone diagram

194. What kind of tool would automate the creation of critical path, float, WBS, and activity sequence?

    A. Project scheduling software

    B. SIPOC-R

    C. PERT

    D. Run chart

195. A vendor has provided an invoice for their time spent on a project, travel expenses and per diem, and the cost of supplies used on the project. What contract is being used here?

    A. Cease and desist

    B. Time and materials

    C. Cost-reimbursable

    D. Fixed-price

196. Roy is struggling with several issues on a project that are overwhelming productivity. He wants to see which issues are causing the biggest disruption to the project. Which tool should he use?

    A. Histogram

    B. Pareto chart

    C. Run chart

    D. Scatter chart

197. A project team has locations in two different cities, and two team members in the different locations are trying to solve a problem. They use software that allows them to share their screens with each other. What type of knowledge management tool are they using?

  A. Intranet sites

  B. Wiki pages

  C. Collaboration tools

  D. Internet sites

198. Miranda is a functional manager whose business will be disrupted with the implementation of a new piece of software. She is invited to vendor demonstrations so that she can see the new production process and offer her opinion before a final selection is made. What role is Miranda assigned for this task?

  A. Consulted

  B. Informed

  C. Responsible

  D. Accountable

199. The project manager is excited to share with the team that they have received the formal authorization to begin the project. What did they receive that gave them this authority?

  A. Request for proposal

  B. Scope statement

  C. Project charter

  D. Project management plan

200. A subject matter expert on a project has been monitoring the distribution of support calls received each hour during the day to determine staffing needs for a project. Which tool is this person most likely using?

  A. Process diagram

  B. Histogram

  C. Run chart

  D. Gantt

201. William works for the public relations office of a government agency. He receives word that construction on a new bridge is complete and that traffic can resume normal operation so that he can issue a press release. What role has William been assigned for this task update?

  A. Consulted

  B. Informed

  C. Responsible

  D. Accountable

202. A buyer knows mostly what they want out of a project, but they are unable to state completely what the product will need to do. Which contract vehicle would make the most sense in this scenario?

   A.   Time and materials

   B.   Cost-reimbursable contract

   C.   The project is not attempted

   D.   Fixed-price contract

203. A customer wants a firm fixed-price for their arrangement with a vendor on a project. Which of the following statements are true? (Choose two.)

   A.   Contract negations will take longer to ensure that the scope is explicit.

   B.   The risk for the contract shifts to the buyer.

   C.   The risk for the contract shifts to the seller.

   D.   There will likely be lots of change orders on this project.

204. A project sponsor is scanning a document that has grades for the status of scope, budget, and schedule on a project, plus some additional KPIs. What document is the project sponsor looking at?

   A.   Key performance parameters

   B.   Balanced score card

   C.   SWOT analysis

   D.   Key performance indicators

205. What does SWOT stand for?

   A.   Strengths, weaknesses, opportunities, threats

   B.   Strengths, work, opportunities, traceability

   C.   Situation, weaknesses, open source, threats

   D.   Situation, work, open source, traceability

Chapter

5

Practice Test 1

This practice exam can be used to simulate the actual CompTIA Project+ exam. The practice exam is balanced in the percentage and number of questions it includes in accordance with the mixture of questions that you will see on the actual exam, although the actual exam may have more questions. That breakdown is as follows:

Domain 1: Project Basics	36%
Domain 2: Project Constraints	17%
Domain 3: Communication and Change Management	26%
Domain 4: Project Tools and Documentation	21%

Set a timer for 75 minutes and attempt to complete this practice test without reference to other materials until the test is over.

1. What are two defining characteristics of a project? (Choose two.)
    A. Reworking an existing project
    B. An organized effort to fulfill a purpose
    C. Has a specific end date
    D. Routine activities to an organization
    E. Blueprints needed to construct a building

2. Why would a buyer issue a purchase order?
    A. To describe the quantity of goods and services needed and what price will be paid.
    B. To outline the intent or actions of both parties before entering a contract.
    C. To stop another company from using their intellectual property and to inform them not to do it again.
    D. The situation requires more flexibility and simplicity than a contract.

3. To which project-centric document would you refer to get a description of the project, find out the key deliverables, and gain an understanding of the success and acceptance criteria for the project?
    A. Project charter
    B. Project schedule
    C. Scope statement
    D. Meeting minutes

4. All of the following are forms of organizational change, EXCEPT
    A. Relocation
    B. Business demerger
    C. Organic shifts
    D. Business merger

5. When the schedule slips on a project because the work is taking longer than planned, what type of common project change does this represent?
    A. Funding change
    B. Timeline change
    C. Risk event
    D. Requirements change

6. Scrum is which one of the following?
    A. A phrase referring to the overcomplication of a project
    B. An Agile technique where backlogs are used
    C. Creating better, more detailed explanations for senior management
    D. The continuous modification and detailing of the project plan

7. The process of assigning numerical probabilities to each risk and the impacts on project objectives is known as which one of the following?

   A. Identify risk

   B. Quantitative risk analysis

   C. Qualitative risk analysis

   D. Risk categorization

8. What type of project management tool is depicted here?

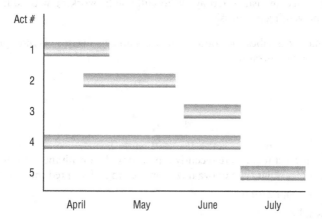

   A. Fishbone diagram

   B. Gantt chart

   C. Collaboration tools

   D. Process diagram

9. Which project role promotes the need and urgency of a project, as well as advertising the project's success?

   A. Project scheduler

   B. Project manager

   C. Project sponsor or champion

   D. Project coordinator

10. The EV for a project is 800, and the AC is 1200. The CPI for the project would be which one of the following?

   A. 1.5

   B. 400

   C. .667

   D. 2000

11. As a part of a daily scrum meeting, the team seeks to share information in three areas. Which set of questions represents the topics of this knowledge sharing?

    A. What did I accomplish today? Who will you be working with today? What obstacles are preventing progress?

    B. What did I accomplish yesterday? What will I do today? What are the necessary next steps?

    C. What did I accomplish yesterday? What will I do today? What obstacles are preventing progress?

    D. What did I accomplish yesterday? Who will you be working with today? What obstacles are preventing progress?

12. Which document describes the goods or services an organization is interested in procuring from outside the organization?

    A. RFI

    B. SOW

    C. RFP

    D. RFQ

13. Members of a project team were recently replaced with consultants with more expertise in the subject matter. What type of organizational change disrupted this project?

    A. Internal reorganization

    B. Business split

    C. Outsourcing

    D. Relocation

14. What does SWOT stand for?

    A. Situation, work, open source, traceability

    B. Strengths, work, opportunities, traceability

    C. Situation, weaknesses, open source, threats

    D. Strengths, weaknesses, opportunities, threats

15. All of the following are common types of project changes, EXCEPT

    A. Scope changes

    B. Requirement changes

    C. Organizational changes

    D. Timeline changes

16. When considering the base communication model, what are the basic elements that are needed? (Choose three.)

    A. Transmission

    B. Receiver

   C. Inbox

   D. Sender

   E. Nonverbal communication

   F. Decoder

   G. Message

17. Cheryl is a technical lead on a project that is wrapping up remote work at a customer site. What is the best method to communicate the work efforts and next steps with the customer?

   A. Closure meeting

   B. Virtual meeting

   C. Kickoff meeting

   D. In-person meeting

18. The approved budget for given work to be completed within a specific timeframe is called which one of the following?

   A. Planned value

   B. Cost variance

   C. Earned value

   D. Actual costs

19. In what step would the make-or-buy decision occur?

   A. During the kickoff meeting

   B. During the design of the product or service

   C. In the execution of the project plan

   D. In the creation of the procurement plan

20. When should an employee's performance expectations be set for a project?

   A. When the functional manager sets annual goals

   B. During the first meeting with a new team member

   C. During the stakeholder identification meeting

   D. During the employee performance review

21. When a project team is assigned to work solely on a project, it is an example of what type of resource?

   A. Dedicated

   B. Collocated

   C. Shared

   D. Physical

22. Developing contingency reserves to deal with risks, should they occur, is known as which one of the following?

    A. Active acceptance

    B. Passive acceptance

    C. Exploit

    D. Transfer

23. A project team based in Europe needs to conduct a job interview with a candidate in India. What is the best communication method to conduct the interview?

    A. In-person meeting

    B. Virtual meeting

    C. Social media

    D. Email

24. What are milestones?

    A. Characteristics of deliverables that must be met

    B. Major events in a project used to measure progress

    C. Checkpoints on a project to determine go/no-go decisions

    D. A measure of the distance traveled on a project

25. What type of project management tool is depicted here?

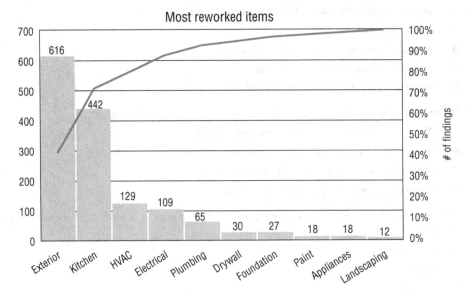

   A. Pareto chart

   B. Project schedule

   C. Histogram

   D. Gantt chart

26. At the beginning of a work period, or sprint, there is a sprint planning meeting. What does this meeting accomplish?

   A. Set a realistic backlog of items to be completed during this iteration

   B. Set the communication and quality plans for the project

   C. Prepare the project charter and kickoff meeting

   D. Get a head start of the work needed on the project

27. Which vendor solicitation method is best to use when more data is needed about the goods and services that need to be procured?

   A. Request for proposal (RFP)

   B. Request for quotation (RFQ)

   C. Request for information (RFI)

   D. Statement of work (SOW)

28. A large company is struggling with inconsistent results in hiring and retention because of a decentralized HR model. What type of organizational change could help this problem?

   A. Business split

   B. Outsourcing

   C. Relocation

   D. Internal reorganization

29. A systematic and independent examination of project procedures, documentation, spending, statutory compliance, and reporting is known as which one of the following?

   A. Audit

   B. Gate review

   C. SCRUM retrospective

   D. Project change

30. All of the following are examples of deliverables, EXCEPT

   A. Blueprints

   B. User documentation

   C. Finished product

   D. Signoff on the project charter

31. Which of the following are types of mutually binding documents? (Choose three.)

   A. SCRUM retrospective

   B. Agreements/contract

   C. Memorandum of understanding

   D. Issues log

   E. Purchase order

   F. Histogram

32. A company is struggling with timely billing of their customers, so they hire a consultant to help determine all of the steps and workflow needed to send a bill. Which tool would the consultant most likely use?

   A. Pareto chart

   B. Process diagram

   C. Project charter

   D. Project scheduling software

33. A company has procurement teams at each of their 22 locations, leading to potentially purchasing the same products from 22 different suppliers. To help save money, the company decides to centralize and standardize the reporting function. What type of business change is this?

   A. Internal reorganization

   B. Staff turnover

   C. Business process change

   D. Outsourcing

34. Once a change request is submitted, where should it be recorded and assigned an identification number for tracking purposes?

   A. Change request log

   B. Risk register

   C. Business process repository

   D. Issue log

35. Which of the following factors present challenges for a global project team located on different continents? (Choose three.)

   A. Language barriers

   B. Level of report detail

   C. Technological factors

   D. Time zones

   E. Cultural differences

   F. Criticality factors

36. All of the following would be updates to the risk register following the qualitative risk analysis, EXCEPT

   A. Watch list of low-priority risks

   B. Risks requiring near-term responses

   C. Causes of risks

   D. Numerical evaluation of each risk

37. What type of project management tool is depicted here?

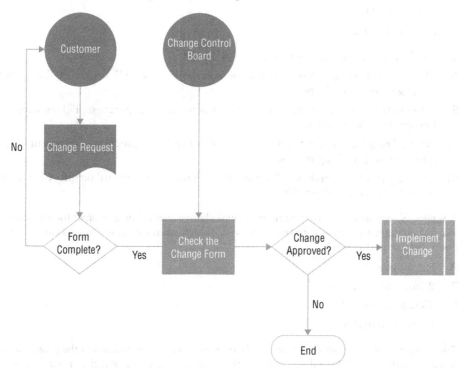

   A. SCRUM retrospective

   B. Fishbone diagram

   C. Process diagram

   D. Risk register

38. What are project assumptions?

   A. Factors considered to be true for planning purposes

   B. Factors considered to be true for control purposes

   C. Internal or external factors affecting the project team

   D. Factors that restrict the project

39. Your friend has hinted that she would like a special gift for her birthday. The following steps are needed for the gift exchange:

   Enjoyment of her gift

   Put card on the gift

   Wrap present

   Choose gift

   Give her the present

   Make purchase

   Fill out the card

   What is the correct sequence for project Happy Birthday?

   A. Choose gift; Make purchase; Put card on gift; Wrap present; Fill out card; Enjoyment of her gift; Give her the present

   B. Give her the present; Put card on gift; Wrap present; Make purchase; Fill out card; Enjoyment of her gift; Choose gift

   C. Put card on gift; Give her the present; Fill out card; Make purchase; Enjoyment of her gift; Choose gift; Wrap present

   D. Choose gift; Make purchase; Wrap present; Fill out card; Put card on gift; Give her the present; Enjoyment of her gift

40. A vendor is very strict on insisting upon formal change control on a project for a customer and few changes are actually getting approved. Which contract vehicle would cause a vendor to behave in this way?

   A. Fixed-price

   B. Request for proposal

   C. Time and materials

   D. Cost-reimbursable

41. The project team is required to attend a daily stand-up meeting to discuss the project activities and roadblocks. Which document lets the project team know that they need to attend this meeting?

   A. Project schedule

   B. Scope statement

   C. Communication plan

   D. Project charter

42. The joining of two businesses to come together and operate as one, single entity is known as which one of the following?

   A. Business acquisition

   B. Business merger

   C. Business process change

   D. Business split

43. A local cable company accidentally cuts the fiber-optic cables going into the project site, thereby disrupting communication. The team requests technicians from the company to repair the damage quickly. What is the trigger for this communication?

   A. Incident response

   B. Task initiation

   C. Risk register updates

   D. Business continuity response

44. An offshore team has issued a holiday schedule consistent with their customs to the project manager. The holiday schedule issued by the team differs from the company's established holiday schedule. This is an example of which one of the following?

   A. Criticality factors

   B. Language barriers

   C. Time zones

   D. Cultural differences

45. A government agency has hired a firm to perform work on its sewer system. As a part of the RFP, the agency requires the successful vendor to carry insurance for errors and omissions. What type of risk strategy is this?

   A. Transfer, negative risk strategy

   B. Exploit, positive risk strategy

   C. Accept, negative risk strategy

   D. Share, positive risk strategy

46. In what stage of team development do team members begin to confront each other and vie for position and control?

   A. Adjourning

   B. Norming

   C. Forming

   D. Storming

   E. Performing

47. A project stakeholder has which of the following responsibilities?

   A. Documentation and administrative support, estimation of task duration, solicit task status from resources, expertise

   B. Documentation and administrative support, provides input and requirements, project steering, expertise

   C. Vested interest, provides input and requirements, project steering, expertise

   D. Vested interest, provides input and requirements, cross-functional coordination, expertise

48. What aspect of project management is shared with Agile and a traditional waterfall approach?

   A. Iterative approach

   B. Adaptive to new/changing requirements

   C. Sprint planning

   D. Self-organized and self-directed teams

49. What type of dependency is the obtaining of sign-off on the design of a product?

   A. Mandatory

   B. Discretionary

   C. External

   D. This is not a dependency

50. At the beginning of a movie project at a production facility, what document would an employee likely be asked to sign?

   A. Cease and desist letter

   B. Service-level agreement

   C. Nondisclosure agreement

   D. Request for proposal

51. What is the best tool for sharing information across an entire organization but shielding that information from those outside the organization?

   A. Collaboration tools

   B. Intranet sites

   C. Wiki pages

   D. Internet sites

52. What is the entity that reviews change requests, evaluates impacts, and ultimately approves, denies, or defers such requests?

   A. CAB

   B. MOU

   C. NDA

   D. CCB

53. A project coordinating the event for a product launch suffered a setback when a plumbing problem flooded the convention hall. Five thousand people are expected to be in attendance at the event, which is scheduled to start in four hours. What factor would influence the communication method?

   A. Relationship building

   B. Criticality factors

C. Language barriers

D. Time zones

54. Measuring the spending to date, determining the burn rate, and accounting for purchases is known as which one of the following?

A. Expenditure tracking

B. Expenditure reporting

C. Estimate to Complete (ETC)

D. Cost accounting

55. Which parts of a SWOT analysis are focused on issues external to the organization?

A. Strengths and weaknesses

B. Opportunities and weaknesses

C. Strengths and threats

D. Opportunities and threats

56. A large, well-established organization that has been in business for many decades would likely have which organizational structure?

A. Weak-matrix

B. Strong-matrix

C. Functional

D. Projectized

57. Which conflict resolution technique produces win-lose results for the parties?

A. Forcing

B. Attacking

C. Avoiding

D. Confronting

58. There is a question about a project decision made earlier in a project. Where should the project manager look to help recall the decision and the circumstances that were discussed?

A. Meeting minutes

B. Project charter

C. Action items list

D. Meeting agenda

59. The architectural design team has completed the blueprints for a new building and communicates this to the project manager. What type of communication trigger is this?

A. Incident response

B. Resource changes

C. Task completion

D. Task initiation

60. The activity that involves determining the usefulness of data gathered to evaluate risk is called which one of the following?

    A. Impact and probability matrix

    B. Risk urgency assessment

    C. Risk data quality assessment

    D. Risk categorization

61. Which project role is responsible for arranging resources between multiple projects?

    A. Project management office

    B. Project scheduler

    C. Project manager

    D. Project coordinator

62. In which document would a project manager refer in order to review the high-level scope, high-level risks, assumptions, and constraints, and to find out who the key stakeholders are?

    A. Project charter

    B. Scope statement

    C. Project management plan

    D. Meeting agenda

63. The project manager just completed a meeting with the steering committee and announces to the team that the project can move forward to the next phase. Which of the following initiated the communication?

    A. Milestones

    B. Business continuity response

    C. Resource changes

    D. Gate reviews

64. In which project phase would the brainstorming, evaluation, and impact of risk be assessed?

    A. Execution

    B. Closing

    C. Monitor and Control

    D. Initiation

    E. Planning

65. Which type of document would be given to a committee during a gate check?

    A. Pareto chart

    B. Communications plan

    C. Status report

    D. Change control plan

66. Which document will ensure the capture of all needed change request information so that it can receive proper consideration?

    A. SIPOC-R

    B. Project charter

    C. Template

    D. Meeting minutes

67. Interpersonal conflicts are starting to develop on a project. What is the best communication method to use when confronting the problem?

    A. Instant messaging

    B. Face-to-face meetings

    C. Email

    D. Videoconferencing

68. What are the two forms of acceptance when considering risk response strategies?

    A. Active

    B. Unintentional

    C. Deliberate

    D. Passive

69. Who is responsible for high-level risk identification?

    A. Project team

    B. Project champion

    C. Project manager

    D. Key stakeholders

70. The types of organizational structures include which of the following? (Choose three.)

    A. Functional

    B. Agile

    C. Co-location

    D. Projectized

    E. Matrix

71. The Closing phase includes all of the following, EXCEPT

    A. Monitoring the risks and issues log

    B. Release of project members

    C. Archiving of project documents

    D. Review of lessons learned

72. What are the three types of estimates used in three-point estimates?

    A. Fastest-Schedule, Least Resources, Most Desirable

    B. Fastest-Schedule, Optimistic, Most Desirable

    C. Most Likely, Least Resources, Fastest Schedule

    D. Most Likely, Optimistic, and Pessimistic

73. An animated movie project requires the following ordered steps: story idea, script, story-board, voice talent, models, and sets construction, to name just a few. Storyboard has what relationship to script?

    A. It is a predecessor task.

    B. It is a discretionary task.

    C. It is a successor task.

    D. It is a mandatory task.

74. After a change in leadership, the new project manager wants to get a sense of the structure and reporting relationships of the project. Which document would give the manager this information?

    A. Lessons learned

    B. Project chart

    C. Meeting minutes

    D. Organizational chart

75. Which of the following are used to conduct virtual meetings? (Choose two.)

    A. Voice conferencing

    B. Face-to-face

    C. Videoconferencing

    D. Impromptu visits

76. What is the activity that determines how soon potential risks might occur and determines responses for those risks?

    A. Risk categorization

    B. Risk urgency assessment

    C. Impact and probability matrix

    D. Risk data quality assessment

77. A project manager has been asked to report on all expenditures to date on the project. What has the project manager been asked to provide?

    A. Expenditures and receipts

    B. Balanced scorecard

    C. Actual cost

    D. Cost variance

78. What factors should be considered when scheduling a video or telephone conference?

    A. Determining whether team members are introverted or extroverted

    B. Recognizing the different time zones and schedules being used

    C. Ensuring writing materials are available in the room

    D. Ensuring that the meeting room has sufficient seating

79. All of the following are cost-estimating techniques, EXCEPT

    A. SIPOC-R

    B. Bottom-up estimating

    C. Parametric estimating

    D. Analogous estimating

80. The work breakdown structure is created during which project phase?

    A. Monitor and Control

    B. Closing

    C. Execution

    D. Initiation

    E. Planning

81. In what organizational structure does a project manager have limited authority over people's time and what they are assigned?

    A. Strong-matrix

    B. Weak-matrix

    C. Functional

    D. Projectized

82. A scope management plan contains which of the following elements? (Choose three.)

    A. Process for creating, maintaining, and approving the WBS

    B. Process for creating the budget

    C. Definition of how the deliverables will be verified

    D. Process for creating the schedule

    E. Process for creating the scope statement

83. Crashing is a project management technique involving which one of the following?

    A. Moving later deliverables to earlier phases to appease stakeholders

    B. Looking at cost and schedule trade-offs, such as adding more resources

    C. Removing critical path activities that are unnecessary

    D. Performing two tasks in parallel that were previously scheduled to start sequentially

84. The communication plan calls for weekly status updates to be emailed, monthly status meetings, and semiannual printed newsletters. This plan is laying out which one of the following?

    A. Criticality factors

    B. Level of report detail

    C. Tailor communication style

    D. Types of communication

85. Total expenditures for completed project work within a specific timeframe is known as which one of the following?

    A. Earned value

    B. Planned value

    C. Cost variance

    D. Actual cost

86. A major car company just completed the launch of a new vehicle. They have discovered a major safety flaw in the new product, and they need to communicate with the general public regarding a product recall. The following methods would be appropriate methods to use. (Choose two.)

    A. Text messaging

    B. Social media

    C. Instant message

    D. Distribution of printed media

    E. Fax

87. In what project phase is the influence of stakeholders the least effective?

    A. Execution

    B. Monitor and Control

    C. Initiation

    D. Planning

88. A construction company is in the middle of a project to build a bridge. The earned value for the project is $9,500, and the actual cost for the project is $7,000. Select the correct cost variance for the project and its meaning:

    A. $2,500 and the project is under budget

    B. $–2,500 and the project is over budget

    C. $2,500 and the project is over budget

    D. $–2,500 and the project is over budget

89. What is the indication of how fast a project is spending its budgeted money?

   A. Planned value

   B. Burn rate

   C. Cost variance

   D. Expenditure tracking

90. All of the following are phases of a project, EXCEPT

   A. Planning

   B. Closing

   C. Development

   D. Execution

Chapter

6

Practice Test 2

This practice exam can be used to simulate the actual CompTIA Project+ exam. The practice exam is balanced in the percentage and number of questions it includes in accordance with the mixture of questions that you will see on the actual exam. That breakdown is as follows:

Domain 1: Project Basics	36%
Domain 2: Project Constraints	17%
Domain 3: Communication and Change Management	26%
Domain 4: Project Tools and Documentation	21%

Set a timer for 75 minutes, and attempt to complete this practice test without referencing other materials until the test is over.

1. What type of project management tool is depicted here?

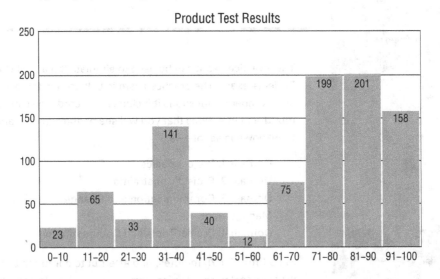

Product Test Results

A. Histogram

B. Gantt chart

C. Pareto chart

D. Process diagram

2. Which of the following is *not* a communication trigger?

A. Project planning

B. Kickoff meeting

C. Milestones

D. Schedule changes

3. A community has a 125-year-old bridge, and a project has been created to restore the bridge and give it historical status. However, the project is in need of funding and support. The bridge is located in a rural area with a large retirement community. What would be the best way to get project information to the community?

A. Instant messaging

B. Text message

C. Distribution of printed media

D. Email

4. What risk tolerance would a startup in the technology industry likely have?

A. Risk taker

B. Risk avoider

C. Gambler

D. Moderate risk tolerance

5. How do stakeholders, sponsors, and management exert influence on a project? (Choose all that apply.)

    A. They do not work on project deliverables.

    B. They lose interest in this project as a newer project begins.

    C. They shift the priorities of the project as it progresses.

    D. They do not attend all meetings.

6. As part of the preparation to begin work on a project, the project manager makes a list: (1) There can be no work on weekends and holidays, (2) overtime is not approved without steering committee consent, and (3) seventy-five percent of the project team must be union staff. This list represents which of the following?

    A. Objectives

    B. Requirements

    C. Constraints

    D. Assumptions

7. What are the defining characteristics of a project? (Choose two.)

    A. It is a part of ongoing operational activities.

    B. It is assigned to a portfolio.

    C. It has a definitive start and end date.

    D. It creates a unique product or service.

    E. It is part of an organization's strategic plan.

8. Where should work produced from the high-level risk assessment be documented?

    A. Risk register

    B. Work breakdown structure

    C. Project charter

    D. Quality control plan

9. Which type of cost estimation uses a mathematical model to compute costs?

    A. Three-point estimating

    B. Bottom-up estimating

    C. Top-down estimating

    D. Parametric estimating

10. What is a user story in the Agile methodology?

    A. Customer survey results after product release

    B. Key information about stakeholders and their jobs

    C. A high level definition of someone using the product or service

    D. Visual representation of product burndown

11. Which type of contract is riskiest for the buyer?

    A. Cost-reimbursable contract

    B. Key performance parameter

    C. Fixed-price contract

    D. Time and materials

12. Which of the following are a means of communication on the current conditions of a project? (Choose three.)

    A. Project charter

    B. Status report

    C. Meeting agenda

    D. Meeting minutes

    E. Communication plan

    F. Dashboard information

13. What is the single role in a RACI matrix where it can only be assigned once per task?

    A. Consulted

    B. Responsible

    C. Informed

    D. Accountable

14. New processes and leadership are introduced to a project after their company joined forces with another company. What type of organizational change disrupted this project?

    A. Business process change

    B. Business merger

    C. Relocation

    D. Business acquisition

15. Which of the following would not receive communication if there was an update to the risk register?

    A. Project sponsor

    B. Project team

    C. PMO

    D. Project manager

16. All of the following are true regarding kickoff meetings EXCEPT

    A. They represent the first time that the project team is introduced to each other.

    B. They happen in the initiation phase.

    C. They occur when project planning is complete.

    D. They communicate the goals, objectives, schedule, and milestones to the team.

17. A risk response plan would most likely be activated in which project phase?

    A. Monitor and Control

    B. Execution

    C. Planning

    D. Initiation

18. An airline engineering company is forced to cut the project budget after poor financial results in the previous quarter. How would this most likely impact the project?

    A. The project will take longer because the number of resources is cut.

    B. The project team goes to the steering committee for more funds.

    C. The project scope is cut back to operate within the new budget.

    D. The project is postponed due to lack of financial resources.

19. A resource shortage means which one of the following?

    A. There are too many resources, leading to underallocation.

    B. There is a shortage of things for team members to work on.

    C. There are not enough resources for the task, leading to overallocation.

    D. There is an abundance of things for team members to work on.

20. A company is located in multiple cities across a continent, and the project will be staffed with team members from various cities. The decision is made to bring the project team to a single location. This is an example of which one of the following?

    A. Insourcing

    B. Collocation

    C. Layoffs

    D. Outsourcing

21. In what type of organizational structure would resources report solely to the functional manager?

    A. Weak-matrix

    B. Projectized

    C. Strong-matrix

    D. Functional

22. Which of the following are ways to organize the WBS? (Choose three.)

    A. Backlog and sprints

    B. Project phases

    C. Subprojects

    D. Major deliverables

    E. Prioritized by risk

23. A project sponsor or champion serves what role on a project?

    A. Develops and maintains the schedule

    B. Serves as the approval authority and removes roadblocks

    C. Sets the standards and practices for projects in the organization

    D. Performs cross-functional coordination

24. Which type of contract allows the seller to recover all allowable expenses associated with providing the goods or services?

    A. Cost-reimbursable contract

    B. Fixed-price contract

    C. Statements of work

    D. Time and materials

25. A popular theme park is doing a major expansion on their property to capitalize on a popular movie franchise. This project has thousands of individuals assigned to the project. The project manager needs to find out which individuals are working on the theming design. Which project-centric document would help give her this information?

    A. RACI matrix

    B. Project charter

    C. Organizational chart

    D. Fishbone diagram

26. As a project is being considered, the steering committee asks to know what environmental variables exist, both internal and external to the company. What is the best tool to complete this scan?

    A. SWOT analysis

    B. Vendor knowledge bases

    C. Process diagram

    D. Histogram

27. What type of organizational change has occurred when a company decides to spin off, or sell off, one of its business units?

    A. Business merger

    B. Business split

    C. Business acquisition

    D. Internal reorganization

28. The documentation strategy for a project calls for each change to be logged at the beginning of each document. This is known as which one of the following?

   A. Risk register updates

   B. Version control

   C. Communication plan

   D. Change request logs

29. A government agency in charge of transportation has completed emergency project work three days earlier than the target they previously communicated. What is the best method to communicate this success to the general public?

   A. Distribution of printed media

   B. Fax

   C. Impromptu media

   D. Social media

30. Which of the following describes a portfolio?

   A. A collection of the sample work a project manager has done that the manager should bring to an interview

   B. A collection of programs, subportfolios, and projects that support strategic business goals or objectives

   C. A group of related projects that are managed together using shared resources and similar techniques

   D. A group of project investments that are maintained to help finance projects

31. What document would be created to outline specific performance criteria or other actions between two parties?

   A. Nondisclosure agreement

   B. Request for proposal

   C. Service-level agreement

   D. Memorandum of understanding

32. The comprehensive collection of documents that spells out communication, risk management, project schedule, and scope management is known as which one of the following?

   A. Project management plan

   B. Dashboard information

   C. Request for proposal

   D. Scope statement

33. What type of project management tool is depicted here?

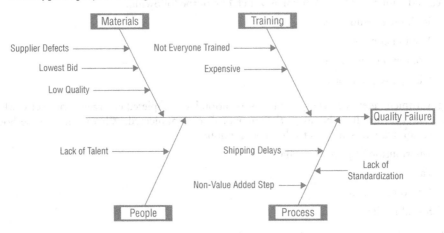

A. Fishbone diagram

B. Process diagram

C. Pareto chart

D. Histogram

34. An organization decides to stop requiring travel receipts and instead will issue per diems. What does this represent for the organization?

A. A business acquisition

B. A business merger

C. A business split

D. A business process change

35. When considering a change, which role would be responsible for analyzing the schedule, budget, and resource allocations to determine how the change impacts the project?

A. Project sponsor

B. Change control board

C. Subject matter expert

D. Project manager

36. Stress testing of a load-bearing bridge has been going on for two weeks. The test completed successfully, and the project manager informs all local departments concerning transportation that the road is ready for painting and final touches. What is the trigger for this communication?

A. Project planning

B. Schedule changes

C. Milestone

D. Task completion

37. A project manager is managing a team located in multiple cities of the same continent. The communication plan calls for weekly status updates. What is the appropriate method for this communication?

   A. Virtual meeting

   B. In-person meeting

   C. Instant messaging

   D. Email

38. What are the standard project phases?

   A. Initiation, Planning, Execution, Monitor and Control, and Closing

   B. Initiation, Preparing, Building, Monitor and Control, and Wrap-up

   C. Discovery, Planning, Building, Quality Check, and Closing

   D. Discovery, Preparing, Execution, Quality Check, and Wrap-up

39. About how much time should a project manager spend communicating?

   A. Up to 27%

   B. Up to 90%

   C. Up to 75%

   D. Up to 50%

40. Project team members are required to report to both the project manager and their functional manager who share authority for the resources. What type of organization is this?

   A. Weak-matrix

   B. Balanced-matrix

   C. Projectized

   D. Strong-matrix

41. A computer electronics company is building a computer chip. The CPI for the project is 0.77, which means which of the following?

   A. The project is over budget.

   B. The project is behind schedule.

   C. The project is under budget.

   D. The project is ahead of schedule.

42. Which of the following are characteristics of an Agile project management approach? (Choose three.)

   A. Up-front, comprehensive requirements gathering

   B. Formally organized teams

   C. Self-organized teams

   D. Sprint planning

   E. Feedback based primarily in lessons-learned meetings

   F. Continuous requirements gathering

43. Teams normally go through a similar development cycle. Which is the correct order of those stages?

   A. Forming, norming, performing, storming, and adjourning

   B. Norming, storming, forming, adjourning, and performing

   C. Norming, forming, storming, adjourning, and performing

   D. Forming, storming, norming, performing, and adjourning

44. As a project manager, you tend to create a plan of the steps to go on vacation. Here are the steps you have decided on:

   Check into resort

   Travel to airport

   Relax and enjoy

   Choose vacation spot

   Take bus to resort

   Book reservation

   Plane ride

   What is the correct sequence for project Relaxing Vacation?

   A. Relax and enjoy; choose vacation spot; travel to airport; take bus to resort; plane ride; check into resort; book reservation

   B. Choose vacation spot; book reservation; travel to airport; plane ride; take bus to resort; check into resort; relax and enjoy

   C. Plane ride; relax and enjoy; take bus to resort; choose vacation spot; travel to airport; check into resort; book reservation

   D. Book reservation; relax and enjoy; take bus to resort; travel to airport; check into resort; choose vacation spot; plane ride

45. What is the activity of determining and documenting any potential risks called?

   A. Risk avoidance

   B. Risk planning

   C. Risk identification

   D. Risk mitigation

46. A government agency has issued a request for quotation (RFQ) for a new fleet of snowplows. What other procurement method is comparable to an RFQ?

   A. NDA

   B. RFI

   C. SOW

   D. RFP

47. Which of the following components is not included in the communication plan?

   A. Report on status of deliverables and schedule

   B. How information will be delivered

   C. When information should be distributed

   D. Stakeholder information needs

48. Primarily used in the federal government and utility industry, what is the performance attribute of a system that is considered critical or essential to the development of an effective capability?

   A. Service-level agreement

   B. Letter of intent

   C. Intergovernmental agreement

   D. Key performance parameter

49. A company is struggling with a lack of flexibility for specialized needs using a centralized model for purchasing and receiving goods. What type of organizational change could help this problem?

   A. Relocation

   B. Outsourcing

   C. Internal reorganization

   D. Business split

50. The original project plan for the uptime of a network to be available is 98 percent of the time. The customer does not want many hassles for their online customers and changes this to 99.5 percent of the time. What type of project change does this represent?

   A. Risk

   B. Quality

   C. Scope

   D. Timeline

51. Who is the target audience, and what is the rationale behind conducting a gate review?

   A. Project governance, to ensure accountability and objective alignment

   B. Project sponsor, to see if they picked a good project

   C. Project manager, to ensure resource availability

   D. Project team, to find out what they are doing wrong

52. Pete is the CEO of a company, and there is an update on a security breach at a customer site. He needs to be notified immediately but is in a meeting off-site. What is the best method to notify him of the problem?

   A. Face-to-face conversation

   B. Text message

   C. Fax

   D. Social media

53. A project is entering the Execution phase, and the project plan has been completed. It is time to introduce the project team members to one another and lay out the objectives, deliverables, and milestones of the project. What is the appropriate form of communication for the next step?

    A. Kickoff meeting

    B. Impromptu meeting

    C. Video conference

    D. Email

54. What do you call the consequence or opportunity that a risk poses to the project?

    A. Risk register

    B. Risk probability

    C. Risk impact

    D. Risk response plan

55. The scope of a project is expanded through the formal change control process, causing the schedule to be extended beyond the original due date. This is an example of which type of influence?

    A. Interaction between constraints

    B. Environmental factors

    C. Constraint reprioritization

    D. Stakeholders, sponsors, and management

56. In what stage of team development do things begin to calm down because the team members become more comfortable with one another?

    A. Adjourning

    B. Performing

    C. Forming

    D. Norming

57. A project management office (PMO) has which of the following responsibilities? (Choose two.)

    A. Provides governance for projects

    B. Markets the project across the business

    C. Establishes key performance indicators and parameters

    D. Manages the team, communication, scope, risk, budget, and time of the project

58. During the Planning phase, all of the following are created, EXCEPT

    A. Change management plan

    B. Lessons learned

    C. Communications plan

    D. Project schedule

59. Cost efficiency of budgeted resources expressed as a ratio is known as which one of the following?

　　A. AC

　　B. CPI

　　C. SPI

　　D. EV

60. The project schedule development should include which critical elements?

　　A. Develop schedule, determine completion date, check stakeholder assumptions, conduct feasibility assessment

　　B. Budget activities, estimate resources, determine milestones, estimate completion

　　C. Define activities, budget activities, estimate resources, estimate completion

　　D. Define activities, sequence activities, estimate resources, estimate duration

61. After establishing the product backlog, what tool would you use to determine the project's velocity?

　　A. Burndown chart

　　B. Fishbone diagram

　　C. Kanban board

　　D. Sprint speed

62. In terms of resource assignments, which best describes how resources are assigned in a projectized environment?

　　A. Resources are assigned on an ad hoc basis.

　　B. Resources must not be collocated.

　　C. Resources are assigned from a functional area to the project.

　　D. Resources must be outsourced.

63. Which type of contract is riskiest for the seller?

　　A. Purchase order

　　B. Time and materials

　　C. Cost-reimbursable contract

　　D. Fixed-price contract

64. How should a project team memorialize what was said and agreed to during project gatherings?

　　A. Create meeting minutes

　　B. Create a business case

　　C. Create a scope statement

　　D. Create a project management plan

65. The dynamite blasting phase of a mountain tunnel project has completed and there were no safety accidents to report. This triggers a call to the project sponsor to report the current status. Which role does the project sponsor have assigned to them on this task?

A. Accountable

B. Informed

C. Responsible

D. Consulted

66. What type of project management tool is depicted here?

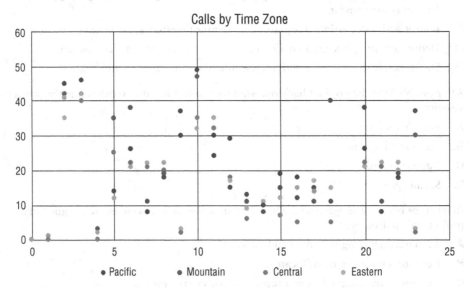

A. Pareto chart

B. Process diagram

C. Scatter chart

D. Histogram

67. An organization decides to use an external firm for their hiring, firing, payroll, and tax functions instead of their internal staff. This is an example of which one of the following?

A. Outsourcing

B. Business demerger/split

C. Relocation

D. Internal reorganization

68. Which risk response strategy attempts to minimize the impact or the probability of a negative risk?

A. Mitigate

B. Accept

C. Transfer

D. Avoid

69. What are the three common constraints found in projects? (Choose three.)

    A. Scope

    B. Personnel

    C. Working Space

    D. Quality

    E. Budget

    F. Time

70. An organization needs to add vendor resources to a project, but they do not have the physical space to house the team. What approach should the organization use for their personnel management?

    A. Use remote teams

    B. Deploy functional teams

    C. Use in-house teams

    D. Deploy projectized teams

71. All of the following are characteristic of an Agile project management approach, EXCEPT

    A. Each release is tested against the customers' needs.

    B. It uses a flexible approach to requirements.

    C. Team members work in short bursts, or sprints.

    D. It follows a strict adherence to a change control process.

72. What is another name for analogous estimating?

    A. Three-point estimating

    B. Top-down estimating

    C. Parametric estimating

    D. Bottom-up estimating

73. What is the definition of a work breakdown structure?

    A. A graphic representation of tasks and their sequence

    B. A task-oriented decomposition of a project

    C. A high-level outline of milestones on a project

    D. A deliverable-oriented decomposition of a project

74. A team is not going to finish a project within the allowed budget, and it has asked for several requirements that are not essential to be moved to a later date. This is an example of which one of the following?

    A. Change

    B. Milestone

    C. Risk

    D. Issue

75. Sharing a positive risk means what will happen?

   A. The project team looks for opportunities to take advantage of positive impacts.

   B. The project team chooses to accept the consequences of the risk.

   C. The project team assigns the risk to a third party who is best able to bring about opportunity.

   D. The project team monitors the probability or impact of the risk event to ensure that benefits are realized.

76. A project team is assigned two individuals who are both approaching or are already on performance improvement plans. The two team members require explicit instruction, require much supervision to accomplish menial tasks, and are often not where they are supposed to be. This is an example of which one of the following?

   A. Resource shortage

   B. Benched resources

   C. Shared resources

   D. Low-quality resources

77. What is the correct formula for schedule variance?

   A. EV – AC

   B. EV – PV

   C. EV / AC

   D. EV / PV

78. The pouring of a foundation for a new building took three days longer than planned. What type of project change would this represent?

   A. Timeline change

   B. Funding change

   C. Quality change

   D. Scoping change

79. An external group has completed an investigation and made recommendations for process improvement to a project team. What type of communication trigger is this?

   A. Business continuity response

   B. Audit

   C. Schedule change

   D. Gate review

80. What best describes a request for information?

   A. A meeting with prospective vendors prior to completing a proposal

   B. Procurement method to obtain more information about goods and services

   C. Procurement document that details the goods and services to be procured from outside the organization

   D. Procurement method to invite bids, review, select, and purchase goods or services

81. A startup company is attempting to compete in an emerging product market. There are constant disruptive technology changes, and the market is shifting in their product tastes. This type of environment would be best served by which one of the following?

    A. Functional environment

    B. Traditional, or waterfall

    C. Agile approach

    D. Projectized environment

82. What is fast tracking a project?

    A. Removing critical path activities that are unnecessary

    B. Moving later deliverables to earlier phases to appease stakeholders

    C. Performing two tasks in parallel that were previously scheduled to start sequentially

    D. Looking at cost and schedule trade-offs, like adding more resources

83. The customer site for a project is located in a rural part of a country, while the project headquarters is located in metropolitan hub. What would be the biggest impediment to face-to-face communication?

    A. Geographical factors

    B. Times zones

    C. Intra-organizational differences

    D. Technological factors

84. What indicates an individual or organization's comfort level with risky situations or decisions?

    A. Risk register

    B. Risk tolerance

    C. Risk avoider

    D. Risk taker

85. A large organization has a finance project that will change purchase requisitions, invoicing, and financial reporting for the entire company. They set up a listserv that emails project updates and allows receivers to set the frequency to daily, weekly, or monthly. This is an example of which one of the following?

    A. Personal preferences

    B. Cultural differences

    C. Criticality factors

    D. Rapport building

86. Which of the following is not a common potential risk to a project?

    A. Scope will change after the project begins.

    B. The costs will exceed the budget.

    C. The budget is left unattended.

    D. Schedule is optimistic, "best case," rather than realistic, "expected case."

87. A project team is located in three different continents. Which of the following would be the biggest factor in scheduling recurring status meetings?

    A. Language barriers

    B. Interorganizational differences

    C. Time zones

    D. Intraorganizational differences

88. All of the following activities are included in risk planning, EXCEPT

    A. Creating a response to each risk

    B. Analyzing the potential impact of each risk

    C. Measuring the SPI and CPI

    D. Identifying all potential risks to the project

89. What is a potential future event that can have either a negative or positive impact on a project called?

    A. A hope

    B. An issue

    C. A requirement

    D. A risk

90. An adaptive method would be preferable to a more rigid project management style in which situation?

    A. In a mature organization with defined processes

    B. When dealing with a rapidly changing environment

    C. When the scope can be easily and thoroughly defined

    D. Where small incremental improvements offer no value to stakeholders

Appendix

Answers and Explanations

Chapter 1: Project Basics (Domain 1.0)

1. **B, E.** A project can be summarized as having the following properties: It is temporary in nature, it creates a unique product or service, it has a definite start and finish, it contains a reason/purpose, and it may be part of a program or portfolio. A group of related tasks is not necessarily a project but could be a to-do list of any kind. Operational activities are activities that take place after a project has been completed. Reworking an existing project is not creating a new product or service, and it doesn't meet the properties of a project.

2. **A.** Providing governance on the project is the responsibility of a project management office, not the project team. The project team is responsible for contributing expertise to the project, contributing deliverables according to the schedule, estimating task duration, and estimating costs and dependencies.

3. **B.** The work breakdown structure is a deliverable-oriented decomposition of a project. It is one of the fundamental building blocks of project planning, such as scheduling activities, and it is used as an input to numerous other planning processes.

4. **D.** The business case is a written document or report that helps executive management and key stakeholders determine the benefits and rewards of the project. It can include justification, alternative solutions, and alignment to the strategic plan.

5. **A, C, D.** Performance Measuring and Reporting, Perform Quality Assurance, and Monitor the Budget are all activities associated with the Monitor and Control phase. In addition to these activities, the Monitor and Control phase includes governance activities, monitoring the risk/issues log, and administering the change control process.

6. **D.** The Communications plan is where all of the elements of the who, what, when, where, and why of communication needs are documented.

7. **C.** Parametric estimating often uses a quantity of work multiplied by the rate formula for computing costs.

8. **B.** Cost Variance is Earned Value – Actual Cost, or $2,500 – $2,275 = $225.

9. **D.** What did I accomplish yesterday? What will I do today? and What obstacles are preventing progress? These are the three questions asked during a stand-up, or SCRUM, meeting.

10. **B.** All of the authority in this example rests with the functional manager who is pulling Marcus back to work on other assignments rather than the project. In a functional organizational structure, resources typically report to a functional manager and the project manager has limited or no authority.

11. **A.** In this scenario, working with the team member to get the desired result is the best course of action. Removing or replacing a team member is not always an option, and thus is incorrect.

12. **D.** The high-level scope definition is documented in the project charter, setting the big picture work that the project hopes to complete.

13. B. The Planning phase is where the majority of the project documents get created. This is where the project goals, objectives, and deliverables are refined and broken down into manageable units of work, such as within the work breakdown structure.

14. A. The project description explains the attributes of the product, service, or result of the project.

15. B. The formula is (Most Likely + Optimistic + Pessimistic) / 3.

16. D. In a functional organization, the authority resides with the functional manager, not the project manager.

17. C. The purchasing of the build site must occur before the construction activity begins.

18. C. The Gantt chart is a type of bar chart that shows task duration and dependencies.

19. D. While stakeholders start out with a lot of influence, it decreases as the project advances because the execution of the project solidifies deliverables at the expense of stakeholders being able to change their minds.

20. C. An external dependency is where an entity or condition outside of the project drives the scheduling for that task.

21. A. This is where one party gets their way, and the other party's interest is not represented.

22. D. A => C => D => E. The critical path has task A (2 days), task C (2 days), task D (2 days), and task E (3 days) for a total of 9 days.

23. D. There is no heroic effort that occurs during an Agile sprint, which is a short burst of activity on a project focusing on a few tasks and working them to a completed state.

24. B. In this scenario, all of the power and authority are present with the project manager and not the functional manager, which is indicative of a strong-matrix organizational structure.

25. B. Performing quality assurance would take place during Monitor and Control, and managing stakeholder expectations should occur throughout the project. The Closing phase is responsible for transition/integration plan, project sign-off, archiving project documents, lessons learned, releasing of resources, and closing of contracts.

26. C. The kickoff meeting is where the project team members and stakeholders are introduced, and it's held at the beginning of the Execution phase.

27. E. Other closing activities would include getting project sign-off, gathering and documenting lessons learned, and conducting training as a part of the transition/integration plan.

28. A. A governance gate is a checkpoint between project phases where approval is obtained to move forward. Usually, project reports are sent to a steering committee to help ensure accountability on the project for time, money, and scope.

29. A, C. The two most correct answers are that the project has a definitive start and end date and that it creates a unique product or service. Projects are considered a success when the goals they set out to accomplish are fulfilled and the stakeholders are satisfied with the results.

30. B. A portfolio is a collection of programs, sub-portfolios, and projects that support strategic business goals or objective. Programs and projects within a portfolio are not necessarily related to one another in a direct way, and projects may independently exist within the portfolio.

31. D. The project charter is prepared and agreed to in the Initiation phase of a project. This document provides formal approval for the project to begin and authorizes the project manager to apply resources to the project.

32. C. This is where the project team members and stakeholders are introduced and the goals for the project are outlined.

33. B. Leadership, time management, team building, and listening are soft skills that are important for a project manager. Critical path diagrams are an artifact, and the creation of them would be considered a hard skill, so answers A and C are incorrect. Following and independence are soft skills, but not typically associated with project management, so D is also incorrect.

34. B. The project charter is where high-level risks should be documented, which occurs in the Initiation phase.

35. D. A project schedule determines start and finish dates for project activities and will also have activity durations and order of precedence.

36. C. This type of estimating can also be called an order-of-magnitude estimate.

37. A. The project manager is not the critical role in this answer. Unless it falls into one of the other three phases, this does not hold true.

38. C. This may include both direct and indirect costs, but it must correspond to the budget for the activity. Actual cost is an example of project cost control.

39. C. Determining activity sequence is an important part of project management, and you will probably see a question like this on the test. For this question, the correct order is: gather bread, peanut butter, and jelly; get a knife; place bread on a plate; spread peanut butter on one slice of bread; spread jelly on the other slice of bread; put both slices of bread together; serve.

40. A, D, and F. Some of the important steps required in the development of the critical path include determining the tasks, determining task start/finish dates, determining task durations and milestones, putting them in sequential order by identifying predecessors and setting dependencies, and identifying the critical path. Scheduling activities also address the allocation of resources, setting baselines, and quality/governance gates.

41. C. Also known as a *person-hour estimate*, this is used in the creation of cost estimates.

42. B. This includes identifying both what resources are needed and when they will be needed.

43. C. This technique may also be called *problem solving*, and it is a superior way to resolve a conflict. The correct solution to a problem can reveal itself, and the facts will contribute to discovering the solution.

44. A, C, E. Using team-building activities, using recognition and rewards, and setting the ground rules are some of the tools that you can use to develop an effective project team.

45. D. This is the ideal state teams are shooting for, where the team is productive and effective. Not all teams are able to achieve this stage of development.

46. B. When quality is a key concern, it means that it is more important than cost. Therefore, it would be beneficial to have the team collocated so that the communication is quicker, corrections are more timely, and the team is not disrupted by time-zone differences.

47. A. When requirements are changing, an Agile approach allows an organization to be readily able to adapt to the environment.

48. D. The project manager has the authority to task team resources and conduct performance evaluations, making this a projectized organizational structure.

49. B. The user story helps focus on how the product is going to be used to help shape how it is designed.

50. D. More established organizations with mature processes and tenured staff would most likely have a functional organizational structure centered around specialties.

51. C. PMP is common shorthand for the project management plan. In the project management world, it can also stand for Project Management Professional, an individual certified from the Project Management Institute (PMI®).

52. B. A backlog is the artifact that is used within an Agile methodology to keep track of all the elements that need to be included in a project but may not be a part of this sprint.

53. C. Initiation, Planning, Execution, Monitor and Control, and Closing are the standard project phases. The project phases are tightly linked, and outputs from one phase usually become inputs of another phase.

54. D. Milestones are major events in a project used to measure progress.

55. B. A work package represents the lowest level of decomposition within the work breakdown structure (WBS). By beginning at the work package level of the WBS, the cost for each activity is calculated and assigned to that work package.

56. A. Although this would be a nice outcome, it is not the purpose of developing a project team.

57. D. In the Agile methodology, tasks can get recorded and identified in a backlog, but it is not a dependency important to task sequencing.

58. B. Remember that a project is temporary in nature, and at times adding too much to the scope changes the temporary aspect of the endeavor. Adding unapproved scope to the project is considered to be scope creep.

59. B. Identification of lower-level WBS components occurs after the major deliverables have been identified.

60. B. Compromising is when each party gives up something to reach a solution in a conflict.

61. B. The framing of the walls must begin before the installation of the network cabling can begin, leading to a start-to-start relationship. The wiring must be in place before dry walling and insulation can begin.

62. B. The critical path has A (2 days), C (2 days), D (2 days), and E (3 days), for a total of 9 days.

63. C. The resource calendar will also let you know the dates resources are active or idle.

64. A, D, F. When there is no harmony within the team, team-building exercises can assist in restoring morale. When a phase is completed, it can be beneficial to celebrate the progress on the project and recognize the contributions of the team. Any kind of change in the team dynamic can impact the project, especially when the leadership is new.

65. D. The space constraints for this organization will force the team to use remote or virtual teams.

66. D. While Nyssa is assigned to the project, it is clear that the power rests with the functional manager, undercutting the project manager's authority.

67. A. Stakeholder expectations having been met is the most critical factor involved when determining whether a project is a success.

68. B. A deliverable can be any tangible or intangible product or service produced as the result of a project.

69. D. The project sponsors' responsibilities include helping define and develop the high-level requirements for the project, functioning as the approval authority, removing roadblocks, marketing the project across the organization, controlling the direction of the project, and defining the business case for the project.

70. D. The business case can include justification, alternative solutions, alignment to the strategic plan, recommended solution, and a feasibility study.

71. A. All projects are constrained by what is typically referred to as the "triple constraints," which include time, budget, and scope as they pertain to quality. Typically, you can manipulate two elements and will have to live with how they constrain the third element. You can have cheap, feature rich, or fast: pick two of three.

72. C. The charter gives formal authorization to begin and to commit resources to the project. Accordingly, project team selection and procurement can begin at this point.

73. D. In addition to archival of project documents, release of team members, and review of lessons learned, Closing consists of the following: transition/integration plan, training, closing of contracts, and project sign-off. Monitoring the risks and issues log is considered to be a process within the Monitor and Control phase.

74. C. The WBS is a project artifact, not resources in the resource management context.

75. A. Top-down estimating, or analogous estimating, is when high-level project cost estimates are used by comparing to a similar project from the past.

76. C. This number is expressed as a percentage.

77. A. Fast tracking is a schedule compression technique that involves completing two tasks in parallel that were previously scheduled to start sequentially. This can come with a higher cost and with increased risk, but it will help the project be completed faster.

78. C. Deliverables are generated during the Direct and Manage Project Work process, during the Execution phase.

79. B. There are not enough resources for the task, leading to overallocation. An individual's workload becomes more severe, leading to longer hours and a higher potential for burnout.

80. E. Adjourning refers to the dissolving of the team when work has been completed.

81. C. When cost is the most important element of the project, virtual teams can help keep costs lower. It can come at the cost of communication efficiency and potentially make quality more difficult to realize.

82. B. This document details how the procurement process will be managed.

83. A. A more solid organization that is working with a fixed budget or other constraints would be best suited for more traditional project management approaches.

84. C. This may be an activity during either the planning or execution phase, depending on the nature of the industry the project is in.

85. A. A change control board (CCB), in conjunction with the change control process, will approve or reject changes to the scope of the project.

86. A. While not listed, this function could also be done by a program or portfolio within those units only. The PMO performs this function across the organization.

87. B. A risk becomes an active issue when it is triggered. For instance, if the cost of materials starts to rise, it might trigger a budget risk that gets moved to the issue log to be actively managed.

88. A. The project manager is attempting to make the conflict appear less important than it really is by implying that they would have to work on the upcoming weekend if they didn't stay that night. No attempt is made to see if there was another solution, like coming in early the next day.

89. D. Whenever a team member joints the project, or at the beginning of the project when multiple people join, is when expectations should be set, including roles, due dates, norms, and team interactions.

90. B. The work breakdown structure is characteristic of a more deliberate, up-front requirements gathering, when many of the requirements are identified early in the project.

91. B. Outsourcing is where work is transferred from employees within the organization to contractors or vendors.

92. B. This is the model that was developed by Dr. Bruce Tuckman, and it is known as the stages of team development.

93. A. Daily standup meetings are typically used with an Agile methodology. As such, a daily standup meeting would not have a governance body in attendance and would normally be attended by project team members.

94. D. This helps keep roles like the project manager and project team accountable from a more strategic standpoint.

95. A. Construction would come after the blueprinting is approved.

96. B, C, E. The three types of organizational structures are functional, matrix, and projectized. In a functional organization, decisions and control are driven by the specialized function (IT, accounting, HR, and so on). With a projectized organization, the project manager has decision-making authority and control over resources. A matrixed organization is a blended model between functional and projectized.

97. D. A positive cost variance (CV) means that the project is under budget, and a negative CV means that the project is over budget. $7,000 - $9,500 = -$2,500; therefore, the project is over budget.

98. A. The primary purpose of the Closing phase is to document the formal acceptance of the project work and to hand off the completed product to the organization for ongoing maintenance and support.

99. B, D, E. The PMO provides guidance to project managers and helps present a consistent, reliable approach to managing projects across the organization. Responsibilities include providing governance for projects, maintaining standard documentation and templates, and establishing key performance indicators and parameters.

100. A. The "champion" role of the sponsor is really important both initially and as the project commences in order to keep the energy and focus of the whole organization committed to its success.

101. C. A program is a group of related projects that are managed together with coordinated processes and techniques. Make sure that you know the difference between a project and a portfolio.

102. C. These are all roles performed by a project coordinator.

103. C. Cost Performance Index (CPI). The formula is CPI = Earned Value (EV) / Actual Cost (AC).

104. C. In a balanced-matrix organization, the project manager and the functional manager both control the budget and share power and authority.

105. C. This lowest level recorded in the WBS is the work package. This is the level where resources, time, and cost estimates are determined.

106. B, E. Smoothing and negotiating are conflict resolution techniques. Storming and norming are stages of group development that were first proposed by Bruce Tuckman. Threatening is an interpersonal response that typically leads to conflict.

107. B. This stage is a process of establishing who is the most influential, and there is jostling for position.

108. C. When a project, or a portion of a project, must be completed prior to another project beginning, it is an example of an interproject dependency.

109. C. The project scheduler gets status updates on the tasks and then communicates the updated timeline and changes to the project team.

110. B. This can be recorded through the use of user stories or short descriptions of the functionality.

111. C. If your project spans multiple time zones and/or there are a variety of schedules being used, take these factors into consideration when scheduling the meeting.

112. B. The project management office's responsibilities include setting standards and practices for an organization, providing tools such as previous project documentation, and delivering standardized documentation and templates.

113. C. Developing the project charter and stakeholder identification are the two activities that occur during the initiation phase. Other activities, like holding a project kickoff meeting and creating the project plan, will take place during the planning and execution phases.

114. D. This document will include the approach to obtaining outside products and services and the rational for choosing whether to insource or outsource the effort.

115. D. Pareto diagramming, or producing a Pareto chart or diagram, is a tool used to focus attention on the most critical issues. It is not used to estimate activity duration.

116. B. Team members are responsible for producing the deliverables spelled out in the project charter and scope statement.

117. C. Parametric estimating often uses a quantity of work multiplied by the rate formula for computing costs.

118. C, E. The issues log and action items are created during the Execution phase. The project charter is created during the Initiation phase. The communication plan is created during the Planning phase. Lessons learned are generally done in the Closing phase, but some projects may choose to do them during Monitor and Control.

119. D. Project managers can spend up to 90% of their time communicating with the stakeholders and the project team.

120. B. Vested interest, providing input and requirements, project steering, and expertise are examples of stakeholder responsibilities. Stakeholder expectation setting and engagement are key elements to project success.

121. A. In this case, Jenny is considered to be a project stakeholder. Remember that a team member is also a form of a stakeholder.

122. A. Project sign-off occurs in the Closing phase, not the Initiation phase.

123. D. Although many roles are responsible for identifying risk, the project team plays a key role because they are more likely to recognize risk as subject-matter experts.

124. B, C, E. The communication plan, organizational chart, and project schedule are all created in the Planning phase. Status reports and action items are developed and communicated during the Monitor and Control phase. Other examples of activities that are a result of the Planning phase are identifying resources, capturing detailed risks and requirements, documenting the change management plan and procurement plan, and developing the budget.

125. D. The project manager is responsible for all artifacts produced during the course of doing project work.

126. B. Characteristics of deliverables that must be met are known as requirements. Distance traveled on a project is good information for expense tracking and reporting. Checkpoints are gate checks on a project. Major events to track progress are milestones.

127. A. Define activities, sequence activities, estimate resources, and estimate duration are all key activities that must occur in order to develop the project schedule.

128. C. The project kick-off meeting is held after the project charter is signed and approved. The project kickoff meeting normally introduces the project team. Project team creation doesn't happen until the Execution phase. *Note*: In the real world, a kickoff meeting can happen in any of the first three phases, but for the test know that it is the Execution phase.

129. A. This activity also includes measuring the project spending to date.

130. C. The sprint planning meeting establishes what can realistically be accomplished during the sprint.

131. D. The burn rate is how fast the project is spending its allotted budget, or how fast the rate money is being expended over a period of time.

132. A, D. The project manager is responsible for managing the team, communication, scope, risk budget, and time of the project, as well as project artifacts and quality assurance.

133. C. The project charter sets the scope, assumptions, budget, and constraints at a high level for the project. As the project advances through the phases, this information will become more precise.

134. B. Creating and verifying deliverables is the key output of the Execution phase. Performance measuring and reporting occurs during Monitor and Control, whereas key stakeholder identification and determining project resources occur during planning.

135. A. This information would generally be found in a responsibility assignment matrix instead of the WBS dictionary.

136. B. The procurement plan explains the decisions made on what will be made and what will be purchased by the organization.

137. B. Program Evaluation and Review Technique (PERT) is a statistical tool used to analyze and represent tasks, not costs.

138. A. The cost performance index (CPI) is EV/AC. Therefore, 900 / 1100 = .84.

139. B. In a projectized organizational structure, the project manager has the most authority, and resources report directly to the project manager.

140. B. Rather than start-to-deferred, the missing relationship is start-to-start, meaning that one task must wait for a different task to start for work to begin.

141. C. A traditional waterfall methodology will be progressively iterative, similar to the iterative approach used with the Agile methodology.

142. B, C, D. The scope management includes the process for creating the scope statement, the definitions of how the deliverables will be validated, and the process for creating, maintaining, and approving the WBS. It also will define the process for controlling scope change requests, including the procedure for requesting changes.

143. D. Confronting is also called *problem solving*, and it is the best way to resolve conflict. By setting out on a fact-finding mission, the correct solution to the problem will present itself to the parties.

144. A. Due to the temporary nature of projects, resources are not permanently assigned to any one project or function.

145. B. A nondisclosure agreement (NDA) helps protect an organization's intellectual property when the project is completed or if there is turnover on the project.

146. D. The other options would not take advantage of the flexible, easily changing environment of the project.

147. C. The Execution phase is where most of the expenditures on materials and labor will occur.

148. C. This is where both parties give up something to help reach a workable solution. The commitment to meeting the deadline and the agreement to allow for time off, while adjusting the timing, are the key decision points.

149. C. Authority and power are shared between the functional manager and the project manager.

150. B, D. This is an example of ongoing operations that are not temporary in nature and do not have an end date. Additionally, the work effort does not produce a unique product.

151. D. With values born out of Lean principles, this is an iterative, incremental approach to managing the activities on a project.

152. C. There are times where the best course of action for the entire project team is to move on without the disgruntled team member.

153. C. Because of the varied time zones, a phone call or video conference would require an additional level of coordination. Therefore, email would be the most efficient what to handle the update.

154. A. Team members are brought together and told why they're working together. Individuals tend to be the most reserved and formal during this stage.

155. A. The use of a third party, like the project manager in the question, can help in producing a positive outcome and the third party's neutrality can assist in reaching an agreement.

156. A. Individuals who are finished with the project but haven't started a new assignment represent benched resources whose skills are not being utilized. This is costly for an organization because team members are being paid, but revenue is not being generated.

157. D. Tiffany is overallocated for the project assignments because there is more work to do than time to work on it.

158. D. Reporting to both the project manager and the functional manager means that Amy is a shared resource.

159. A. A discretionary dependency is defined by the project management team, and they are normally process or procedure driven.

160. D. The high-level scope definition documents the reason for the project and the problem you're trying to solve and provides a high-level description of some of the deliverables needed to make the project a success.

161. D. Option D is not correct since this is an example of alternatives identification and analysis. Risk assessment is done on the proposed project, not the alternatives.

162. B, C. A project coordinator supports the project manager and performs time and resource scheduling. This individual also provides cross-functional coordination and documentation and administrative support, and checks for quality.

163. D. This is a form of a lessons-learned meeting used in the Agile methodology to help improve future sprints.

164. E. During the transition from the project to normal operations, training of the new specifications will occur.

165. B. With an Agile approach, the result is that requirements can be adjusted as results are developed during the iterations.

166. E. The project manager is asserting his or her will without consideration of Jessie's position. Although this is a permanent solution, it is not a particularly good one.

167. B, C, E. This meets the requirements for a project because Wigitcom is creating a new product or service, and the effort is temporary in nature. It would also be a part of a program, or related projects, that share resources. In this case, the security team's resources would be shared with this project.

168. B. Commonly a bar chart, the burndown chart depicts the progress made with each iteration approaching the completion of the project.

169. C. With the aid of email, videoconferencing, and other technologies, providing the ability to communicate with team members all over the globe, projects are able to be completed successfully using virtual teams.

170. A. A resource shortage might be a tempting answer here, but the key is the involvement of multiple projects. Hence, resource contention exists between projects.

171. C. After the team has formed and stormed, this is where familiarity with one another helps to settle things down and individuals begin to deal with project problems instead of people problems.

172. B. Avoiding never results in problem resolution, and it is potentially the least effective technique.

173. C. Benched resources often occur in projectized organizations where there are resources on the payroll but they are not currently assigned to a project.

174. B. The project manager has full authority and controls time and tasks. As a project manager, you need to be wary of having low-quality resources assigned to a project, because sometimes functional managers will try to give you their lowest-caliber individuals.

175. B. An example of a mandatory dependency might be pouring the concrete foundation and letting it cure prior to framing a building.

176. B. The WBS is developed during the Planning phase. The WBS is a deliverables-oriented hierarchy that defines all of the work of the project.

177. B. Predefined acceptance criteria help ensure quality and minimize work. They can be used in both the Agile and waterfall methods.

178. B, C, E. The ways to organize the WBS are by subprojects (where the project managers of the subprojects each create a WBS), by project phases, or by major deliverables.

179. D. This is also known as withdrawal, and it never results in a resolution of the problem. It is also an example of a lose-lose conflict resolution technique.

180. D. The communication plan sets out who needs to be informed of what types of project changes, and it will direct which method of communication should be used.

181. D. Project sponsors should use their influence to help remove obstacles like nonparticipation on the project.

182. C. Effective team building can help create efficient and effective groups focused on getting the work done, oftentimes with team members enjoying the work immensely.

183. D. Collocation is when team members are physically working in the same place. Remember, this is not restricted just to consulting resources. In-house resources, or those who work for the same company, even in the same building, might be collocated to work in the same room or suite for a project.

184. B. When an employee is not meeting expectations, it is important for the project manager to intervene, making sure that the expectations are clear, inquire if there is a problem, and enforce the expectations.

185. D. The project team contributes their expertise to the project and gives their estimates for task duration, cost estimates, and dependencies.

186. B. This helps depict the differing levels of decomposition depending on the expected date of work.

187. C. Level 1 of the WBS is the project level. The first level of decomposition can commonly be the second level of the WBS (deliverables, phases, projects).

188. B. Expenditure reporting includes a breakdown of expenditures to date, and it will compare the financial outcome with the budget projections and remaining budget on the project.

189. D. The burndown chart is a visual representation and measurement tool showing the completed work against a time interval to forecast project completion.

190. A, C, D. Among items contained in a WBS dictionary are the list of scheduled millstones, criteria for acceptance, and descriptions of the work components.

191. A. This is not an element of the scope baseline but a management skill used to help get teams unstuck.

192. C. The iterative nature of an Agile approach, which emphasizes continuous feedback and interactions, would be the best approach in this situation.

193. A. This is indicative of a more traditional waterfall approach where the scope is controlled with a more rigid change process.

194. C. Assumptions are events, actions, or conditions that are believed to be true for planning purposes.

195. C. The sprint planning meeting sets what can realistically be accomplished during the sprint.

196. A, B, E. Agile is characterized by self-organized and self-directed teams, sprint planning, and continuous requirements gathering. Projects using a waterfall technique would have characteristics of formally organized teams and saving feedback for lessons learned meetings at the end of the project.

197. A. A high-level scope definition creates a shared understanding of what is included and excluded from the project. This information will serve as the basis for the development of the project charter.

198. A, B, E. Option C is not correct because that is the responsibility of the project management office. Option D is the role of a project stakeholder, and option F is the function of the project manager.

199. D. No real or permanent solution is achieved. This can be an example of a lose-lose result as neither side achieves resolution of their issues.

200. B. Crashing is a schedule compression technique that typically allocates additional resources to complete tasks quicker. Adding more resources will increase the costs of the project.

201. C. Lessons learned occurs during the Closing phase of the project.

202. C. A CPI over 1 means that the project is spending below the budget forecast at the measurement date.

203. A. The project scheduler is responsible for communicating the timeline and any changes.

204. C. Low-quality resources do not have the required experience, are not accomplished with the skill set, have poor passion for the project, or carry a bad attitude to work. Low-quality resources can sometimes be replaced, but they will always need to be managed in some form.

205. B. A project is represented by the individuals on the team, and ensuring the correct skills, level of experience, availability, and interest are all part of the team selection process.

Chapter 2: Project Constraints (Domain 2.0)

1. C. Influences can manipulate or impact existing constraints or may bring about new constraints.

2. B. Constraint reprioritization is a shifting of which constraint is unmovable, thereby setting how the other constraints are manipulated. "You can have it cheap, right, or fast—you get to pick two out of three" illuminates the interplay between the triple constraints.

3. C. Strengths, weaknesses, opportunities, threats (SWOT) is a tool used to perform a moment-in-time environmental scan.

4. B. Remember that a risk can be either positive or negative, and it represents an opportunity or threat that did not exist earlier in the project.

5. B. The risk register is the tool used to document all potential risks for future analysis and evaluation.

6. D. Risk analysis is the process of figuring out what risks might happen and what the results would be if each risk did occur.

7. B. Risk impact details the consequence or result that will occur if the event actually happens. Typically, this is categorized with a rating of High, Medium, and Low.

8. **A, D, F.** Commonly referred to as the "triple constraints," almost all projects are constrained by time, budget, and scope as they impact quality.

9. **B.** Similar to the availability of people with certain skills, equipment availability and *scheduling* can also lead to a constraint on a project.

10. **B, C.** Two of the triple constraints are represented in the options, a predefined budget and a fixed, or mandated, finish date. These constraints will impact the options available in terms of scope, and they should be considered in terms of creating the scope statement.

11. **A.** The scarcity of this particular type of skill set, or when they have restricted availability or cannot be on the project on time, can all represent a constraint on the project.

12. **A.** Change requests, scope creep, and interactions between constraints are some of the influences that can impact a project.

13. **D.** All three of these roles can contribute to the identification of risk on a project.

14. **D.** There are no changes to the existing project, but a new project is competing for the same resources at the same time as the existing project. The stakeholders' focus has changed.

15. **A, D, E.** Standard information on a risk register might include an identification number, description, probability and impact, score, and owner as they all relate to risk.

16. **B.** This is an example of a cease and desist letter, where there is an attempt to get a purportedly illegal activity halted and not continued again in the future.

17. **B.** Enhancing a risk involves increasing the probability or impact of the risk event to ensure that benefits are realized. This could come in the form of the construction company telling you that they could complete the building of a new gym early if there was a monetary reward for doing so.

18. **D.** Acceptance is choosing to live with the impact that a risk would have on the project.

19. **C.** The risk response plan outlines the course of action that will occur should the risk materialize and start impacting the project.

20. **D.** Risk probability is the likelihood that a risk event will occur, and it is typically expressed as a number between 0.0 and 1.0.

21. **B.** Opportunities are external conditions that contribute to positive risks on a project, like a bull market in the product area, better weather conditions than expected, or a drop in materials costs.

22. **C.** SWOT involves analyzing the project by strengths/weaknesses, which are internal to the organization, and opportunities/threats, which are external to the organization.

23. **B, D, F.** The techniques of brainstorming, interviews, and facilitated workshops can all assist in creating an initial risk list. The estimating techniques are used in activity estimation for a task, and a fishbone diagram would help create cause and effect relationships.

24. D. An integrated master schedule is a networked and cross-referenced schedule containing the detailed work packages and plans to support a project.

25. C. Environmental factors are actual constraints rather than influences of a constraint.

26. A. A change request can create impact on any existing constraints or cause a new constraint. Consider if the change request causes a change to the project due date; then the scheduling constraint would be affected.

27. C. Scope involves the specific goals, tasks, and deliverables of a project. It helps to provide boundaries for the project so that it does not expand and go on forever. Remember, when altering one of the triple constraints, at least one of the others is affected. Therefore, adjusting scope is sure to impact either schedule or budget.

28. A. Weather conditions form an environmental constraint that will influence when and often how a project can be completed.

29. D. Staffing is not an automatic constraint on a project—it is more of an environmental factor to an organization. The other answers represent the triple constraints of time, budget, and scope, as they pertain to quality.

30. B. Determining how a risk might positively or negatively impact a project, and just how likely the risk is to occur, is risk analysis.

31. B. Constraints like a fixed timeframe or budget, small windows in weather, or scarce resources limit the options the project team can pursue.

32. C. The Wigit Construction bridge project is limited by time, budget, and scope, which are the elements of the triple constraints.

33. B. SWOT stands for strengths, weaknesses, opportunities, threats, and it is an exercise in performing an environmental scan at a moment in time. This environmental scan can help reveal project risks.

34. D. C&D is shorthand for cease and desist, where documents are sent to a business or individual in order to halt a supposed illegal activity and to prevent it from being resumed.

35. A. To share a positive risk, the project seeks to assign the risk to a third party who is best able to bring about the opportunity—for instance, a company that already has a working factory in a country where the materials are going to be sold, reducing costs of the project.

36. B. Transference is the strategy of moving the liability of the risk to a third party by purchasing insurance, performance bonds, and other tools.

37. A. Expert judgment is where subject matter experts, stakeholders, and project team members contribute their expertise on similar projects to help make a recommendation.

38. A. The probability and impact matrix is a tool used to calculate an overall risk score, and to help organize, prioritize, and present information to determine what is needed in the risk response plan.

39. C. The area of weaknesses looks at the elements in the company where it can improve, which may introduce risk to a project. Negative risks are also associated with weaknesses.

40. A. Teams not attending status meetings would be an example of an active issue, not a potential future consequence that will impact the project.

41. A. Measuring the Schedule Performance Index (SPI) and the Cost Performance Index (CPI) are a part of monitoring and controlling the project and not directly an activity of risk planning.

42. C. A memorandum of understanding is an agreement between two parties that indicates a common expression of action. It does not imply a legal commitment by the parties.

43. A. RACI stands for responsible, accountable, consulted, and informed, and it is a tool to help designate roles and responsibilities on a project.

44. A, B. Project stakeholders, sponsors, and management can influence the constraints of a project in a variety of ways, including shifting the priorities and/or resources, losing interest in a project in favor of newer efforts, and contributing to scope creep.

45. B. Deliverables represent a constraint because they spell out detailed requirements or measurable results that direct the actions of the project team.

46. A. The scope of the project has changed but not the schedule, so costs will increase. This is an example of the triple constraints driving what is important in a project.

47. B. The project scope is cut back to operate within the new budget is the most likely impact on this project. The schedule would not be affected, since there is no call to lengthen or shorten the project time.

48. B. Budget is the cost constraint, and the team will not be able to work unlimited hours on the project without it affecting budget, scope, or quality.

49. D. The risk register may contain additional elements, including the response plan or where the plan may be located.

50. A. The tool used to determine how likely a risk is to disrupt the project and what the total impact on the project would be is the probability and impact matrix.

51. B, D. The risk score is the risk probability, typically expressed as a number between 0.0 and 1.0, multiplied by the risk impact. Projects may choose different quantifiable measures for probability and impact, and that would be spelled out in the risk plan.

52. C. The critical path method can also be defined as finding the longest path through the network diagram.

53. C. Risk triggers are a sign that a risk event is about to or has occurred, and that action may be needed.

54. D. When seeking to exploit a positive risk, you should look for opportunities to take advantage of positive impacts, ensuring that the risk materializes. For instance, the price of oil drops and the project is able to purchase all of the required oil at a significantly reduced price than was planned.

55. D. Avoiding the risk attempts to bypass the risk altogether, including the elimination of the cause for a risk event.

56. D. Threats are external to the organization and have negative impacts on the project, such as a softening product market, labor unrest, or trade barriers.

57. C. When work is ready to begin is the appropriate time to hold a kickoff meeting, after all of the planning has been completed.

58. D. Risk identification is brainstorming and recording all potential risks that might occur during a project.

59. A. International Standards Organization develops and publishes international standards for many industries. You may also see it as the International Organization for Standardization.

60. B. It stands for responsibility, accountable, support, and inform. This is an alternative form of a RACI chart, with "consulted" replaced by identifying who serves in a supporting role.

61. B. This example shows the interrelationship of how one constraint—in this case schedule—is influenced by the change of another constraint—scope.

62. D. Scope creep is where the project definition is constantly expanding, and control over being able to finish the project lessens.

63. A, C, D. These are common influences that can impact a project: change requests, scope creep, and reprioritization of constraints.

64. C. A constraint is anything that limits the options of the project team or dictates a specific course of action.

65. D. The wedding costs will be increased as people are added to meet the deadline. The trade-off between time, cost, and scope is at play here. The only variable that has changed is time or schedule. Since the scope is the same, costs will increase.

66. C. The conditions for dealing with the changing seasons, including how the final product's care would influence the construction, are examples of environmental constraints.

67. D. This is a scheduling constraint because the timing and availability of a resource is restricted because of the skill set scarcity.

68. B. A memorandum of agreement helps indicate the goodwill on the part of both parties and keeps track of commitments. It is not a legal document, nor does it have any enforceability in court.

69. B. A good practice when identifying project risks is to have a set of questions to ask during the brainstorming step.

70. D. The risk management plan outlines how the project will define, monitor, and control risks throughout the project.

71. A. Cost of quality (COQ) represents the costs needed to bring a substandard product or service produced by the project within the standard described by the quality plan or other criteria.

72. D. During the Monitor and Control phase, the project team observes whether a risk is triggered and takes the planned course of action should that occur.

73. A. Mitigate is a risk response strategy for a negative risk. An attempt is made to minimize either the probability of risks happening or the impact.

74. C. The probability and impact matrix will also include a calculated final risk score that can be used to prioritize the risk's severity.

75. A. The strategies used to deal with negative risks are avoid, transfer, mitigate, and accept.

76. A. This technique does not change the critical path or project completion date, but it balances specific schedule dates when there is concern about resource availability.

77. D. Normally, one of the triple constraints is more restrictive than others, in this case budget. However, if Wigitcom doesn't remain relevant in the marketplace, they run the risk of going out of business. Therefore, scope becomes more important regardless of the cost.

78. A. Much like the organizational breakdown structure, the resource breakdown structure lists the different resources by categories like labor, heavy equipment, materials, supplies, and so forth.

79. A. This is an internal dependency where one part of a company is waiting for another part to finish their work before they can begin the next step.

80. A. Milestones can also represent the completion of major deliverables on a project.

81. B. The company is checking to see that a project could be successful. A feasibility study might also look at personnel availability, costs, or timelines.

82. A. The company is trying to mitigate the impact by monitoring the probability that the risk will happen so they can act quickly to reduce negative results.

83. C. An organizational breakdown structure (OBS) is a hierarchical model setting or describing the established organizational framework for project planning and resource management.

84. D. Subject matter experts have expert judgment and experience in the topic or project area that should be consulted.

85. B. The Project Management Institute (PMI®) published *A Guide to the Project Management Body of Knowledge®*, which is a cross-industry framework of good practices in project management.

86. A. Since the need for success on her current project is probably desirable for job security, Katie would most likely try to avoid risky decisions because the margin of error is so low.

87. D. Risk tolerance is the threshold of comfort one has accepting a risk and its consequences.

88. C. This would be an example of the scope continuing to grow while the project is underway. A change control process will provide a formal way to handle these issues.

89. B. When there is a preset project end date, as when a law sets a date by which an activity must be completed, schedule compression can be used to shorten the project schedule.

90. A. This technique modifies the project schedule when accounting for unforeseen issues or resource availability.

91. C. Alternative analysis gauges the different options that might be considered to accomplish the assignment with the resources that are available.

92. B. Discretionary dependencies are also known as preferred logic, soft logic, or preferential logic.

93. D. Assumptions are those conditions that are assumed to be true in relation to the project.

94. C. Fast tracking is a schedule compression technique where activities or phases decided to be done in sequence are instead done concurrently.

95. C. The software company is seeking to share the positive risk with a third party that can act on the opportunity.

96. B. A statement of work formally captures and defines work activities, timeframes, milestones, and deliverables that a vendor must meet in the performance of work for a customer.

97. D. A request for quotation is generally more involved than just a price per item response. It can also be called an invitation for bid.

98. D. Key performance parameters identify the desired operational capability in a threshold and objective format.

99. D. Because of the stability within her job due to great performance, Karen probably has a bigger cushion to gamble and take more risks.

100. D. Contingency reserves are set aside to deal with risk consequences, and management reserves cover future situations that are unable to be predicted.

101. C. Overwhelming individuals on a project can lead to burnout, project turnover, or task slowdowns that will all negatively impact a project.

102. B. A resource calendar describes the timeframes in which resources (equipment and team members) are available for project work.

103. B. The 95 percent phenomenon is where the project seems to stagnate or be unable to complete the last step or steps so that the project can be completed.

104. A. Organizations where the project managers have authority over personnel and other resources is a projectized organizational structure.

105. D. The 3.5 mile a week target is a key performance indicator to help track the success of a particular project outcome.

106. A. Service-level agreements spell out the thresholds that must be maintained in providing services, such as response times, defect rates, and other qualities.

107. D. Key performance indicators can be used at different levels of a project or organization to help determine the success of reaching particular outcomes.

108. C. The company's survival is dependent on the team gambling or having a high risk tolerance to remain competitive. Not taking chances could doom the company's future.

109. B. If you only have a structural engineer or senior programmer's time for a small window, the schedule is engineered to make use of that resource window.

110. C. Factors that are outside the project team's control, but are needed for project success, are known as external dependencies.

111. D. A signal that a dependency is mandatory is when the activities have physical limitations, such as flattening a road before paving.

112. A. Crashing is a technique where resources are added to the project at the lowest possible cost, reflected in the decision to use overtime instead of adding team members.

113. C. The unexpected nature of a natural disaster elsewhere impacting this project would lead the project team to reprioritize the risks in an attempt to respond.

114. B. Stability is the name of the game, and it is unlikely that Richard's organization is willing to accept uncertainty in their decisions.

115. A. The critical path has zero float or slack time, and it is the shortest amount of time in which a project can be completed.

116. C. Progressive elaboration represents the iterative nature of project planning, where prior artifacts get updated and improved as the project progresses.

117. A. Wigit Construction is accepting the consequences of the risk should it happen instead of attempting to avoid, transfer, or mitigate it.

118. C. A purchase order is an official offer issued to a seller indicating types, quantities, and agreed-upon prices for products and services.

119. D. Contingency reserves are calculated for known risks and are paired with documented mitigation response plans.

120. A, C. Avoidance and acceptance are both risk response strategies used to address negative risks.

121. B. The formation of a hurricane that could make landfall and impact the cost of materials is a risk trigger.

122. B. The software company is taking advantage of the positive risk facing them by acting to merge, which is an example of exploiting a risk.

123. C. A request for proposal is a formal document that an organization posts to solicit bids from potential suppliers and vendors.

124. A. When an organization needs help in figuring out what is available in the marketplace, they release a request for information (RFI).

125. C. The company's survival is dependent on the team gambling or having a high risk tolerance to remain competitive. Not taking chances could doom the company's future.

126. A. The project team is avoiding the risk altogether by choosing to use a known material that meets quality specifications.

127. C. The key is actually setting money aside to deal with the risk should it occur.

128. C. This strategy watches for and emphasizes risk triggers to help enhance the probability or impact of certain risks.

129. B. The project team has shifted the risk and consequences of material defect to the third party with the use of a warranty.

130. A. The probability ranking in this analysis would be high, medium, and low, and getting expert judgment on what the impact would be. Qualitative risk analysis may use other techniques and may not necessarily use high/medium/low scores.

131. C. A Gantt chart is a tool that displays activities and represents visual task duration along with activity precedence.

132. D. With the safety component of the project in a stable industry, the company's reputation and public safety role would make them avoid or be reluctant to accept uncertain outcomes.

133. D. Although the CompTIA Project+ objectives do not state this, it is perfectly reasonable to accept the consequences of a positive risk as much as it is for a negative risk.

134. A, D. Passive acceptance is when the project team is not able to eliminate all of the threats to a project. Active acceptance includes developing contingency reserves to deal with risks should they occur.

135. B. Exploiting looks for opportunities for positive impacts to make certain the desired outcome will occur.

136. C. This process takes the more subjective results from the qualitative risk analysis and ties them to more numerical measures for evaluation and prioritization purposes.

137. C. The project team is closest to the work that needs to get done, should bring some expert judgment to the project, and will be on the hook for project success.

138. B. Risk identification, probability and impact analysis, and risk response would all take place during the Planning phase of the project.

139. B. Community acceptance of the project is a key success indicator, and community outreach should lessen the possibility of dissatisfaction or protests over the project.

140. A. The project team is unable to eliminate the risk to the project, but it is willing to accept the consequences of the impacts.

141. B. Wigitcom, through the use of insurance, is transferring the negative risk consequences to a third party.

142. A. The urgency assessment uses risk triggers, time to develop and implement a response, and overall risk ranking as inputs for the analysis.

143. D. Probability and impact is a prioritization tool, and not a category that might be included in a resource breakdown structure.

144. D. As the project progresses, the Monitor and Control phase would be looking for risk triggers and then engaging a risk response plan should the need arise.

145. B. The choice is just to let the risk happen since the team can live with the consequences in the unlikely event it occurs.

146. D. By requiring the successful vendor to carry the insurance, it allows the consequences of negative risk to be transferred to the third party.

147. D. Quantitative risk analysis would add more concretely measured items such as the numerical score for each risk.

148. C. This assessment checks to ensure that the data is unbiased and accurate.

149. A. The industry plus the fact that the company is relatively new would suggest a more aggressive, gambling type of risk tolerance for the company to grow and succeed.

150. C. This helps create the differing levels of decomposition.

151. D. In a functional organizational structure, the functional manager has the authority to dictate what the employee does.

152. B. Milestones are major events that are used to measure progress on a project.

153. A, C. A risk becomes an active issue should it materialize, and the appropriate risk response should be implemented.

154. C. The issues log contains a list of issues with IDs, descriptions, and owners of the issue, and it starts to develop as the execution of the project gets underway.

155. C. Governance gate meetings help to ensure accountability and that the project is proceeding according to plan.

156. A. Agile is a methodology, not an organizational structure.

157. A. A SCRUM introspective is a form of lessons learned that is done with the Agile methodology at the end of each sprint.

158. D. Early in the process is when individuals will be shy and reserved and treat each other formally.

159. D. During the kickoff meeting, formal approval for the project might occur in the form of project sign-off.

160. A. The criteria for approval are those conditions that must be in play for the customer to accept the end results of the project.

161. A. Deliverables are specific items that must be produced in order for the project to be complete, and they are usually tangible in nature.

162. C. Assumptions are those things believed to be true for planning purposes. It is important to communicate assumptions with key stakeholders so there are no missed expectations.

163. D. The timeframe, need for a mobile app, and security are all example of a project's requirements.

164. C. An action items list depicts all of the project actions that should be resolved in order to fulfill deliverables.

165. D. When the project work wins out over the functional work, it is a strong-matrixed organizational structure.

166. B. Constraints are those conditions that restrict or dictate the actions of the project team.

167. D. Activities that monitor the progress of the project and require corrective actions occurs in the Monitor and Control phase.

168. B. The more stable the industry and the company, the greater the likelihood that a traditional project management methodology would be successful.

169. A. Formal approval is normally a requirement for purchase orders to be created, for team members to be assigned to the project, and for work to begin.

170. C. This is a key performance indicator that helps track success at reaching desired outcomes.

171. B. Rework needing to be performed due to substandard product represents the costs to make the product meet standards.

172. B. There is interplay between time and cost on the project, meaning that the scope will need to be adjusted accordingly.

173. D. It is important to communicate to stakeholders and the project team what the risks are and how the team will respond, and to let everyone know should a risk turn into an issue.

174. C. Mitigation of a risk is reducing the chance that the risk could happen, or lessening the impact in the event that the risk gets triggered.

175. D. Strengths and weaknesses focus on what the organization does or does not do well.

176. A. Risk identification is not the correct answer because it captures only a third of the activities on which Valdene is working. To capture the complete picture, risk planning includes identification, risk assessment, and risk response planning.

177. B. This is the activity that compares costs and expenses to date against the cost baseline so that the stakeholder can see the variance between what was planned for and what actually occurred.

178. A. Best practices and internal processes are known as preferred or soft logic from a dependency standpoint. The three types of dependencies are mandatory, discretionary, and external. Therefore, internal would not be the correct answer, as tempting as it might seem.

179. D. In terms of the triple constraints, the results would be the project taking longer with the resources that have been assigned to the project.

180. A. Additionally, the team could choose to accept the risk that might occur and its consequences. Moreover, acceptance can also be used as a strategy for positive risks.

181. D. The banking industry generally leans toward low risk tolerance and looks for long-term, low-yield investments, such as government bonds.

182. C. The risk register will become more detailed through progressive elaboration as the project matures.

183. A. It is important to set expectations that these funds are not for extra functionality or enhancements, but to deal with circumstances, like cost overruns and variances in estimates, and to deal with specific risk situations.

184. A. This is a memorandum of agreement, and it generally does not have any court enforcement capabilities.

185. B. Depending on the analysis supporting the risk response plan, sometimes action may not be taken at all. At other times, a deliberate action is called for to deal with the risk.

186. B. The elements of the project plan, including the schedule, estimates, and responses to risk, will get more detailed and updated as the project team works through the planning steps of a project.

187. D. The management reserve is different in the spending authority, and its purpose is to cover unforeseen costs.

188. C. Weather conditions are examples of dependencies that are external to the organization, but they need to happen for a project or activity to proceed.

189. C. Although the two companies could merge, the probability that they will do so would yield a score between 0.0 and 1.0 in assessing its likelihood.

190. A. The entire R&D industry would likely have a very high risk tolerance because they need to challenge the status quo constantly in order to stay relevant.

191. A. The person is not the influencer, but the needed change request leading to more scope influences the variables of the project.

192. C. Opportunities and threats are conditions like the weather or political climate that affect the organization or project but are not within the control of the organization.

193. C. The management team is looking for both the threats and opportunities the project might experience so that the appropriate risk response can be enacted.

194. A. The strengths portion designed for project management work can quickly generate expenditure reports for stakeholders, including management.

195. A. Strengths looks at the positive attributes and/or positive risks associated with the project.

196. A. The project team will not have to compete with functional assignments in the course of the project.

197. C. This is a method of the Agile methodology to create a list of all of the activities that need to be completed, whether or not they are included in the next sprint.

198. C. A rapidly changing environment like that found in a startup would be the ideal benefit for using an adaptive approach.

199. D. A nondisclosure agreement will spell out the confidentiality expected on the project, giving legal protections to the company.

200. B. The business case helps to provide justification as to why resources should be assigned to a project and what the return could be on the project.

201. A. It is important to include the direct and indirect costs as they correspond to budgeted activities.

202. B. Sign-off on the project charter would be a milestone, not a deliverable.

203. A. Gate checks would be more representative in a waterfall approach to project management, whereas Agile uses a more adaptive approach to requirements and execution.

204. B. When a company augments their own staff with resources outside of the company, it is known as outsourcing.

205. A. The team member is not given a chance to tell his or her side of the story, and the project manager does not inquire as to why the behavior is happening. These solutions can be short-lived.

Chapter 3: Communication and Change Management (Domain 3.0)

1. **C, D.** Allowing teleworking, or allowing employees to work remotely, is a form of relocation that can definitely impact a project. Additionally, allowing employees to elect not to work in an office is an example of a business process change.

2. **A.** Although many project team members will think that documentation is just busy work, these documents are vitally important for many reasons, including auditing performance.

3. **C.** The Change Control Board (CCB), not the SME, would have the responsibility to approve or reject the change.

4. **D.** A change request log can be a simple spreadsheet that has the ID number, date, description, and so forth of the change.

5. **D.** After approval, the next step would be to implement the change. At that point conducting a quality check and updating documentation can occur.

6. **A.** Remember that resources can be people, materials, or equipment.

7. **D.** This is especially true when tasks are along the critical path, or when there is no float for that activity.

8. **A.** Key stakeholders can change due to a variety of factors, and this would need to be communicated to all stakeholders on the project, including the project team.

9. **D.** Distribution of printed media is a communication method rather than a communication trigger.

10. **B.** This incident would require corrective action to repair the damage and prevent future recurrence of the problem.

11. **B.** The plan lays out the communication methods as well as the frequency.

12. **A.** The confidential nature of HR issues, plus the need to handle a situation delicately, would invite a face-to-face conversation. A good rule is to praise publicly and criticize privately.

13. **B.** When multiple organizations are involved in the project, the different norms and practices of each company need to be considered so that the expectations of both companies are met.

14. **D.** Strong relationships can improve communication and trust on the project. Individual and group relationship building can improve morale and therefore the quality and timeliness of the project.

15. D. Even a separation of one mile in a city can produce lots of wasted time in traveling and parking. Wide spacing of a project within a city makes it difficult to schedule an impromptu meeting due to the distances among the team members, unless a video or voice conference is used.

16. C, E. Of the options listed, the only methods appropriate for mass dissemination to the public are social media and printed materials. The other forms represent more one-on-one forms of communication.

17. D. For most organizations, the need to have a fax copy of original signatures is important for legal purposes. However, the use of scanned and emailed documents, or digital signatures, is also gaining acceptance.

18. B. When there is a significant change in the situation, interrupting the meeting and letting the CEO know with an in-person meeting would be the best choice due to the urgency of this matter.

19. C. Text messaging allows Mickey's boss to get an update in the middle of another meeting, and if he deems the update important enough, the text notification allows the boss to step out of the meeting to get more information.

20. C. The use of external resources, instead of using internal resources or increasing permanent staffing, is called *outsourcing*.

21. C. A change in the routine or form of how an organization conducts business is a business process change.

22. B, D, E. Other forms of organizational change include relocation, mergers/acquisitions, and demergers/business splits.

23. A. Communicating changes is a key function of status meetings so that expectations are communicated, input can be gathered, and updated assignments can be given.

24. B. During any change where the team starts with a working product and the change disrupts its availability, it makes sense to reverse the changes. In some Agile practicing software companies, they may only roll forward to the next, future version of the software rather than reverse any changes. In this example, due to the availability of the phone's security component, it would make it important to roll back.

25. D. A subject matter expert (SME), with input from the project manager, should evaluate the impact of the change to determine if it should be attempted, what is the impact on the triple constraints, what would be the benefits, and so on.

26. B. After all documentation is updated, it is important to disseminate the updated information of the change to all applicable parties so that they understand that a change has been made, what the impact of the change will be, and what the new expectations of the project team are.

27. B. Key stakeholders, project staff, sponsors, or governance/CCB members can all submit a change request for consideration.

28. C. The quality metrics on the project were adjusted for fewer defects.

29. B, D. The scope and funding are the common elements that changed in this example.

30. A. Organizational changes would come from the functional side of the organization, not the project side.

31. B. One of the most common risks to any project can be staff turnover, and when this happens, it needs to be communicated to the project team and the project manager.

32. A, C, E. Auditors are a project-independent group who wouldn't need to be communicated with during the project. Product end users would only be communicated with when the product was ready. Shareholders are not normally involved in a project where minute details like milestone completion would be communicated.

33. A. A review by an internal team, such as security or even an internal audit division, is an audit with a recommendation to fix the finding.

34. B. Because the report reflects a routine update, the criticality does not dictate that MaryAnn be disturbed. She can be updated at noon or later.

35. A. Based on the mission of each work unit, practices can vary wildly between different groups within a company.

36. C. Different cultures may observe occasions that will differ greatly from one another. It is important to take these differences into account when you have an international team, whether or not they are offshore.

37. B. The project team's communication method allows for individual personal preferences to be set in how frequently they receive communication.

38. A. Language barriers can present huge obstacles in communication, sometimes even when the same language is being spoken in different dialects.

39. D. A closure meeting would wrap up the project activities associated with the audit, allow the audit findings to be presented, and raise questions about the recommendations.

40. A. When schedules do not align, and there is a need to share a detailed message about what is going on, what is being done to address an issue, and what alternatives are available, an email would be the best way to share the information. The next day, it would also be okay to follow up with an in-person meeting to make sure that the boss received the information.

41. A. Social media would allow for broad notices to go out to the general public, including traditional forms of media, to let everyone know about the work and closed highway.

42. B. There is a safety aspect to this change where Phil or Fernando could come to bodily harm. Therefore, getting them on the phone and ensuring that they know that the delay is happening is the best method of communication.

43. D. For an impromptu meeting where the team is dispersed, a virtual meeting, such as a conference call, would be preferable so that the team in the field can remain on site and get back to work when there is a resolution. Moreover, the problem in the field might need someone on site for observation to report to the team.

44. D. Outsourcing is the replacement of internal resources with external resources to perform the same business function.

45. A. This is also known as a *business demerger*.

46. B. Other types of organizational change recognized by CompTIA include business process change, internal reorganization, and outsourcing.

47. A. To take a subject matter expert or project team member off their project work to analyze a change will disrupt the planned work. It is important to scope the project as completely as possible prior to work beginning, and then regulate any change requests that come through. Or, if scope of the project is completely unknown, using an Agile methodology might make more sense.

48. A. Before updating the project management plan or communicating with the stakeholders, validate that the change is the next logical step. CCB approval would occur prior to the change being enacted.

49. B. A template will allow for a standard submittal in the change control process that includes all of the information that is needed on the purpose and impact of the change.

50. B. This is an example of an issue that should be captured in the issue log, and then the project manager should address the issue with the individual or the functional manager.

51. A, B, C. Technological factors, times zones, and interorganizational differences are examples of communication methods rather than triggers that would initiate communication to occur.

52. C. Anyone working on or associated with the project can submit a change that is then reviewed by a change control board or other process. As such, an executive sponsor is not needed for a change request.

53. C. The practices of the two organizations will dictate how they tend to operate and what norms they follow. There can be a clash of these norms when two organizations work together on a project.

54. C. The executive team is expressing their personal preferences in terms of communication. This could be problematic when there are critical items that need to be discussed but the executive team doesn't want to receive updates.

55. A, B, E. Of the provided list, time zones, cultural differences, and language barriers are factors that would influence the project the most. The level of report detail, criticality factors, and technological factors would not be unique to an international project.

56. B. To help clarify facts and have the ability for people to refer to the information again in the future, the distribution of printed media would be the best method.

57. C. Instant messaging is less disruptive than an impromptu meeting where Bridget's concentration might be disrupted beyond just answering the question. Instant messaging allows Bridget to respond and return to her work, and it is also more expedient than email.

58. B. When there are interpersonal problems, or strife/conflict on the project, it is best to address those issues in-person so that nonverbal communication can be observed and individuals can be encouraged personally to ensure the resolution of the problem.

59. D. Know the difference between a merger and an acquisition. The former is where two businesses come together to operate as one, whereas the latter is where one organization takes over the other one.

60. C. The addition of more resources, the modification of scope, or the adjustment of the timeline are examples of some of the changes that might be requested.

61. D. A regression plan, or rollback plan, will identify the steps and level of effort to return to the original state.

62. D. The personnel on the project have switched so this is a resource change.

63. C, D. A virtual meeting is where everyone is not in the same location, and the use of technology allows the meeting to occur.

64. B. The project management office offers standardization for a project, but it does not get involved in the details of individual projects.

65. D. The loss of expensive equipment, injuries or fatalities, or public relations incidents would override Mo's desire not to be uninterrupted.

66. C. Companies typically have organization-wide practices even when they are a global firm. When the practices have different nuances within the same company, it is known as intraorganizational differences.

67. B. Sometimes the confidentiality of a project or product would prevent the sharing of information, even within the same company.

68. B, D. Giving the project team a phone call or sending a text message are preferable because they immediately alert the recipients that you are attempting to communicate with them.

69. A. The hope of the marketing campaign is that some of their videos will go viral where they repeatedly shared and viewed based on virtual "word of mouth."

70. A. Based on the information in the question, technological factors are affecting the choice of communication methods.

71. D. The more involved nature of instructions would allow written, detail communication to reach the trailer. Other electronic forms of communication would not be reliable in this situation.

72. A. For routine meetings for project teams that are not collected, a virtual meeting utilizing either teleconferencing or video conferencing would be the best choice.

73. C. Internal reorganizations can disrupt a project if resources are no longer available to work on the project.

74. A. Using an incremental naming convention is a great way to keep track of versions. Also don't forget to make updates within the document itself to capture the version and the changes made in that version.

75. C. Once approval is granted, the next step is to go ahead and act upon the approved change—in this case, starting work on the improved landscaping.

76. A. Change requests should always be captured in writing to document the request and the response to the change, and to keep a paper trail to show why the project's timeline, budget, or scope might have changed.

77. A, B. To ensure maximum participation by Don on the project, aligning the communication approach with his preferences will help gain his engagement.

78. A. Safety issues, public relations issues, and certain risk factors are critical to communicate to key stakeholders so that responses can be coordinated and executed.

79. D. Regularly scheduled meetings would be the ideal format to share this type of information. Including a portion to discuss routine updates on the standing agenda is a good practice.

80. C. The closure meeting will allow for status updates of all activities; for the project team to turn in any property, such as ID badges/key cards; and to bring that phase of the work effort to an end.

81. D. The kickoff meeting typically happens at the beginning of the Execution phase, and it is a primary means of introducing the project team members to each other.

82. B. An acquisition is when one business takes over another. Be sure to know the difference between a business merger and an acquisition for the test.

83. C. Remember that a risk event on a project can be either positive opportunities or negative events that affect the project.

84. C. The project will no longer be able to keep to the current schedule due to the emergency leave of the key programmer.

85. D. It is important to attempt to meet stakeholder preferences in terms of communication so that you get an active response and high levels of participation from that stakeholder.

86. B. Different time zones can complicate getting status meeting scheduled because of the variance in start and quit times, as well as lunch breaks, which do not always align to provide a good window to meet.

87. B. Voice conferencing, or teleconferencing, would be the ideal choice as it would not require Greg to travel, allows for back-and-forth communication, and wouldn't be interrupted by poor Internet quality.

88. A. Relocations in the middle of a project have the potential to cause schedule delays.

89. A. Due to the geographic separation of the project team, the most efficient way to get the communication to the entire project team would be email. Attempting to schedule a virtual meeting would be troublesome due to the different time zones of the project team.

90. C, D. In practice, the step most often skipped is updating the project management plan of the change. A diligent project manager should ensure that this doesn't get missed. There are times where a project team or team member just starts working on a change that hasn't been approved at all. Make sure that there is a process, people are trained on it, and that it is enforced so that a successful and timely completion of the project can occur.

91. B. The requirements to be met for the project have changed, but have not fundamentally added to the scope of the project.

92. C. Due to the compliance nature of this topic, formal documentation of this communication is needed. As such, both sending an email explaining the compliance requirement and asking for an email in return, acknowledging receipt and understanding, will help to create an audit trail.

93. D. Version control helps create the audit trail of changes to documentation, when decisions change, and when was the last update to certain documents.

94. A, D. Adding more work to the project that is not part of the baseline is a scoping change. The added time would be a timeline change.

95. B. In a collocated environment, it would be ideal to pull everyone into a conference room or community area and hold an impromptu meeting to communicate the urgent news.

96. D. What is described in the question is an example of a risk event. Since it was previously identified in the planning of the project, the next step would be to enact the risk response to handle the event.

97. D. The content of the message will oftentimes cause you to tailor the method of communication.

98. C. If the team is not collocated, routine announcements and updates can be distributed via email as a weekly newsletter or something comparable. Some organizations use collaboration software like Microsoft SharePoint, where a list of all updates is posted as they are gathered and the audience is invited to read the updates.

99. A. The project manager looks to the factors of how the change would disrupt the schedule, budget, resource team, and quality of the project.

100. A. Distribution of printed media, either delivered door to door or via a mailer, would be an appropriate communication method based on the demographic.

101. B. A change control board (CCB) is the body that evaluates and approves changes.

102. C. Taking time to celebrate accomplishments is important, and it helps the morale of the entire project team. Please remember not to drink and drive.

103. A. Using some form of teleconferencing, such as videoconferencing or a phone call, would make the most sense from an economic perspective. An in-person meeting would be cost prohibitive for on a candidate who may not join the team. Email would not allow for verbal communication to be assessed and would drag the interview out over an unacceptable time period. Social media would not keep the discussion confidential, so it isn't a good fit.

104. A, E, F. The basic communication model is sender-message-receiver.

105. A. Task completion is communicated to the project manager and/or coordinator so that they can signal the next activities to begin.

106. D. Gate reviews are presented to a governance board or steering committee to validate cost models, schedule, risks, and objective obtainment.

107. B. When a task is complete, especially on loud equipment that normally signals an emergency, the project team should communicate to the affected stakeholders that work has been completed.

108. C. Changes in schedules will warrant communication as well as an explanation of how this will affect budget and scope.

109. C. Since the project team is working on the proposed project schedule, the trigger is project planning. If the situation was adjusting the schedule after the project was already underway, then the answer would be schedule changes.

110. B. Audits typically occur at the conclusion of a project and can be interpreted as a form of lessons learned performed by an independent group.

111. A. Text messages are excellent for quick, simple updates. In this instance, there is not a lot of information that needs to be conveyed.

112. A. The norms and practices of different work units within an organization can make project scheduling a challenge.

113. D. The CEO is stating her personal preferences regarding frequency and how the information is to be tailored to fit her style.

114. C. When project teams are separated by large distances, mountains, canyons, rivers, oceans, or other factors, geographic issues can influence how and when communication will occur.

115. B. Well-formed, written communication such as email is a great format to share complex information because the recipient can digest and process the information, refer back to it, and send follow-up questions as needed.

116. D. A closure meeting is where final hand-off of the project is conducted, including closing out any contracts and sometimes conducting lessons learned. Lessons-learned meetings can be separate from closure meetings.

117. A. For routine messages, or for very complex messages, email is the best method as it allows the project team to consume the information when they choose and minimizes the disruption of project work.

118. B. To help control costs and to minimize disruption of project work, a virtual meeting would be the ideal choice to handle routine meetings.

119. D. During the execution of the activity, the expectations that were set had to be changed. This should invite the project manager to reset communications with all stakeholders so that they will know when the service will be restored.

120. B. With the identification of new risks, the information should be captured in the risk register and stakeholders need to be informed so that mitigation plans can be developed.

121. B. Communication occurs throughout the project planning process in the creation of plans for risk, quality, communication, schedule, budget, and scope, to name a few.

122. D. Audits are reviews to obtain evidence to ensure that good practices are followed, that the project team is behaving in an ethical and legal fashion, and that no fraud, waste, or abuse is occurring.

123. C. When dealing with a cutting-edge technology project, secrecy can play a key role in being the first to market and/or protecting intellectual property. Confidentiality constraints would prevent the team member from sharing information with the rest of the industry until the project is complete.

124. A. This message does not carry any urgency or criticality, and it does not need to be communicated immediately. Therefore, it can wait until a routine status meeting or an email communication.

125. A, C. Oftentimes in remote locations there is no umbrella of mobile phone or satellite coverage, since some canyons or mountains create blackout areas where coverage cannot occur. In this case, the geographic terrain impacts the technological options at a project team's disposal.

126. B, C, F. When dealing with any team on a different continent, or even on opposite sides of the same continent, time zones will impact communication. The project team also needs to account for language barriers and cultural differences when planning communication.

127. A. Faxing, or scanning and emailing documents, are common, legally accepted forms of sending documents with original signatures. Electronic signing of documents is also gaining acceptance.

128. D. Even one lost day can be impactful on a project, especially if the tasks are along the critical path. Having an impromptu meeting, getting the direction clarified, and resolving differences in approach is the best method for achieving project success.

129. E. The kickoff meeting typically occurs at the beginning of the execution phase, not the initiation phase.

130. B. The project manager is sending the signal to the organization that work is commencing on the telephone switch. To the best of their ability, they should also communicate when the phone service should be restored.

131. D. Project managers spend up to 90 percent of their time communicating, and coordinating during the planning of a project relies on high communication.

132. B. Due to the complex nature of the message, the project manager was influenced to write out a complete message to explain all of the circumstances.

133. B, D. Sometimes, the urgency or importance of certain communications can override a stakeholder's personal preferences because the project team can be at a standstill unless a decision is made.

134. B. Even when different countries speak the same language, it can sound foreign when one is not used to hearing someone from that part of the world speak that language. Don't forget that the difficulty in understanding each other is probably mutual for individuals on both sides of the communication.

135. D. Instant messaging allows for quick back-and-forth communication with minimal distraction to others in attendance at the board meeting.

136. A. To help keep a project on schedule, the key is to minimize disruptions to the project during work time. As such, a voice conference or other type of virtual meeting will allow the team to participate in the impromptu meeting without stopping work to travel, deal with traffic, and park.

137. B. Notification of passing an inspection would be a milestone. Do not be confused with it being task completion because the task in this example would have been wiring and terminating the electrical in the building.

138. F. Depending on the nature of the findings, an audit's target audience could be any stakeholder or project team member on a project. Typically, you will see steering committee members and the project manager as the target audience for an audit.

139. D. Social media, and old-school media like TV and newspapers, are the best and quickest ways to disseminate information to the general public.

140. C. Technology can be a great tool to help collaboration and communication, but it can sometimes take more time than it is worth when it doesn't work correctly.

141. D. The shift in time zones on any continent, not just North America, can create challenges in finding appropriate times to meet. This is especially true for projects with teams on different continents.

142. B, D. The correct answer would be any form of instant communication, such as radio communication, calling a mobile phone, or text messaging. The communication plan should direct the method of communication used when corresponding with members in the field.

143. C. Face-to-face meetings, or in-person meetings, are the superior choice for working on conflict resolution, giving performance appraisals, and working on team building.

144. A. Any time the scope, budget, or schedule changes, the information needs to be discussed and communicated. At this point, the project manager should disseminate this information to stakeholders.

145. B. In the IT world, software audits are routine to see if there is any true up or true down (that is to add more licenses if needed, or remove licenses that you are not using) that needs to happen after a large project is complete.

146. B. A disability is not an example of a personal preference, so the correct answer is technological factors. If the technology does not exist, then the project team will need to adjust their communication approach with Cynthia to accommodate her disability.

147. C. Working on three different continents would mean that one work team is likely off-duty/sleeping at any given time during the day. As such, the best method would be email so that the off-duty team would get the information when they begin their shift, whereas the other teams would get the information instantly.

148. D. The project scope has been altered through the change control process, and the project team needs to be informed and the plan needs to be adjusted.

149. B. Along with nondisclosure agreements, personnel actions are confidential and are not shared beyond the employee and management. As such, it can appear to those not in the know that nothing is happening to correct the problem.

150. A, C. When dealing with a varied constituent base, remember that some individuals will have a communication preference one way or the other. So including both electronic and nonelectronic forms of communication may be vital to getting the message out to everyone.

151. A. There can be both internal and external audits; either one should be independent in authority and practice.

152. D. The viability and conditions of the project have dramatically changed warranting some form of communication to the project sponsor even while she is away on vacation.

153. C. Placing flyers on cars that park on the street, mailing the information to residents, and posting signs will help ensure that everyone knows about the parking disruption so that the project can continue.

154. A. Highly detailed information that requires time to digest is best suited to be delivered in writing. Hence, the work lead tailored the message delivery based on the content of the message itself.

155. C. As the parent organization makes functional changes, it can cause a shift away from project work toward more administrative time until new work patterns can be established on the new processes.

156. B, C. Some companies might choose to move their operations to a country with more lax tax laws, whereas other companies might cease doing the activities that are causing the increased tax burden and shift that liability to a different company that isn't as concerned about the change.

157. D. Wigitcom should look for some type of demerger and seek to sell off that business unit so that it can focus on its core competencies.

158. C. Implementing a standardized set of processes, forms, and reports will help to eliminate the inconsistent results the organization is getting.

159. B. Be sure to consider how the relocation of all or part of an organization can disrupt your project.

160. A. The adjustment of work assignments and staff within the same organization is an internal reorganization.

161. C. Also known as a demerger, be mindful of how this can impact a project with parts of the organization that are no longer there.

162. B. Including additional features on a project that was not scoped originally would represent an alteration in the requirements.

163. D. The practice of adding initials at the end of a filename allows readers to see who has added comments or changes to a document.

164. A. Resource changes should be communicated to the project team as quickly as possible so that there are no missteps in task delivery.

165. C. Large-scale, probable scenarios should have a response plan in place informing team members what their responsibilities are to work.

166. C. A functional manager would be the ultimate owner of the final product in their area, so her absence could lead to decisions with which she doesn't agree, or the pursuit of a direction that will not ultimately work.

167. C. Since all email addresses, possible fax numbers, or social media tags for a specific geographic area are not known, these factors led to the use of distribution of printed media as the communication method to get the word out.

168. B. Wigit Construction was acquired by a different company when it agreed to be sold.

169. C. Instead of taking on the overhead of hiring and training staff, which is not the company's core competency, outsourcing would provide the best choice to get the needed service.

170. B. Moving the operational headquarters and the majority of the construction equipment would improve visibility and reduce costs.

171. C. To help keep people and property safe, the company made a change to their business processes so that accidents are not repeated.

172. A. To achieve so drastic a change in quality might require the project team to look at all aspects of the business: hiring, training, processes, and materials to achieve the CEO's goal.

173. C. Version control creates a trail of what changes were added, by whom, and at which point in the document's history.

174. A. Early in a project is when risks are most likely to occur, and accordingly, they can have bigger impacts on the project.

175. B. A localized event that is minor in scale to a business continuity event is known as an *incident response.*

176. B. The business continuity response is a plan on how the company will continue to operate in the event of disaster.

177. B. Work slippages can impact the timeline, especially when that work is along the critical path.

178. A. The mutual joining of two companies to do work as a single company is a merger. This can disrupt the project as the new organization struggles with the activities of joining cultures and processes.

179. C. People are any organization's biggest expense, and the temporary nature of this funding means that it cannot hire permanent employees. The agency would not be able to pay these employees after the grant expires. Temporary hires would also work in this scenario.

180. A. The mutual joining of two organizations where leadership and elements of each culture are retained is a merger.

181. B. Remember that a demerger and a business split are different names for the same type of change.

182. D. Any addition, subtraction, or change of a resource is reflected with this type of change.

183. A. The company is preparing to fulfill its mandate, even in the event that the hurricane makes landfall. The response plan will spell out where and when people are to report in the event of disaster.

184. A. Any adjustment to common practices would be considered a business process change.

185. D. Relocation of resources can often disrupt a project, even if those individuals remain assigned to the project.

186. A. Reorganizing by centralizing this function would increase consistency and control for the organization.

187. D. Since one company is purchased wholly by the other, this is an acquisition. If the two companies mutually joined and kept elements of each organization, it would be a business merger.

188. D. Moving business functions around within the same organizational umbrella is a business reorganization.

189. D. Alterations in the way business is conducted, information is routed, and approvals are given are all business process changes.

190. B, D. Two changes need to be communicated: the cutback in budget, and the change in resource assignments. Be as transparent as your company allows in the sharing of information by keeping your team informed.

191. C. Key stakeholder changes can influence the support and direction of a project. It will be important to bring the new sponsor up to speed on the objectives, status, and importance of the project.

192. D. The audit findings led to corrections in business processes to ensure that there are better controls so that theft does not occur in the future.

193. C. Joining forces, and thus combining talent and regional market strengths as a new organization, is the best choice from this list.

194. D. Finding a location where the team can share the same facility should greatly reduce the identified problems.

195. B. Projects can have business processes just like functional units. This was a change to how a project's business process works.

196. D. An incident response has similarities to a business continuity response, but it is smaller in scale and localized to a particular part of the business.

197. B. When there is a change in project resources, there needs to be communication with the project team. The addition or subtraction of a team member may cause a change in the chemistry and morale of a project team.

198. A. Altering how an organization is structured to conduct business is a form of reorganization.

199. C. Conforming to government requirements can oftentimes introduce mandated business process changes, like having the CFO sign off on the accuracy of financial reports.

200. B. Using another company's resources and expertise to perform a function that previously was done internally is called *outsourcing*.

201. D. Defects, rework, and their related costs are all related to the quality plan or a quality change.

202. A. Fundamentally changing how an organization does business is a change in the business process.

203. B. The quality of the network, in this case the network's availability, was changed from the original request.

204. B. Seeking out a smaller or struggling company and investing in their purchase could greatly improve DewDrops position since they have the cash (liquid assets).

205. A. The key to this answer is the approval to move forward. Gate reviews are check-in points where authorization to proceed must be given.

Chapter 4: Project Tools and Documentation (Domain 4.0)

1. B. Ralph's role on the project is that he is accountable for all actions on the project and those of the project team. He has the authority to task, delegate, and ensure the quality of the deliverables.

2. D. Collaboration tools allow for instant messaging, sharing work screens among team members over the network, and other areas including videoconferencing. A wiki page might be used as a collaboration tool, but the collaboration tool set is much broader than just wiki pages.

3. B. It is critical to capture any assignments that have been handed out, who owns the assignment, and when the task is due. This helps make sure that there is no lapse in completion due to unclear assignments and a lack of clarity on what needs to be completed and by when.

4. A. A status report is a written document that captures the progress being made on a project, what challenges have materialized, and data on tracking to complete the project on time and on budget.

5. A. A process diagram is a visual representation of the steps in a process. Other names for process diagrams include process maps and workflow diagrams.

6. D. The project charter is the document that authorizes the project to commence.

7. A. Publishing a meeting agenda and disseminating it in advance allows team members to be prepared and meetings to be on time and focused and improves the use of team members' scarce time on a project.

8. A, B, C. Meeting agendas, communication plans, and project charters would all fall into the category of planning documents at various levels. Project condition information, or status, can all be gleaned in different forms from dashboard information, status reports, and meeting minutes.

9. D. Standard tools like Microsoft Project or Primavera, plus an exploding market of cloud-based tools, help to automate the creation and updating of the project schedule. More simplistic projects can use Microsoft Excel or a comparable tool.

10. B. Intranet sites are information sites internal to an organization, and they are normally protected by a firewall that requires a form of authentication to gain access to the information. These are great hubs for communicating organizational information.

11. B. RACI stands for responsible, accountable, consulted, and informed. At a task or activity level, it identifies who needs to do what action based on the individual's role.

12. C. Being consulted means that there is a two-way communication that will take place prior to a decision or action being taken for a particular task or decision. This will often vary in a RACI matrix from activity to activity.

13. D. A key performance indicator to meet the publisher's target is to complete 1/12 of the books each day, which would be 8,333. Meeting this target would let Carl know that they are on track to complete the job on time. Missing this number would mean that Carl would have to change the speed of the process, add more personnel, or add more shifts.

14. B. The scope statement is a more detailed explanation of what the project will deliver compared to the project charter, which contains a high-level scope definition.

15. A. Action items routinely get assigned during meetings, and they are key to capturing what needs to get done, who will do it, and when it needs to get done. This information should be shared with the team after the meeting so that work can be done and follow-up can occur. Action items are those activities that must be completed in order to fulfill the project's deliverables.

16. C. The project charter will also contain high-level information about assumptions, constraints, and risks. Remember, it is also the formal authorization to begin project work.

17. C. The organizational chart is a graphic representation of how the project is structured, and it contains the reporting relationships for the project.

18. B. The project schedule, commonly displayed in the form of Gantt chart, shows the order of tasks, start and end dates, duration, and when using project software can automatically help keep track of the percentage of work completed on a task.

19. A. A dashboard is a form of a status report that will display conditions of different data elements and key performance indicators to communicate the progress and challenges of the project.

20. B. According to *A Guide to the Project Management Body of Knowledge (PMBOK Guide®)*, Fifth Edition, published by the Project Management Institute (PMI®), a histogram is a special form of a bar chart used to describe central tendency, dispersion, and shape of a statistical distribution.

21. C. This defines a status report. Although this is a specific type of communication, the need for the report and who it will be sent to would be included in the communication plan. The actual report itself is a different project artifact.

22. B. Having someone assigned to capture what occurs in a meeting and create a written record is very helpful to the efficiency of the project.

23. C. The project charter includes information such as high-level risks, requirements, budget, assumptions, and constraints. Much of this information can be captured within a business case document, which can serve as a starting point for developing the project charter. Remember that the project sponsor is responsible for creating and signing the project charter.

24. D. Meeting agendas are distributed in advance of the meeting to allow people to be prepared during the meeting. Some organizations have a standard for delivering the agenda a certain period of time in advance, such as two business days prior to the meeting. This standard can be added to the communications plan to ensure uniformity on the project.

25. C. Project scheduling software, especially for complex projects, can aid in the ease of tracking data and producing reports. Remember, there is a learning curve for all users whenever a new software tool is introduced on a project.

26. B. For any given task, there must be one, and only one, position that is accountable. Being accountable in a RACI context means that one person is ultimately answerable for the correct and thorough completion of a deliverable or task.

27. B. A dashboard is either an electronic or paper report that shows lots of information in the format of a dashboard display with different "instrumentation panels" showing key performance information from different project areas.

28. B. The scope statement is a reference for what the product needs to do, what assumptions and constraints have been identified, and what key performance indicators will be used to track and measure the project's success.

29. D. This plan sets the written communication, meeting schedule, and escalations that should occur to keep the identified stakeholders up to date on project events.

30. C. Key performance indicators are the critical and quantifiable measures needed to track success factors for a project, product, or an organization. There should be a limited number of "key" indicators that need to be tracked.

31. A, B. It is possible for someone to be both responsible and accountable. Remember that there can be only one person who is accountable, but multiple people can be responsible. Where an individual gets assigned to multiple participation types is dependent on the number and quality of staff assigned to the project.

32. C. Action items are comparable to a "to-do" list of activities that need to occur for product completion. Remember that this is a dynamic list that can often grow during the course of the project, specifically in meetings.

33. A. Project authorization is a component of the project charter, and therefore it is not a component of the organizational chart.

34. D. A status report or dashboard would allow the stakeholder to get the information on the current conditions of the project. Other performance measurement tools like a balanced scorecard could help give a glimpse into the project.

35. D. Meeting minutes help to memorialize details of conversations and decisions that were made in the moment. Often during the course of a project, so much time passes with so many other decisions made that it can be difficult to recall what was done and why. Meeting minutes are a tool to help address those challenges.

36. A. Process diagrams are often called workflow diagrams, which show all of the steps from start to end in a process.

37. C. With a RACI matrix, it is easy to get accountable and responsible mixed up, particularly when first creating the matrix. Those who must see the task completed are *accountable*, whereas the people who will actually do the work are *responsible*. Keep a sharp eye out to make sure that you don't get confused.

38. B. The project charter also gives formal authority to begin the project, and it allows the project manager to begin applying resources to the project.

39. D. A fishbone diagram, also called an *Ishikawa diagram*, is a visualization tool for categorizing the potential causes of a problem in order to identify its root causes.

40. D. Specific actions that need to get completed are added to the action items list. This list is great during meetings to maintain an accurate track of the tasks that come up during discussion so that they can be successfully undertaken and completed.

41. B. A histogram can be used to show the frequencies of problem causes to help understand what is needed for preventive or corrective action.

42. B. Famous sites like Wikipedia are examples of simple web tools that allow users to create content for websites. Often, content can mean the difference between a popular website and one that doesn't get much web traffic.

43. A. When you are assigned to be responsible, it means that you are assigned to do the work to achieve the task. There should be at least one role of responsible for every task or activity, but multiple people can be assigned to do work. Be sure not to get this confused with accountable.

44. D. The project management plan consists of all project planning documents, including the approved scope statement, schedule, communication plan, and more.

45. A. The project sponsor is responsible for publishing, signing, and approving the project charter. The document includes high-level elements of requirements, milestones, budget, assumptions, constraints, and risks.

46. B. The issues log will maintain a unique identifier for each issue along with a description of the issue, owner, and due date.

47. C. A Pareto chart contains both a line graph and bars where the individual values are represented in descending order by the bars and the cumulative total is represented by the line.

48. D. Dashboards allow users to select which elements they want displayed and reported on. *Note*: For the exam, look for the electronic delivery of information, but remember that nondynamic dashboards can be effective in meetings as one-page brief sheets.

49. A. Meeting minutes are used to provide a recap of what was discussed in a meeting.

50. B. The scope statement documents the deliverables required to produce the product or service that the project is creating.

51. C. The resource conflict with the needed aircraft is an issue that needs to be actively managed, so this would get added to the issues log.

52. D. The project schedule will have task dependencies and durations for the project manager to compute whether it is on the critical path. Using project software, the critical path can get created automatically.

53. D. Fishbone diagrams are also called Ishikawa diagrams based on the causality diagrams created by Kaoru Ishikawa. Fishbone diagrams are a tool used to show causes of specific events.

54. D. This stakeholder is designated to be informed, which is a one-way communication that takes place after an action or decision has already been completed.

55. A. The issues log is a numbered list of issues that contains descriptions and the other attributes detailed in the question.

56. D. It is critical to memorialize meetings, especially action items and decisions that were made so that there is a record of lessons learned for audit purposes.

57. C. The project management plan is the collection of plans created to address budget, time, scope, quality, communication, risk, and other project elements.

58. D. A dashboard gives a snapshot of many different elements of the project in "instrumentation panels" on a screen. *Note*: A dashboard does not have to be electronic, and a single page, printed dashboard can be an effective communication method.

59. A, D, F. A RACI chart is a matrixed-based chart used to identify roles and responsibilities on a project. It stands for responsible, accountable, consulted, and informed.

60. A. A run chart is a graph that displays observed data in a time sequence.

61. C. The project schedule would contain the information for activity start and finish dates.

62. A. The project schedule sets the timing plan for the project of what needs to be done, how long it will take, and in what order.

63. B. An agenda allows for forethought and preparation to occur, and it enables the best use of the scarce time of the project team and stakeholders.

64. B. The Pareto principle implies that 20 percent of problems take up 80 percent of a team's time to deal with them. A Pareto chart is a bar chart that shows the largest concentration of values from greatest to smallest.

65. C. Vendor knowledge bases can come in two forms: those accessible to all web users and those where only company representatives can access the information. In either case, they help the user to self-service to try to solve a problem without calling a help center.

66. C, E. Action items are a tactical item used to record a "to do" list in the course of meetings, and a request for proposal is a procurement vehicle to help obtain goods and services. The procurement plan might be a part of the project management plan, but the RFP would ultimately be added to archived project documentation.

67. A. The communication plan sets the frequency, nature, and content that needs to occur for the project to be successful. It also can include who owns the tasks needed for each communication item.

68. A. An effective tool in meetings is to make sure that there are assignments on who is running the meeting, who is the timekeeper, and who will keep the minutes. When a single individual has multiple roles in a meeting, it lessens the quality of the meeting deliverables.

69. A. Especially valuable at the beginning of a project, a run chart helps identify information about a process before there is enough information to set dependable control limits.

70. C. The project schedule will serve as a guide throughout the entire project to help track toward completing the project on time. When activities and tasks cause delays, it is important to update the project schedule. Be sure to keep a baseline of the schedule to compare the planned completion time versus the actual time to complete.

71. B. The communication plan documents the types of information needs the stakeholders have, when the information should be shared, and the method of delivery.

72. A. The project management plan is a term that refers to all of the planning documents, including the budget and schedule. Other elements might include a quality plan, resource plan, and procurement plan, to name a few.

73. D. A scatter chart depicts pairs of numerical data to help the analyst look for a correlation or relationship.

74. C. The organizational chart would have a breakdown of the hierarchy for the project and show where the assignments are for each project function and resource.

75. D. A scatter chart can also be called a *scatter diagram*, and it is used to help identify a correlation between the dependent and independent variables.

76. D. When asked to see the project management plan, there are a lot of people who incorrectly think that this is the project schedule. The project management plan includes the different project plans needed for project success.

77. C. Named after the American engineer and management consultant, Henry Gantt, a Gantt chart allows users to see at a glance information about various activities, start and end dates, duration, activity overlaps, and when the project will start and end.

78. D. The project organizational chart helps to clarify involvement on the project, and it can be used to help create a decision-making matrix indicating who has authority to make certain decisions.

79. D. The project manager needs to ensure that the project management plan is complete to allow for turnover and lessons learned and to create a project documentation repository.

80. C. Mitigation is associated with the prediction and response to risk where an issues log is tracking active incidents. A correct answer could be tracking what action is to be taken.

81. D. It is possible that action items are also kept in an electronic list, or on flip chart paper kept in the project room. Regardless of how the list is kept, remember to make sure that each item is assigned to a team member and that they are clear on what needs to be done and by when.

82. C. The World Wide Web component of the Internet has transformed how users expect to get information about a company's products and services.

83. C. The organizational chart will spell out who reports to whom and what teams might exist within the project.

84. B. The organizational chart for the project sets the hierarchical reporting structure of the project. All other options describe the project charter.

85. B. The issues log helps to manage items that need to be monitored and/or escalated to minimize the impact on the project team.

86. C. A dashboard is a form of a status report that displays summary information from lots of different areas of the project to present a snapshot of key information for analysis and discussion.

87. B. For longer and more complex projects, status reports become critical to making sure that stakeholders stay current on the progress, risks, and issues facing the project.

88. A. The organizational chart describes the project team member organization and identifies reporting structures.

89. C. A status report explains high-level detail on the progress and challenges the project is experiencing. The cadence, or frequency, of the report will be set by the communication plan.

90. D. The scope statement will document the product description, key deliverables, success and acceptance criteria, and key performance indicators.

91. D. The method, cadence, target audience, and subject matter for various communications are spelled out in the communication plan.

92. A. Meeting agendas are distributed in advance of the meeting to allow for people to be prepared during the meeting.

93. C. Especially valuable at the beginning of a project, a run chart helps identify information about a process before there is enough information to set dependable control limits.

94. B. There can be one, and only one, person who is accountable per task in a RACI matrix.

95. B. A purchase order is a legally binding agreement that guarantees the delivery of goods and services along with the agreed upon compensation.

96. D. Time and materials contracts set an hourly rate for a contract worker. *We are here for you!* would get compensated only for the hours the two administrative assistants work for the project or organization.

97. A. A MOU is a binding agreement between multiple parties. A legal agreement between two government organizations is also known as an *intergovernmental agreement,* but that will likely not be on the test.

98. D. This document would be a legally enforceable contract that guarantees service, payment, and delivery.

99. B. When there is inadequate information to make a determination to pursue a purchase, a request for information (RFI) can help the buyer gather information to make an informed decision. An RFQ is not an appropriate response in this scenario because Hugh's company is not ready to purchase, at which point a time-limited quote would be useful. They are only investigating at this point.

100. C. In order for a vendor proposal to be accurate and meaningful to the organization that publishes an RGF (request for proposal), there must be a complete written explanation of the goods or services that are needed. This is known as a statement of work, or SOW.

101. C. An RFI will provide information to Wigitcom to help them make a determination as to what solutions are available, which vendors can help, and the order of magnitude estimate to the costs.

102. D. Plotted points on a scatter chart indicate the type of relationship, or the absence of a relationship, between two variables—one dependent and one independent.

103. C. Once accepted by the seller, this becomes a legally binding document for goods and services to be provided and for compensation to be given at the listed price.

104. B. An RFQ is a tool used to help determine estimates for time and cost through bids for specific products or services.

105. B. Warranties help allay the concerns of the buyer that the stated quality will be backed by the company, and if there is a problem, the seller will make the buyer whole with their purchased product or service.

106. B. An organization issues an RFP when they are ready to begin work and are ready to procure goods and services in support of that work.

107. C. A contract is legally enforceable, and it typically falls into three categories: fixed-price contracts, cost-reimbursable contracts, and time and material contracts.

108. C. Key performance parameters define the boundaries that comprise the scope of a project and identify the capability that must be delivered in terms of quantity, quality, coverage, timeliness, or readiness.

109. C. Project scheduling software can help keep track of start and end dates and durations, produce Gantt charts, and track progress through the project.

110. A. A letter of intent is a negotiable document, and it can be thought of as an agreement to agree to certain terms and conditions should the parties create a contract.

111. A. A request for information (RFI) is used when there is not enough information or expert judgment to know what a good or service will cost, or to understand how many vendors there are who can meet this demand.

112. B. Service-level agreements (SLAs) spell out the expected performance levels to be followed and adhered to.

113. C. The letter should let *We are here for you!* know to stop using DewDrops' name and to not engage in using it again in the future.

114. C. As outlined in the contract, the seller can recoup costs that are allowable in the contract terms.

115. C. As an example, two parties might create service levels in a project around deliverables being produced on time, how quickly problems would get created, and what incentives or penalties occur because of performance.

116. C. As Jeff has completed the SOW, the organization knows what they need to procure and are ready to move forward. Therefore, this scenario describes a request for proposal.

117. A. An RFI will give a sense of the number of providers or contractors who can provide the goods and services in question. An RFI will also help to give a ballpark for the costs.

118. D. Although this example shows a technology company protecting their intellectual property, a cease and desist letter is not limited to technology companies or intellectual property concerns.

119. A. Wiki pages allow users to freely create and edit web page content using a web browser.

120. A. The people would do the work become responsible in the RACI matrix for that task.

121. A. A purchase order creates the binding arrangement between buyer and seller, guaranteeing service to the buyer and compensation to the seller.

122. A. Key performance parameters (KPPs) are vital characteristics, functions, requirements, or design considerations that have a major impact on a product or service. Failure to meet these parameters would trigger a review by a validating body to ensure compliance.

123. A. A warranty will normally be time-limited and will expired once that time limit is reach. For example, car manufacturers might have a warranty on the vehicle powertrain for a certain number of miles or a certain period of time.

124. B. RFQ generally means the same thing as an invitation for bid (IFB). An RFI is similar to an RFQ in that they both serve the same purpose, and most organizations use one or the other of these methods to help determine estimates.

125. D. Though similar to an RFI, one way a request for quotation (RFQ) is different is in the delivery of a quote that the procuring organization can act on.

126. B. RACI stands for responsible, accountable, consulted, and informed, and it is used to help clarify roles and responsibilities. It is not a procurement vehicle.

127. B. Some projects become impossible to manage without the aid of software to help keep track of information and automate the various reports the stakeholders require.

128. B. A memorandum of understanding (MOU) is used when a legal agreement can't be created between the two parties.

129. C. To protect their intellectual property, Wigitcom should send a cease and desist letter. If the other company does not comply, then Wigitcom can follow up with other legal actions.

130. B. Letters of intent can help assure the parties of the actions each party would take, like agreeing to contractual terms and conditions prior to negotiating a contract. It helps to show and share the good faith of each organization.

131. C. A nondisclosure agreement assures that what's discussed, revealed, or created is kept within the organization.

132. C. This process includes submitting a SOW, receiving bids from vendors and suppliers, evaluating proposals, and making a selection.

133. B. A bidder's conference typically occurs right after an RFP is published to help improve the quality of the proposals submitted. Moreover, vendors can get a better sense of whether or not they have the information they need to decide to provide a bid.

134. B. A nondisclosure agreement assures that what's discussed, revealed, or created is kept confidential for Wigitcom.

135. A. As outlined in the contract, the seller can recoup costs that are allowable in the contract terms. This also allows flexibility to the buyer when the final outcome is not well defined.

136. A. Fixed-price contracts are good agreements when the statement of work is clear and concise.

137. C. This is riskiest type of contract for the buyer because the total costs of the project are unknown until the project is completed. It does have the advantage, however, to the buyer of easily changing the scope.

138. D. An RFI and an RFQ are similar in the gathering of data to help an organization make an informed decision. The differentiator is the agency's desire to move forward with a purchase once the information is gathered and analyzed.

139. A, B, E. Documents that are binding between two parties, meaning that they can be legally enforced to deliver service, payment, or other attributes, are agreements/contracts, memorandums of understanding (MOUs), and purchase orders. Other forms include nondisclosure agreements, cease and desist letters, letters of intent, service-level agreements, and warranties.

140. A. Because Wigitcom is paying for time and expenses and not for a defined deliverable, they will be able to change their mind as often as they are willing to pay for doing so.

141. C. As the seller of the service continues to work on a project, the greater the chances for certain outlined costs to be reimbursed. This becomes a trade-off between flexibility and uncertainty.

142. D. The SOW specifies in detail the goods and services the organization is purchasing from outside the organization. This is a common prerequisite when issuing an RFP.

143. D. A request for information can have a similar meaning to a request for quotation in some companies. An RFQ can also invite a cost quote that would be valid for a certain period of time.

144. A, C. Because MOUs are simpler with straightforward language, they allow more flexibility and does not require either party to obtain the services of an attorney. A good time to use an MOU is when you are dealing with government entities or agencies that cannot enter into certain contractual relationships.

145. D. Fixed-price contracts are good agreements when the statement of work is clear and concise.

146. B. A fixed-price contract is risky to Wigit Construction as the seller because if there are problems on the project and it takes longer to complete, Wigit Construction must still pay for the labor and increased costs of materials to fulfill the contractual obligation.

147. C. A bidder conference helps the buyer sell their interest in the project and helps sellers determine if it is worth the investment to submit a proposal.

148. A, D. The RFI and RFQ may be used interchangeably, but may also have different meanings in different organizations. Ask questions to learn what these terms mean in your organization.

149. A. As outlined in the contract, the seller can recoup costs that are allowable under the terms of the contract.

150. A. The RFP will be published with the statement of work as well as other terms and conditions of both the procurement and the agreement that will need to be reached to do business with Wigit Construction.

151. A. A request for proposal (RFP) is issued when an organization is ready to begin work and needs to procure goods and services.

152. B. A purchase order guarantees payment for goods and services. Once accepted by the seller, it becomes a legally binding document.

153. A. The statement of work (SOW) specifies in detail the goods or services an organization is interested in purchasing from outside the organization.

154. C. Service-level agreements (SLAs) spell out the expected performance levels to be followed and adhered to. For instance, an electrical utility may have a requirement with their customers to restore power within a certain period of time in case there is an outage.

155. C. A fixed-price contract is risky to the seller because if there are problems on the project and it takes longer to complete, the seller still must pay for the labor and increased costs of materials to fulfill the contractual obligation.

156. A. A memorandum of understanding (MOU) is used when a legal agreement can't be created between the two parties. It is common for government agencies to create MOUs between each other to provide services or performance criteria to one another.

157. D. Collaboration tools would allow screen sharing, joint document editing and sharing, video calls, task lists, and calendars.

158. C. A process diagram can be used in two forms: mapping the process as it is, and then reworking it to how it should be.

159. C. Action items would be developed in the creation of the scope statement, or they could make up a list generated during project meetings.

160. B. With a fixed-price contract, the risk is on the seller. When changes to a project increase their costs but not their revenue, they stand to lose money. Accordingly, they would likely allow very few changes to the project's scope.

161. A. A SWOT analysis looks at strengths, weaknesses, opportunities, and threats where strengths and weaknesses are internal-facing and opportunities and threats are external-facing.

162. A. Time and materials contracts set an hourly rate for a contract worker, such as a painter to finish an interior, instead of a fixed price. The total cost is not known at the outset, and it will depend on the amount of time spent to produce the product or service.

163. D. When someone has a role of informed, it means that they are informed after a decision has been made or a result has been achieved.

164. A. Vendor knowledge bases can be great sources of information, but access is restricted to employees of that company.

165. D. This document shows values from a variety of areas of the project to show a balanced view of the project.

166. C. Wiki pages can be edited though a web browser and do not require special software. Using Wiki pages would allow all three managers to add to a single page to keep a log of events and progress.

167. A. The best document to gain an understanding of the project and structure would be the organizational chart.

168. A. To help determine if the project should move forward, a status report would provide a snapshot of the work done to date, status of budget and schedule, and issues facing the project.

169. D. NDAs are common contract vehicles for jobs in both the government and private sector that would require a security clearance.

170. A. Process diagrams are often called workflow diagrams. They show all the steps from start to end in a process.

171. A. The project sponsor is looking at a single variable on the project—that is, the budget. That variable will probably not tell the complete story of the project, including that the increased cost was from increasing the scope and not cost overruns. A balanced score card helps provide that bigger picture.

172. D. Time and materials is tied to a rate and a number of hours. If the buyer is willing to forgo the task the contract worker was meant to do in favor of other work, or if the buyer would like to have additional work done at their cost, this contract vehicle allows that type of flexibility.

173. C. When someone has a consulted role, they have input either to the work or to the decision prior to it being completed.

174. B. A Gantt chart is a type of bar chart that illustrates a project schedule.

175. A. Intranet sites are protected by a password or network firewall, and they can contain both information and functionality for the business to operate.

176. D. Meeting minutes capture the details of why decisions were made, what was discussed, and any assignments/due dates that materialized out of the meeting.

177. D. There are lots of reasons a cease and desist letter might be sent. In this instance, it could be that the wall is being built on the wrong side of the property line or that it is in violation of a land-use covenant.

178. C. Time and materials contracts are great to use for staff augmentation situations. The customer is only on the hook for whatever time they use, so it gives the customer maximum flexibility.

179. C. Project scheduling software can aid in the tracking and reporting of tasks, schedule, and critical path.

180. B. Key performances indicators are a performance measurement tool to help track progress toward a goal or objective.

181. B. An NDA is used to assure that what's discussed, discovered, or developed between the two parties is kept within the partnership.

182. B. Dashboards are like the instruments in the dashboard of a car, with different indicators presenting information on different aspects of performance.

183. B. The project schedule reflects activity start and end dates, task durations, and a representation of predecessors of each task. Project schedules are often represented through a Gantt chart.

184. B. A run chart, or a run-sequence plot, creates a graph that displays observed data over a period of time.

185. D. A SWOT analysis looks at the strengths and weakness of the organization and compares it with the opportunities and threats the external environment holds for the company.

186. D. Internet sites are an almost expected knowledge management tool today, and they are a great way to communicate services, products, and what a company stands for to the general public.

187. D. A letter of intent is a negotiable document, and it can be thought of as an agreement to agree to certain terms and conditions should the parties create a contract.

188. D. Run charts often represent some aspect of the output or performance of a manufacturing or business process.

189. A. Make sure that each issue has an identifier, an owner, and a due date to resolve in order to help keep the project on track.

190. D. A fishbone diagram is used to help determine and define the different factors that could cause a problem and to perform an analysis to determine the root cause.

191. C. The monitoring of a staff hours in this example means that staff hours are a key performance indicator to staying on time and on budget.

192. A. If someone's activities are encroaching on the rights of another organization, like trespassing, violating copyright, or overreaching on mineral rights, a cease and desist letter would be used to attempt to correct the behavior.

193. B. A histogram can be used to show the frequencies of problem causes in order to help understand what is needed for preventive or corrective action.

194. A. Use of project scheduling software can increase the amount of time during setup, but it can save lots of time in managing the project in later phases.

195. B. Time and materials will allow the vendor to provide invoices at an interval prescribed by the contract for approved time and appropriate expenses. Make sure that the rules governing what can be invoiced and how often are spelled out in the contract.

196. B. A Pareto chart shows the values in a bar chart in descending order from left to right, and it then adds a line chart to show the cumulative score. This will allow the analyst to see which issues are causing 80 percent of the disruption and to focus on them first.

197. C. Collaboration tools, like videoconferencing, screen sharing, and sites that allow for the joint sharing of documents, tasks, and calendars, can be invaluable to a project.

198. A. Miranda is assigned the role of consulted as her opinion is needed to help make a good selection and to help with acceptance of the final product from a change management perspective.

199. C. The signing of the project charter allows for resources to be applied to the project and for work to begin.

200. B. Most likely, this analyst is using a histogram, which can be used to show the frequencies of problem occurrences to help understand what is needed for preventive or corrective action.

201. B. William is informed that the bridge work has now been completed.

202. B. This contract type allows for flexibility when the scope is unclear, but it comes with the risk of increasing and unknown final costs to the buyer.

203. A, C. A fixed-price contract puts some risk on the seller that any problems on the project will cut into their revenue. Accordingly, they will likely want to make sure that every detail of the scope is spelled out and not allow many changes without an increase in the budget.

204. B. A balanced score card looks to a variety of project factors to help determine a grade for the entire project.

205. A. This is a tool to do a moment-in-time environmental scan looking at issues both within the organization and those that are external to the organization.

Chapter 5: Practice Test 1

1. B, C. A project is an organized effort to fulfill a purpose and has a specific end date. Additional project properties include that it is temporary in nature, has a specific start and end date, and it exists to provide a unique product or service.

2. A. Once accepted by the seller, this becomes a legally binding document for goods and services to be provided, and for compensation to be given at the listed price.

3. C. This is a more detailed explanation of the project's scope as compared to the project charter, which contains a high-level scope definition.

4. C. Other types of organizational change recognized by CompTIA include business process change, internal reorganization, and outsourcing.

5. B. This is especially true when tasks are along the critical path, or when there is no float for that activity. *Float* is the amount of additional time a task has to complete before it begins to disrupt the critical path of a project.

6. B. The elements of the project plan, including the schedule, estimates, and responses to risk, will get more detailed and updated as the project team works through the planning steps of a project.

7. B. This process takes the more subjective results from the qualitative risk analysis and ties them to more numerical measures for evaluation and prioritization purposes.

8. B. A *Gantt chart* is a type of bar chart that illustrates a project schedule.

9. C. The "champion" role of the sponsor is very important both initially and as the project commences to keep the energy and focus of the whole organization committed to the project's success.

10. C. The Cost Performance Index is Earned Value/Actual Cost. Therefore 800 / 1200 = .667.

11. C. A scrum meeting is typically held in the morning at the same time, in the same place, and it sets the context for the team's work.

12. B. The statement of work (SOW) specifies in detail the goods or services that you are purchasing from outside the organization.

13. C. Outsourcing involves the contracting out of work to another party.

14. D. This is a tool used to perform a moment-in-time environmental scan, looking both within and external to the organization.

15. C. Organizational changes would come from the functional side of the organization, not the project side.

16. B, D, G. The basic communication model is sender-message-receiver.

17. A. The closure meeting will allow for the status of all activities; for the project team to return any property, such as ID badges or key cards; and for bringing that phase of the work effort to an end.

18. A. Planned value is the total cost of work planned as of the reporting date, and it is calculated by multiplying the hourly rate by the total planned or scheduled hours.

19. D. During the creation of the procurement plan is where this document is developed, and it explains how decisions will be made and what will be purchased by the organization.

20. B. Whenever a team member joints a project, or at the beginning of the project when multiple people join a project, is when expectations should be set, including their role, due dates for tasks, norms, and team interactions. Because this question addresses "project work," the annual goal expectation session would not be correct, since it would not account for the specific expectations on the project. This could be influenced by what type of organizational structure is being used (functional, projectized, or matrixed).

21. A. A dedicated project team will not have to compete with functional assignments in the course of the project, allowing team members to focus exclusively on project work.

22. A. The key is actually setting money aside to deal with the risk should it occur during the course of the project. Failing to plan in this way can lead to project disruption or cancelation.

23. B. Using some form of teleconferencing like videoconferencing or a phone call would make the most sense from an economic perspective. An in-person meeting would be cost prohibitive for a candidate who may not join the team. Email would not allow for verbal communication to be assessed, and it would drag the interview out over an unacceptable amount of time. Social media would not keep the discussion confidential, so it isn't a good fit.

24. B. Milestones are used in project management to mark a specific point along a project timeline, such as the project start and end date, completion of a phase, or gate checks.

25. A. A Pareto chart contains both a line graph and bars where the individual values are represented in descending order by the bars, and the cumulative total is represented by the line.

26. A. A ScrumMaster typically coordinates this meeting, which is a collaborative effort to detail all of the work that needs to be completed and each item's respective acceptance criteria.

27. C. An RFI will give a sense of the number of providers or contractors who can provide the goods and services in question. An RFI will also help provide a ballpark for the costs.

28. D. Reorganizing by centralizing this function would increase consistency and control for the organization on HR practices such as hiring and retaining employees.

29. A. Audits are reviews to obtain evidence to ensure that good practices are followed, that the project team is behaving in an ethical and legal fashion, and to ensure that there is no fraud, waste, and abuse occurring.

30. D. Signoff on the project charter would be a milestone, not a deliverable.

31. B, C, E. Documents that are binding between two parties, meaning that they can be legally enforced to deliver service, payment, or other attribute, include agreements or contracts, memorandums of understanding (MOU), and purchase orders. Other forms include nondisclosure agreements, cease and desist letters, letters of intent, service-level agreements, and warranties.

32. B. Process diagrams, often called *workflow diagrams*, show all of the steps from start to finish in a process. Another process improvement tool a consultant could use would be SIPOC-R to identify the suppliers, inputs, processes, outputs, customers, and requirements.

33. A. Internal reorganizations can disrupt a project if resources are no longer available to work on the project, or if there are new or changed stakeholders with whom the project team will need to work to achieve project success.

34. A. A change request log can be a simple spreadsheet that has the ID number, date, name, and description of the change.

35. A, D, E. When dealing with any team on different continents, or even on opposite sides of the same continent, time zones will impact communication. The project team also needs to account for language barriers and cultural differences when planning communication.

36. D. Quantitative risk analysis would add more concretely measured items like the numerical score for each risk, whereas qualitative risk analysis uses expert judgment to prioritize the project risks using a predefined rating scale.

37. C. A process diagram is a visual representation of the steps in a process. Other names for process diagrams include *process maps* or *work flow diagrams*.

38. A. Assumptions are events, actions, or conditions that are believed to be true. Another way to look at it is that they are things that must be true in order for the project to be a success but that are outside the control of the project team.

39. D. On the exam, it is likely that there will be a scenario-based question that will test your critical thinking skills to reason through the correct activity sequencing of a project. This question should help give you a taste of what you might encounter.

40. A. With a fixed-price contract, the risk is on the seller. When changes to a project increase their costs but not their revenue, they stand to lose money. Accordingly, they would likely allow very few changes to the scope.

41. C. The communication plan documents the types of information needed by the stakeholders, when the information should be shared, and the method of delivery.

42. B. Know the difference between a merger and an acquisition. The latter is where one organization takes over the other one.

43. A. An incident response has similarities to a business continuity response, but is smaller in scale and localized to a particular part of the business.

44. D. Different cultures will take time out to reflect on certain occasions, which will vary greatly from one another. It is important to take these differences into account when you have an international team, whether or not they are offshore.

45. A. By requiring the successful vendor to carry the insurance, it allows the consequences of negative risk to be transferred to the third party.

46. D. In the storming stage, the process of establishing who is the most influential occurs and there is jostling for position.

47. C. A project stakeholder understandably has a vested interest in the outcome of the project and therefore needs to provide input and requirements to the project. Other roles for stakeholders might include project steering and providing subject matter expertise.

48. A. A traditional waterfall methodology can be progressively iterative, similar to the sprints used with the Agile methodology, which creates a backlog of work to be completed in a specific time period; that process is repeated until the product is completed.

49. B. A discretionary dependency is defined by the project management team, and they are normally process or procedure driven. This is typically a logical relationship between two activities.

50. C. NDAs are common contract vehicles for jobs in both the government and private sector that would require a security clearance or where information needs to be protected from competition.

51. B. Intranet sites are protected by a password or network firewall, and they can contain information and functionality for the business to operate such as project status updates, time keeping, and employee self-service.

52. D. A change control board (CCB) is the body that evaluates and approves changes. The specifics are defined in the change control process that would be set up as a part of a project.

53. B. It is critical to communicate safety issues, public relations issues, and certain risk factors to key stakeholders so that responses can be coordinated and executed.

54. A. This is the activity that compares costs and expenses to date against the cost baseline so that a stakeholder can see the variance between what was planned and what actually occurred.

55. D. Opportunities and threats are conditions like weather or political climate that affect the organization or project but are not within the control of the organization.

56. C. More established organizations with mature processes and tenured staff would most likely have a functional organizational structure centered around specialties like human resources, finance, research and development, and so on.

57. A. Forcing is where one party gets their way, and the other party's interest is not represented.

58. A. Meeting minutes help to memorialize details of conversations and decisions that were made in the moment. Often during the course of a project, so much time passes with so many other decisions made that it can be difficult to recall what was done and why. Meeting minutes are a useful tool to help address those challenges.

59. C. Task completion is communicated to project managers and/or coordinators so that they can signal the next activities or project phase to begin.

60. C. This assessment checks to ensure that the data is unbiased and accurate.

61. A. The project management office performs the function of coordinating resources across the organization.

62. A. The project charter also gives formal authority to begin the project, and it allows the project manager to begin applying resources to the project.

63. D. The key to this answer is the approval to move forward with the project. Gate reviews are check-in points where authorization to proceed must be given.

64. E. Risk identification, probability and impact analysis, and risk response would all take place during the Planning phase of the project.

65. C. To help determine if the project should move forward, a status report would give a snapshot of the work done to date, status of the budget and schedule, and issues facing the project.

66. C. A template allows for a standard submittal in the change control process that includes all of the information needed on the purpose and impact of the change.

67. B. Face-to-face meetings, or in-person meetings, are the superior choice for working on conflict resolution, giving performance appraisals, and working on team building.

68. A, D. Active acceptance includes developing contingency reserves to deal with risk should it occur. Passive acceptance is when the project team is not able to eliminate all of the threats to a project.

69. A. The project team is closest to the work that needs to get done, should bring some expert judgment to the project, and will be on the hook for project success.

70. A, D, E. The three types of organizational structures are Functional, Matrix, and Projectized. Agile is a project management methodology, and co-location is a logistical setup of a project team rather than an organizational structure.

71. A. Monitoring the risks and issues log occurs during the Monitor and Control phase and is not an activity of the Closing phase.

72. D. The formula used is (Most Likely + Optimistic + Pessimistic) / 3.

73. C. It is a successor task, because storyboarding would come after the development of the script. In the creation of an animated movie, many more steps than these are required to create the final product.

74. D. The best document to gain an understanding of the project structure would be the project's organizational chart.

75. A, C. A virtual meeting is where everyone is not in the same location, and the use of technology, such as video or audio conferencing, allows the meeting to occur.

76. B. The urgency assessment uses risk triggers, time to develop and implement a response, and overall risk ranking as inputs for the analysis.

77. C. Actual cost represents the true total and final costs accrued during the process of completing project work for a specific time period. It is important to include the direct and indirect costs, since they correspond to budgeted activities.

78. B. Recognize the different time zones and schedules being used. If your project spans multiple time zones or there are a variety of schedules being used, take these factors into consideration in scheduling the meeting.

79. A. SIPOC-R is a process improvement method, and the acronym stands for Suppliers, Inputs, Process, Outputs, Customers, and Requirements. It is not used for cost estimating.

80. E. Creation of the work breakdown structure involves organizing the team's work by breaking it down into manageable chunks or sections. This effort needs to happen before work begins, and therefore it occurs in the Planning phase.

81. C. In a functional organization, the authority resides with the functional manager, not the project manager. This can create difficulty for project assignments and task completion.

82. A, C, E. The scope management includes the process for creating the scope statement, the definitions of how the deliverables will be verified, and the process for creating, maintaining, and approving the WBS. It will also define the process for controlling scope change requests, including the procedure for requesting changes.

83. B. Crashing involves adding more resources to a project so that it can be completed faster.

84. B. The plan lays out the communication methods as well as the frequency and audience.

85. D. Actual cost may include both direct and indirect costs, but it must correspond to the budget for the activity. This can include labor costs, cost of materials, and use of equipment.

86. B, D. Of the options listed, the only methods that are appropriate for mass dissemination to the public are social media and printed materials. The other forms represent a more of a one-on-one form of communication.

87. B. The Monitor and Control phase sees a decrease in stakeholder influence. Although stakeholders start out with a lot of influence, it decreases as the project advances because activities are underway or completed and the ability to change one's mind is diminished.

88. A. The formula for cost variance (CV) is $CV = EV - AC$. The calculations would produce a value of $2,500, indicating the project is under budget. A positive cost variance (CV) means that the project is under budget, and a negative CV means that the project is over budget. $9,500 - $7,000 = -$2,500$; therefore, the project is under budget.

89. B. The burn rate is how fast the project is spending its allotted budget, or the rate that money is being expended over a period of time.

90. C. This may be an activity during either the Planning or Execution phase, depending on the nature of the industry the project is in.

Chapter 6: Practice Test 2

1. **A.** According to *A Guide to the Project Management Body of Knowledge* (PMBOK® Guide), Fifth Edition by the Project Management Institute (PMI®), a histogram is a special form of a bar chart used to describe the central tendency, dispersion, and shape of a statistical distribution.

2. **B.** A kickoff meeting is a form of communication rather than a trigger of communication.

3. **C.** Distribution of printed media, either delivered door-to-door or via a mailer, would be an appropriate communication method based on the demographic.

4. **C.** The industry plus the fact that the company is relatively new would suggest a more aggressive, gambling type of risk tolerance for the company to grow and succeed.

5. **B, C.** Project stakeholders, sponsors, and management can influence the constraints of a project in a variety of ways including shifting the priorities and/or resources, losing interest on a project in favor of newer efforts, and contributing to scope creep.

6. **C.** Constraints are those conditions that restrict the project in certain ways, like resources, timeframes, schedules, or budget.

7. **C, D.** A project can be summarized as having the following properties: is temporary in nature, creates a unique product or service, has a definite start and finish, contains a reason/purpose, and may be part of a program or portfolio. By definition, operational activities are, well, operational and take place after a project is completed. Inclusion in a portfolio or being a part of an organization's strategic plan are not limited just to projects and are therefore not the correct answer.

8. **C.** A high-level overview of the risks of the project would be included in the project charter.

9. **D.** Parametric estimating often uses a quantity of work multiplied by the rate formula for computing costs.

10. **C.** Short stories help focus on how the product is going to be used, which helps shape how the final product is designed.

11. **A.** This is riskiest for the buyer because the total costs of the project are unknown until the project is completed. It does have the advantage to the buyer of easily changing the scope.

12. **B, D, F.** Meeting agendas, communication plans, and project charters would all fall into the category of planning documents at various levels. Project condition information, or status, can all be gleaned in different forms from dashboard information, status reports, and meeting minutes.

13. **D.** There can be one, and only one, person who is accountable per task in a RACI matrix.

14. **B.** The mutual joining of two companies to do work as a single company is a merger. This can disrupt the project as the new combined organization struggles with the activities of joining cultures and processes.

15. C. The project management office (PMO) offers standardization for a project, but it does not get involved in the details of individual projects.

16. B. The kickoff meeting typically occurs at the beginning of the execution phase, not the initiation phase.

17. A. As the project progresses, the Monitor and Control phase would be looking for risk triggers and thereby engaging a risk response plan should the need arise. Remember, Execution and Monitor and Control occur simultaneously, but from an identification standpoint, the risk response plan would be categorized with Monitor and Control functions.

18. C. The project scope being cut back to operate within the new budget is the most likely impact on this project. The schedule would not be affected, because there is no reason to lengthen or shorten the project time.

19. C. There are not enough resources for the tasks assigned, which leads to overallocation of the staff working on the project.

20. B. Collocation involves moving the project team to the same location and work space.

21. D. In a functional organizational structure, the functional manager has the most authority and resources report directly to their functional manager.

22. B, C, D. The ways to organize the WBS are by subprojects (where the project managers of the subprojects each create a WBS), by project phases, or by major deliverables.

23. B. Two of the responsibilities of the project sponsor are serving as the approval authority for the project and helping to remove roadblocks that are in the project team's way.

24. A. As outlined in the contract, the seller can recoup costs that are allowable in the contract terms.

25. C. The organizational chart describes the project team member organization and identifies reporting structures.

26. A. A SWOT analysis looks at the strengths and weakness of the organization and compares them with the opportunities and threats the external environment holds for the company and, therefore, the project itself.

27. B. Also known as a demerger; be mindful of how this can impact a project when parts of the organization are no longer there.

28. B. Version control allows for a trail of what changes were added by whom and at which point in the document's history.

29. D. Social media and old-school media like TV and newspapers are the best and quickest ways to disseminate information to the general public.

30. B. A portfolio is used to help support strategic business goals or objectives, and it may have a manager to control resources across the group of programs and projects to ensure success.

31. D. A memorandum of understanding (MOU) is used when a legal agreement can't be created between the two parties. It is common for government agencies to create MOUs between the parties to provide services or performance criteria to each other.

32. A. The project management plan is the collection of plans created to address budget, time, scope, quality, communication, risk, and other project elements.

33. A. A fishbone diagram, also called an *Ishikawa diagram*, is a visualization tool for categorizing the potential causes of a problem in order to identify its root causes.

34. D. A change in how an organization conducts business is a business process change.

35. D. The project manager looks to the factors of how the change would disrupt the schedule, budget, resource team, and quality of the project.

36. D. When a task is complete, the project team should send a communication to that effect to the appropriate stakeholders.

37. D. For routine updates, email can be an excellent method to communicate remotely, especially if no decisions or discussions need to be made as a part of the update.

38. A. The five project phases as identified in CompTIA Project+ objectives are Initiation, Planning, Execution, Monitor and Control, and Closing.

39. B. Project managers can spend up to 90 percent of their time communicating with the stakeholders and the project team on status updates, getting information, and giving assignments.

40. B. In a balanced-matrix organization, the project manager and the functional manager both control the budget and share power and authority.

41. A. The project is over budget. A CPI under 1 means that the project is spending more than was forecast for the measurement date.

42. C, D, F. Agile is characterized by self-organized teams, sprint planning, and continuous requirements gathering that leads to a more flexible management approach.

43. D. Forming, storming, norming, performing, and adjourning is the mode of group development that was developed by Dr. Bruce Tuckman.

44. B. On the exam, it is likely that there will be a scenario-based question that will test your critical thinking skills to reason through the correct sequencing of activities on a project. This question should help give a flavor of what you might encounter.

45. C. Risk identification is brainstorming and recording all potential risks that might occur during a project.

46. B. A request for information can have a similar meaning to a request for quotation in some companies. An RFQ can also have a cost quote that would be valid for a certain period of time.

47. A. This defines a status report. Although it is a specific type of communication, the need for the report and to whom it will be sent would be included in the communication plan. The actual report itself is a different project artifact.

48. D. Key performance parameters are vital characteristics, functions, requirements, or design considerations that have a major impact on a product or service. Failure to meet these parameters would trigger a review by a validating body to ensure compliance.

49. C. If reorganizing by decentralizing this function, each of the business units would increase flexibility and potentially improve the speed of getting the services and materials for this function.

50. B. Defects, rework, and their related costs are all related to the quality plan or a quality change.

51. A. Gate reviews are presented to a governance board or steering committee to validate cost models, schedule, risks, and objective obtainment.

52. B. The content of the message will often cause you to tailor the method of communication.

53. A. The kickoff meeting typically happens at the beginning of the Execution phase, and it is a primary means of introducing the project team to each other. Remember, in real-world project management, it is not uncommon for the kickoff meeting to be held in the Initiation, Planning, or Execution phase. For the exam, remember that the kickoff meeting occurs in the Execution phase.

54. C. Risk impact details the consequence or result that will occur if the event actually happens. Typically, this is categorized with a rating of High, Medium, and Low.

55. A. This example shows how one constraint, in this case the schedule, is influenced by a change in another constraint, the scope.

56. D. After the team has formed and stormed, this is where familiarity with one another helps to settle things down and individuals beginning to deal with project problems instead of people problems.

57. A, C. A third responsibility that a PMO might have is to maintain standard documentation and templates.

58. B. Lessons learned occurs during the Closing phase of the project.

59. B. Cost performance index (CPI) is expressed as a ratio of Earned Value/Actual Costs.

60. D. To develop the project schedule, the following task/activities should be completed: define activities, sequence activities, estimate resources, and estimate duration.

61. A. The burndown chart is a visual representation and measurement tool showing the completed work against a time interval to forecast project completion.

62. A. Due to the temporary nature of projects, resources are not permanently assigned to any one project or function.

63. D. A fixed-price contract is risky to the seller because if there are problems on the project and it takes longer to complete, the seller still must pay for the labor and increase costs of materials to fulfill the contractual obligation.

64. A. Meeting minutes capture the details for why decisions were made, what was discussed, and any assignments or due dates that materialized out of the meeting.

65. B. When someone has a role of informed, it means that they are informed after a decision has been made or a result has been achieved.

66. C. A scatter chart graphs pairs of numerical data to help the analyst look for a correlation or relationship.

67. A. Outsourcing is the replacement of internal resources with external resources to perform the same business function.

68. A. Mitigation of a risk is reducing the chance that the risk would happen, or lessening the impact in the event that the risk does get triggered.

69. A, E, F. Commonly referred to as the Triple Constraints, almost all projects are constrained by time, budget, and scope as they impact quality.

70. A. Using remote teams can alleviate the space constraints for this organization.

71. D. Strict adherence to a change control process is indicative of a more traditional waterfall approach, where the scope is controlled with a more rigid change process.

72. B. Top-down estimating, or analogous estimating, is where high-level project cost estimates are used by comparing them to a similar project from the past.

73. D. The work breakdown structure breaks the project down into small, manageable chunks of work.

74. A. The addition of more resources, the modification of scope, or the adjustment of the timeline are examples of some of the changes that might be requested.

75. C. To share a positive risk, the project seeks to assign the risk to a third party who is best able to bring about the opportunity. For instance, a company already has a working factory in a country where the materials are going to be sold, reducing costs on the project.

76. D. Low-quality resources do not have the required experience, are not accomplished with the skill set, have poor passion for the project, or carry a bad attitude to work. Low-quality resources can sometimes be replaced, but they will always need to be managed in some form.

77. B. Schedule Variance (SV) is calculated by taking Earned Value (EV) and subtracting the Planned Value (PV).

78. A. Work slippages can impact the timeline, especially when that work is along the critical path.

79. B. A review by a team, either internal or external, is conducting an audit with a recommendation to fix the findings.

80. B. A request for information (RFI) is used when there is not enough information or expert judgment to know what a good or service will cost, or to understand how many vendors there are who can meet this demand.

81. C. When requirements are changing, an agile approach allows the organization readily to be able to adapt to the environment.

82. C. Fast tracking is a scheduled acceleration technique where two tasks that are scheduled in parallel are started at the same time.

83. A. When project teams are separated by large distances, mountains, canyons, rivers, oceans, or other factors, geographic factors can influence how and when communication will occur.

84. B. Risk tolerance is the threshold of comfort one has for accepting a risk and its consequences.

85. A. The project team's communication method allows for individual personal preferences to be set in how frequently they receive communication.

86. C. The project manager not controlling costs is an issue in project management, whereas the other options represent potential future problems, or risks, that could impact the project.

87. C. Different time zones can complicate getting status meeting schedules because of the variance in start and quit times.

88. C. Measuring the schedule performance index and the cost performance index are a part of monitoring and controlling the project, and they are not directly an activity of risk planning.

89. D. Remember that a risk can be either positive or negative, and it represents an opportunity that did not exist earlier in the project.

90. B. When dealing with a rapidly changing environment, the ability to react to new information and feedback is essential. The other options would not take advantage of the flexible, easily changing environment of the project.

Index

C

Q

R

Comprehensive Online Learning Environment

Register on Sybex.com to gain access to the comprehensive online interactive learning environment and test bank to help you study for your CompTIA Project+ certification.

The online test bank includes:

- **Practice Test Questions** to reinforce what you learned
- **Bonus Practice Exams** to test your knowledge of the material

Go to http://www.wiley.com/go/sybextestprep to register and gain access to this comprehensive study tool package.